Chairman Mao Talks to the People

Talks and Letters: 1956–1971

The Pantheon Asia Library

New Approaches to the New Asia

No part of the world has changed so much in recent years as Asia, or awakened such intense American interest. But much of our scholarship, like much of our public understanding, is based on a previous era. The Asia Library has been launched to provide the needed information on the new Asia, and in so doing to develop both the new methods and the new sympathies needed to understand it. Our purpose is not only to publish new work but to experiment with a wide variety of approaches which will reflect these new realities and their perception by those in Asia and the West.

Our books aim at different levels and audiences, from the popular to the more scholarly, from high schools to the universities, from pictorial to documentary presentations. All books will be available in paperback.

Suggestions for additions to the Asia Library are welcome.

Also by Stuart Schram

Mao Tse-tung
The Political Thought of Mao Tse-tung
Authority, Participation and Cultural Change in China
La Théorie de la "révolution permanente" en Chine
Protestantism and Politics in France

By Stuart Schram with Hélène Carrère d'Encausse
Marxism and Asia

Stuart R. Schram is Professor of Politics (with reference to China) in the University of London and Head of the Contemporary China Institute of the School of Oriental and African Studies.

Chairman Mao Talks to the People

Talks and Letters: 1956–1971

Edited with an introduction by
Stuart Schram

Translated by
John Chinnery and Tieyun

PANTHEON BOOKS
A Division of Random House, New York

Copyright © 1974 by Stuart Schram

All rights reserved under International and Pan-American
Copyright Conventions. Published in the United States
by Pantheon Books, a division of Random House, Inc.
Originally published in Great Britain as *Mao Tse-tung
Unrehearsed: Talks and Letters: 1956–71* by Penguin
Books, Ltd., London.

Library of Congress Cataloging in Publication Data
Mao, Tsê-tung, 1893–
    Chairman Mao Talks to the People.

(The Pantheon Asia Library)
    Includes bibliographical references.
1. Mao, Tsê-tung, 1893–   I. Schram, Stuart R.,
ed. II. Title.
DS778.M3A2513   1974   335.43′4   73–18731
ISBN 0-394-48688-9
ISBN 0-394-70641-2 (pbk.)

Manufactured in the United States of America

First American Edition

Contents

Introduction

The Great Proletarian Cultural Revolution launched by Mao Tse-tung in 1966 was marked by many surprising developments. One of the most unexpected repercussions, and perhaps not the least significant, was the divulgence of complete or partial texts of many statements and directives by Mao, and by other leading figures in the Chinese Communist Party, hitherto known only within a restricted circle. The bulk of these materials dates from the period since the establishment of the Chinese People's Republic in 1949, though some go back to the anti-Japanese War of 1937–45, or even to the 1920s. A few such items or fragments, previously treated as confidential, were officially published in China during the Cultural Revolution. Most of them, however, appeared only in the tabloids and other periodicals and documentary collections put out by the various 'Red Guard' and 'Revolutionary Rebel' organizations which flourished in the years 1966–9. It is from sources of this kind that I have selected the texts translated in this volume.*

There are some who have doubts as to the propriety of publishing documents such as these, or indeed of reproducing any versions of Mao's writings not authorized by the Chairman himself. For the most part, the speeches and writings which appear here are not generally accessible within China, and there are grounds for believing that Mao and the Chinese authorities would rather foreigners did not read them either. Under the

---

* For details regarding the Chinese sources used, and the other available translations of some items, see the note at the end of this introduction.

circumstances, does not publishing them amount to meddling in the internal affairs of the Chinese people?

This view is, in my opinion, invalidated by the fact that the originals of the items included here are to be found in many university libraries, and the majority of them have already been translated elsewhere. Under the circumstances, it would be merely burying one's head in the sand to pretend that they do not exist, and to refrain from enjoying them, and learning from them. Moreover, the real flesh-and-blood Mao revealed in these uncensored utterances, Rabelaisian in speech and forthright in his criticism both of himself and of others, is not only more believable, but far more impressive, than the plaster saint worshipped by some of his self-appointed disciples. For all these reasons, it seems abundantly worth while to make these documents conveniently available to English-speaking readers.

These texts can be appreciated in at least three different perspectives: firstly, as the expression of Mao Tse-tung's thinking about various political, economic, and philosophical problems, secondly, as historical documents contributing to our knowledge of events in China in the years 1956–71, and, thirdly, as lively and entertaining prose which, as suggested above, projects a vivid image of one of the most remarkable personalities of our times. The present volume, though reasonably ample in scope, is not an attempt at an exhaustive scholarly compilation of all available texts of Mao for the period under consideration. My aim has been to bring together a number of the most important and characteristic texts, while making the book, in so far as possible, accessible to those with no detailed knowledge of China. Thus, I have omitted the vitally important directive called the 'Sixty Articles on Work Methods', written (or put into final form) by Mao Tse-tung in January 1958, which requires for its comprehension a considerable range of information about Chinese economic policies at the time, and is written in what is (at least for Mao) a rather drab, bureaucratic style.

As regards the substance of the materials included, emphasis has been put on Mao's ideas rather than on factual information, both because such texts are of broader relevance, and because very detailed discussions of events require much heavier annotations to make them intelligible to the general reader. Since most of Mao's available utterances for the past two decades take the form of commentary on pressing policy issues, it was, of course, not possible to select items containing only statements of a high degree of generality, unaccompanied by concrete detail. Moreover, it is the essence of Mao's style of speaking and writing that he constantly illustrates even the most abstruse points by examples drawn either from current affairs, or from Chinese history, which often require elucidation for the Western reader. I have, nevertheless, endeavoured to keep annotations to a minimum, and have refrained from writing a history of China since the 1950s in the form of a running commentary. The number of notes required might have been reduced by cutting out some of the more obscure and esoteric passages in the speeches, but this would have defeated the purpose of this book, which is to give the reader as complete and unvarnished a picture as possible of Mao the man and the thinker. Every item has therefore been translated *in extenso* from the best and fullest Chinese text available to me; I have made no cuts in any of them. (Any suspension points which may be encountered are to be attributed to the editors of the Chinese sources.)

While this book has been compiled in the first instance for a broad public, it should also be of some use to China specialists, who would otherwise have to seek out these documents in a number of different sources. Three of the speeches included here (Text 2, and the first two of those making up Text 4) and substantial parts of three others (Texts 10, 11 and 15) have never before been translated into English. The others can all be found in one place or another, but no single source includes more than approximately a quarter of the 80,000-odd words making up this anthology, and the whole of the available texts are scattered among eight or ten books, pamphlets, and periodical issues. This edition also offers the advantage that all of the speeches have been newly translated by John Chinnery and Tieyun. Without wishing to disparage the many others who have laboured over the interpretation of these often rather off-hand and cryptic utterances, I have no hesitation in saying that the standard of accuracy and of literary quality attained here is higher than in any of the other existing translations. There is also the advantage, by no means negligible in the case of ideological texts such as these, that all the materials have been translated by the same hands, with an effort to employ as far as possible a single English equivalent for each Chinese term.

In evaluating the substantive interest of these materials, one of the first questions which suggests itself is: 'What distinguishes these texts from the *Selected Works* for the period 1926–49, or from the post-1949 items officially published, such as the speech of July 1955 on agricultural cooperativization, or the speech of February 1957 on contradictions among the people?' As might be expected, the style is considerably racier, containing a number of the earthy metaphors which Mao used in the 1920s, but edited out of the official canon.* While this makes for entertaining reading, the more important difference lies deeper. The Mao of the 1950s, and especially of the 1960s, is older, more experienced, perhaps wiser, certainly more self-confident than the Mao of earlier years. As a result, his thinking is both more concrete and more speculative than in most of his previously known works. At the same time, one is struck by the basic continuity and consistency of Mao's approach to politics, and to life, over the past half-century and more.

My aim in this introduction is not to impose some rigid pattern on the rich and varied materials which follow, still less to put forward a closed and definitive interpretation of Mao Tse-tung's thought. I propose merely to single out a few themes which may serve as guiding threads to aid the reader in his own exploration of these speeches. I have grouped them under the main headings of organizational principles, education, patterns of economic development, and foreign relations.

* For examples of such bowdlerization, see S. Schram, *The Political Thought of Mao Tse-tung* (Penguin, 1969), *passim.*

Organization: the Party and the masses

For Mao, as for every other revolutionary, the central problem which subsumes all the others is that of combining effective leadership with broad participation, in order to achieve a radical transformation of society. As a disciple of Lenin, he formulates this dilemma in terms of the concept of democratic centralism. One can, however, discern in his exposition of this concept certain peculiarities which offer clues to the essential originality of his approach to revolution.

Lenin coined the term 'democratic centralism' to define the proper functioning of the Communist Party itself, and in the Soviet Union today it is still used primarily in speaking of the Party, though the same principles are supposed to apply to other political and economic organizations, such as the trade unions or the state bureaucracy.* Mao, on the other hand, though he uses the term in discussing the Party, also employs it much more broadly to characterize the spirit of Chinese society as a whole, and the relations between the leadership and the masses. This difference in usage stands in fact as a symbol of the crucial difference between Mao Tse-tung's thought and orthodox Leninism. Lenin utterly distrusted the spontaneous tendencies of the population as a whole, and even of the working class, unless they were guided and controlled by a conscious vanguard in the guise of a Communist Party. Mao Tse-tung, for his part, is by no means free of Leninist elitism, but he is none the less prepared, to a far greater extent than Lenin, to trust the masses and to involve them actively in shaping their own fate. Logically, the result is not very tidy, and in practice it may lead to chaos, as Mao discovered during the Cultural Revolution, but this approach is also responsible, in the last analysis, for the great creative upsurge which has struck so many recent visitors to China.

* For a concise summary of Soviet usage dating roughly from the same period as the Mao speeches contained in this volume, see the entry 'Democratic Centralism' in the second edition of the *Politicheskii Slovar'* (*Political Dictionary*) (Moscow: Gospolitizdat, 1958), p. 163.

The most extended discussion of these issues in this volume, and indeed the fullest discussion to be found in any single work by Mao, is contained in Text 8, Mao's speech of 30 January 1962 to the '7,000 cadres conference' (so called because the audience was made up of 7,000 cadres from various levels, who had been called together in Peking to discuss basic policy issues, in the context of the continuing re-adjustment following the difficulties encountered in the course of the 'Great Leap Forward' of 1958–9). This text, which revolves around the question of democratic centralism to such an extent that in many collections of materials this concept serves as a title for the whole speech, illustrates eloquently both the reality of the impulse towards mass participation to be found in Mao Tse-tung's thinking, and the limitations on this impulse.

Lenin had defined democratic centralism in terms of organizational principles: freedom of discussion, but absolute acceptance of decisions once adopted; consultation with the rank and file, but absolute obedience of lower organs to higher organs. Mao, too, accepts these principles, but characteristically he poses the problem not only in terms of organization, but in terms of communications. 'Without democracy', he declares, 'there cannot be any correct centralism because people's ideas differ, and if their understanding of things lacks unity then centralism cannot be established. What is centralism? First of all it is a centralization of correct ideas ...' This 'centralization of ideas', Mao makes plain, has two aspects. On the one hand, it refers to the flow of information from the grass roots without which the 'processing plant' at the centre will lack the raw material out of which correct decisions and policies are made. But at the same time it implies that only if people are consulted will they subsequently be in the right frame of mind to accept the decisions of the leading organs once they are elaborated, and to work willingly and wholeheartedly for their implementation.

The manner in which Mao discussed these issues in 1962 was not unrelated, as he makes perfectly clear himself, to the situation in China at the time. A year earlier, the scarcity of food had reached such a point that in certain areas of the country deaths occurred as a result of malnutrition. There were still, Mao declared, 'many difficulties', and these could only be overcome by encouraging the masses to speak out and thereby mobilizing their enthusiasm. It is no doubt this context which explains the relatively heavy emphasis, in the speech to the 7,000 cadres conference, on the importance of democracy rather than centralism. Twenty years earlier, at a time when his concern had been to unify the Party under his leadership, he had declared: 'The Communist Party not only needs democracy, but needs centralization even more.'* But the real hallmark of his thinking is the conviction that in the last analysis it is not necessary to choose between the two. Liu Shao-ch'i referred in 1941 to democracy and centralism as 'two contradictory concepts', and analysed the 'contradiction between leaders and led' as a permanent trait of the Party organization.† Mao Tse-tung also perceived these contradictions, which he analysed at length in his speech of 27 February 1957, but he was persuaded that it was somehow possible to maximize both aspects simultaneously. The continuity of his views on this point is illustrated by the formulation which he put forward in the summer of 1957, quoted in his speech of 1962, inserted with only minor verbal changes in the Party Constitution adopted at the Ninth Chinese Communist Party Congress in April 1969, and retained likewise in the new Party Constitution adopted at the Tenth Congress in August 1973: 'We must bring about a political climate which has both centralism and democracy, discipline and freedom, unity of purpose and ease of mind for the individual, and which is lively and vigorous.'‡

Only the very naïve would contend that the reality of Chinese

---

*Speech of 1 February 1942; see the relevant extract in *The Political Thought of Mao Tse-tung*, p. 313. He made the same point in 1962, despite his emphasis on democracy on that occasion.

†In his lectures of 1941 on 'Organizational and Disciplinary Self-Cultivation'. See the analysis in *The Political Thought of Mao Tse-tung*, pp. 94–5. The reference to 'two contradictory concepts' occurs on p. 142 of the Chinese text cited there.

‡See below, p. 163. The text of July 1957 in which Mao originally made this statement is not included in this volume, because only brief extracts are available.

society under Mao's leadership has always lived up to this credo, but that is no reason for going to the opposite extreme and postulating that such statements are necessarily mere hypocrisy and sham. Perhaps the most striking evidence of Mao's genuine concern with these problems is provided by his long-standing war against bureaucracy. This, too, is of course an ambiguous tendency since it can be interpreted as a vendetta against others in the leadership of the Chinese Communist Party not in sympathy with the Chairman's policies. It is worth pointing out, however, that one of the most sweeping proposals in this domain prior to the Cultural Revolution is to be found in Mao's speech of April 1956 on the 'Ten Great Relationships', in which he advocated streamlining Party and state organs, and cutting away two thirds of them (Text 1, p. 75). There is no evidence that Mao was, at this time, in sharp conflict with the Party leadership as a whole, though statements such as this may not have increased his popularity with some of his comrades. The 'streamlining', when it came, was to be even more drastic than Mao had suggested; according to Chou En-lai, five sixths of the state bureaucracy in the capital had been cut away in the course of the Cultural Revolution – though many of the cadres involved had gone to lower levels, in the context of a policy of decentralization, rather than losing their jobs altogether.*

More significant, in a sense, than such quantitative criticisms of the proliferation of the bureaucracy are Mao's attacks on bureaucratic arrogance, and here again his speech of January 1962 to the 7,000 cadres conference shows him at his most eloquent and biting. 'Those of you who . . . do not allow people to speak, who think you are tigers, and that nobody will dare to touch your arse . . . will fail. People will talk anyway. You think that nobody will really dare to touch the arse of tigers like you? They damn well will!' Or again, in somewhat less highly coloured, but none the less telling, language: 'Let other people speak out. The heavens will not fall and you will not be thrown out. If you do not let others speak, then the day will surely come when you are thrown out' (Text 8, pp. 167, 187).

*Interview of February 1971 with Edgar Snow. *The Long Revolution* (New York: Random House, 1972; and London: Hutchinson, 1973), p.14.

Four years later, Mao decided the time had come to take a hand himself in the fulfilment of this prophecy. His method for throwing out the bureaucrats, the Great Proletarian Cultural Revolution, appeared to some, at least in the early stages, to smack of pure anarchy. A comparison of the statements he himself made during the years 1966–9 regarding 'rebellion' against Party control shows that, although he was prepared to go very far indeed in this direction in order to achieve his tactical aim of weakening his adversaries in the bureaucracy, in the end he remained more firmly committed to the central axioms of Leninism than many people (myself included) had imagined.

In July 1966, on the eve of the first great outbreak of Red Guard violence directed against Party cadres, Mao declared: 'To use the excuse of distinguishing between "inner [Party]" and "outer [Party]" is to fear revolution' (Text 16, p. 254). That is to say, Party members should not regard themselves as qualitatively different from the masses and superior to the masses. The students in particular should be given their heads; Party cadres who tried to suppress the Red Guards were like the conservative northern warlords of the May Fourth period, and would come to no good end. A natural corollary of this view was that violence plays a positive role in the political process, since getting beaten up by the right-wingers 'toughens up the left-wingers' (Text 17, p. 258).

Already in his letter of 1 August 1966 to the Red Guards of Tsinghua University Middle School, Mao began to spell out the limits to his endorsement of rebellion. Replying to a missive from the Red Guards transmitting to him the texts of two big-character posters making use of the slogan he himself had coined, 'To rebel is justified!', he subtly transmuted this to read: 'It is right to rebel against reactionaries.'* In other words, rebellion is *not* justified merely as a form of self-expression, directed against anyone and everyone in authority; it is legitimate

---

*For the text of these Red Guard posters, see *Peking Review*, No. 37 (9 September 1966), pp. 2–21. For Mao's original statement, in 1939, that 'to rebel is justified' (then attributed to Stalin), see *The Political Thought of Mao Tse-tung*, pp. 427–8.

only when it serves politically correct ends. The subtlety
– and difficulty – of Mao's tactical position at this point is
eloquently illustrated by the fact that the slogan 'To rebel is
justified!' continued to be used publicly in its original form for
a further two years, even though Mao had given a clear hint
that the validity of this principle was subject to certain limitations. By October 1966, he had reached the stage of recognizing that, in calling forth the Red Guard movement, he had not
realized how shattering its impact would be. 'Since it was I who
caused the havoc,' he said, 'it is understandable if you have
some bitter words for me.' He also began to stress the way in
which Party cadres should learn from the Red Guards and
correct their work style, rather than emphasizing the role
of the Red Guards themselves (Text 21, pp. 271–3). At the
same time, he repeated the point, which he had made a decade
earlier in the 'Ten Great Relationships', that the democratic
parties participating in the United Front retained their use-
fulness, and that some non-communists were better revolutionaries than many Party members (Text 20, pp. 268–9).

In February 1967, Mao explicitly repudiated those ultra-leftists within China (and among his followers abroad) who imagined that the masses, under the guidance of correct ideology,
could do without leadership. Noting that the Shanghai People's
Committee had demanded the abolition of 'heads', Mao remarked: 'This is extreme anarchism, it is most reactionary. If
instead of calling someone the "head" of something we call him
"orderly" or "assistant", this would really be only a formal
change. In reality there will still always be "heads" ' (Text 23,
p. 277). This interview marked in fact the decisive, symbolic
turning-point in Mao's thinking, regarding not only abstract
problems of political theory, but also the concrete form which
China's new polity, after victory (if it could be achieved) in the
Cultural Revolution, should assume. In January, he had appeared to be wavering, and perhaps to be somewhat tempted
after all by the 'Paris Commune' models promoted by Ch'en
Po-ta, but by early February he had set his face resolutely
against any such solution, and had turned towards the formula
of the 'Triple (or Three-way) Alliance', in which the young

activists who had come to the fore during the Cultural Revolution were made to unite with, and ultimately to subordinate themselves to, representatives of the People's Liberation Army and the older and more experienced Party cadres. Now, in his conversations with Chang and Yao, the leaders of the Shanghai Commune which had been set up on 5 February 1967, he made his position quite clear.* Thereafter, the evolution both of the situation, and of Mao's thinking about it, continued basically in the same direction of retreat from 'extended democracy', with overtones of anarchism, towards something more like the Leninist conception of the relation between the leaders and the masses. This process reached its culmination when, in April 1969, at the First Plenum of the new Central Committee elected at the Ninth Congress of the Chinese Communist Party, Mao reiterated the Leninist axiom that the Party is *the* decisive leadership organization, the locus of consciousness and authority in society. 'You are communists,' he said, 'you are that part of the masses which is more conscious, you are that part of the proletariat which is more conscious.' (Text 25, p. 288.)

Adding up all these statements, and considering them in the context of the policies espoused by Mao in the course of the past two decades, and especially during the Cultural Revolution, one can see clearly that he is not prepared to turn over control of the revolutionary process to the spontaneous impulses of the people themselves. But one can also see how repugnant to him is the idea of social and economic change moving tidily along under the control of the bureaucrats, without the active participation of the citizens.

If Mao Tse-tung strives to minimize the gap between the cadres and the masses, it is no doubt with the object of combating bureaucracy, but also because, like those late nineteenth-century Chinese thinkers who first taught him how Western liberalism could be made to serve China's resurgence, he is

---

*For a fuller discussion of Mao's attitude during the period from the autumn of 1966 to the spring of 1967, and of the issues involved, in the light of Mao's previous thinking about democracy and centralism, see my introduction to *Authority, Participation and Cultural Change in China* (Cambridge University Press, 1973), especially pp. 95–6.

persuaded that the energy of the people as a whole can be maximized only by releasing the initiative of every individual. Only by mobilizing these energies can the country be effectively industrialized, so as to increase both national power and the well-being of the population. Underlying Mao's conviction that this *can* be done are certain ideas about the possibility of educating the masses for their role in social change.

Education, culture, and revolution

Talking to Edgar Snow in December 1970, Mao Tse-tung said that he wished to be remembered by only one of the four titles given him in the early stages of the Cultural Revolution (Great Teacher, Great Leader, Great Supreme Commander and Great Helmsman), that of Teacher. He had, he recalled, been a primary-school teacher in his youth.* At first glance, this would appear to be merely a gesture of modesty. Yet there is a sense in which a concern with education stands at the centre of Mao's career. His approach to revolution stresses the importance of cultural change, and education, in the broadest sense, is the instrument by which he seeks to create new men and women.

One can discern three strands in Mao's conception of education as it is spelled out in particular in some of the talks contained in this volume. Education, to be effective, must break with traditional patterns of rote learning, scholasticism, and meek submission of the pupil to the authority of the teacher; it must be linked to practice, and specifically to production; it cannot be separated from class struggle. Moreover, the whole process must, as already suggested, serve to re-shape the ideas and habits which the Chinese people have inherited from the past. In other words, education goes hand in hand with political revolution, economic revolution, and cultural revolution.

In his remarks on education, especially since 1958, Mao has called into question the traditional Chinese form of elitism – an exaggerated reverence for scholars and intellectuals – just as he has called into question elitism in its Leninist guise of the mys-

* *The Long Revolution*, p. 169.

tique of the Party as the locus of consciousness. And yet, once again, it is necessary to avoid taking these iconoclastic statements too literally. As Mao put it in his Hunan peasant report of 1927, 'To right a wrong it is necessary to exceed the proper limit; the wrong cannot be righted without doing so . . .'* Mao's statements mocking those with 'book learning' must be read in this light – though it must be acknowledged that, however one interprets them, they remain in some cases very extreme.

'In history it is always those with little learning who overthrow those with more learning,' declared Mao at Chengtu in March 1958 (Text 4c, p. 118). This comment was made in the context of a discussion of how new schools of thought arise; Mao has even less regard for the contribution of intellectuals to politics. Discussing the problem, as he so often does in these talks, in the light of examples from Chinese history, he said in 1964:

> Only two of the emperors of the Ming Dynasty did well, T'ai-tsu and Ch'eng-tsu. One was illiterate and the other only knew a few characters. Afterwards . . . in the Chia-ch'ing reign when the intellectuals had power, things were in a bad state . . . To read too many books is harmful.

The learning of these emperors and officials of earlier centuries was, of course, the traditional learning, but Mao is sceptical of those who immerse themselves in Marxist lore as well. 'We shouldn't read too many books. We should read Marxist books, but not too many of them either. It will be enough to read a few dozen. If we read too many we can . . . become bookworms, dogmatists, revisionists.' (Text 10, pp. 204, 210.)

Mao's rejection of the traditional fetishism of learning is closely related to his affirmation of the advantages of youth over age. In a society such as that of China in which reverence for one's elders was a cardinal virtue, the creative role of youth was understandably one of the first ideas put forward when the Confucian order came under attack in the early twentieth century. It has remained a favourite theme of reformist and revolutionary writers alike ever since China's first 'cultural

*Selected Works, Vol. I, p. 29.

revolution', the May Fourth Movement of 1919, and Mao Tse-tung has always laid particular stress on it. 'The whole of the Chinese revolutionary movement found its origin in the action of young students and intellectuals,' he declared on the twentieth anniversary of the May Fourth Movement, in 1939.* In his Chengtu speech of March 1958 Mao re-affirmed his faith in youth in ringing terms:

From ancient times the people who have created new schools of thought have always been young people without great learning. Confucius started at the age of twenty-three; and how much learning did Jesus have? ... Marx was also very young when he first created Dialectical Materialism. His learning was also acquired later on ... When young people grasp a truth they are invincible, and old people cannot compete with them.

The decisive superiority of young people over old, in Mao's view, is that the young have 'the ability to recognize new things at a glance' and, having grasped them, 'open fire on the old fogeys'. Mao's admiration for youth is rooted in a consistent intellectual position based on hostility to the acceptance of authority and routine which characterized traditional Chinese society, but statements like that just quoted are also inspired by an emotional attachment to his own earlier experience, as the continuation of the passage makes abundantly clear:

As soon as they have grasped the truth the young founders of new schools embarked on discoveries, scorning the old fogeys. Then those with learning oppressed them. Isn't that what history is like? When we started to make revolution, we were mere twenty-year-old boys, while the rulers of that time ... were old and experienced. They had more learning, but we had more truth [Text 4, pp. 118–20].

While intensely aware of the virtues of youth, Mao recognizes that old people still have a role to play. 'The older you get the less useful you are,' he declared in 1958, but he added: 'Of course we still need old people; they must also take the helm.' The future 'Great Helmsman' of the Cultural Revolution could say no less, though he clearly felt that old men were useful only

*The Political Thought of Mao Tse-tung, p. 354.

if they were attuned to the needs of youth. Moreover, old people after all do have experience, which young people lack. This point, which he had made in the 1930s,* Mao re-affirmed in 1966, on the eve of the Cultural Revolution, in talking to his nephew, Mao Yüan-hsin:

> Formerly, I was principal of a primary school, and a teacher in a middle school. I am also a member of the Central Committee, and was once a department chief for the Kuomintang. But when I went to the rural areas and spent some time with peasants, I was deeply struck by how many things they knew. I realized their knowledge was wide, and I was no match for them, but should learn from them. To say the least, you are not a member of the Central Committee, are you? How can you know more than the peasants? [Text 15, p. 251].

The talks included in this volume from the period of the Cultural Revolution show graphically Mao's evolution from an emphasis on the virtues of youth to a stress on the need to educate young people. On 21 July 1966, as already noted, he identified a positive attitude towards the Red Guards as the touchstone of a true revolutionary, likening those who suppressed the student movement to the militarists of the 1920s (Text 16, p. 253). By October, he was already thinking more of the need for cadres to redeem themselves and thus continue to play a useful role. 'If one wants to educate others, the educationist should first be educated,' he declared, implying that young people could and should be educated by their elders, provided only that the latter adopted the proper approach for doing this (Text 20, p. 264). To be sure, Mao still saw the overall contributions of the young rebels as positive. 'There are many things which the Propaganda Department and the Ministry of Culture were unable to cope with,' he said on 9 January 1967. 'Even you [pointing to Comrade Ch'en Po-ta] and I could not cope with them. But when the Red Guards came they were immediately brought under control.' (Text 22, p. 276). But he was also resolved that young people should not imagine they were in sole charge of events. In early 1967, a quotation from an article written by Mao during the May Fourth

* *The Political Thought of Mao Tse-tung*, p. 353.

Movement of 1919 was widely used by the Red Guards: 'The world is ours, the nation is ours, society is ours.'* In February 1967, in talks with the Shanghai leftists Chang Ch'un-ch'iao and Yao Wen-yüan, the Chairman said he didn't altogether remember these words, and they shouldn't be used any more (Text 23, p. 279). The implication was clearly that these young people should not imagine that the world belonged exclusively to *them*, rather than to the Party cadres or even to the Chairman himself.

This evolution found its logical culmination in Mao's directive of December 1968 according to which educated young people should go to the countryside 'to be re-educated by the poor and lower-middle peasants'.† Although this measure was inspired in part by a desire to get undisciplined elements among the Red Guards out of the cities, where they had been fighting bloody battles with one another, it was also in complete harmony with Mao's deep-seated conviction that the education required by the younger generation cannot merely be book learning, but must be linked to the class struggle and to production.

Turning now to Mao's ideas on education in a narrower sense, it is worth noting, first of all, that the most important recent texts on this theme among those available to us are from 1964 (Text 10, the first part of Text 15, and others not included here). This is no accident, for it was in 1964 that the problem of 'bringing up successors' to carry forward the revolution was first raised explicitly and publicly, at the congress of the Youth League, and in the ninth Chinese reply to the Soviet open letter of 1963.‡

In his discussion of educational methods at the 'Spring Festival Forum' in February 1964 (Text 10) Mao stressed practicality, and the need to minimize the distance between students and teachers, in terms which make plain the link

---

*For a complete translation of this article, written by Mao in July and August 1919, see the *China Quarterly*, No. 49 (1972), pp. 76–87. The sentence in question appears on p. 84.
†*Peking Review*, No. 52 (1968), pp. 6–7.
‡See *Peking Review*, No. 28 (1964), pp. 6–22, and No. 29 (1964), pp. 23–32.

between these two aspects of his thought. Though praising Confucius because he taught only a limited number of subjects (and had known, in his youth, something of the suffering of the masses), Mao proceeded to condemn the Confucian learning both on class grounds, and because there was nothing in it about industry or agriculture. 'People's limbs were not exercised and they could not distinguish between the five grains.' This lack of *rapport* between the traditional education and productive activity was obviously related to the fact that scholars derived their status from the mastery of esoteric learning, and regarded manual labour as beneath them. Mao sees such attitudes persisting in the present Chinese educational system, with its examinations which are 'a method of surprise attack, asking oblique or strange questions'. This, he complains, is 'still the same method as the old eight-legged essay' (a composition written to a rigid set pattern by candidates aspiring to officialdom in the old imperial examinations). The important thing, he declares, is to understand the issues and to give original and creative answers, rather than to 'memorize and learn by rote'. In a conversation with his nephew Mao Yüan-hsin in July 1964, he elaborated on this criticism of teachers, urging them not to make such a mystery of their knowledge, but to hand out notes on their lectures in advance. 'With university students, especially the senior students, the main thing is to let them study and work out problems. What is the point of talking so much?' It is because the teachers are not really sure of their own mastery of the subject that they 'put on arrogant airs to frighten people off'. Hence, 'the problem of educational reform is primarily a problem of teachers' – that is, of persuading teachers to divest themselves of the attitudes of scholar–bureaucrats (Text 15, p. 248).

The theme of class struggle is implicit in Mao's observations regarding the need to link education and production, which have as their corollary the rejection of old ideas regarding the superiority of mental over manual labour, but Mao repeatedly places this concept explicitly at the very centre of his discussions of education. 'Class struggle is your most important subject, and it is a compulsory subject,' he remarked to his nephew Mao Yüan-hsin in July 1964. Students, he added, should go to the countryside and to the factories to participate in revolutionary movements there. 'Only when you have completed such a course of political training can I consider you a university graduate ... If you don't even know about the class struggle, how can you be regarded as a university graduate?' (Text 15, p. 246.) In August 1964, talking to Ch'en Po-ta and K'ang Sheng, he returned to the same theme, in the context of a discussion of philosophy:

> ... To get some experience of class struggle – that's what I call a university. They argue about which university is better, Peking University or People's University. For my part I am a graduate of the university of the greenwoods, I learned a bit there [Text 11, p. 213].

'The greenwoods' in Chinese parlance, as in English, evokes the habitat of heroic outlaws in revolt against an unjust society. Mao is here referring, of course, to his years of guerrilla warfare in the countryside, in the days of Chingkangshan and Yenan, the emphasis being on the lessons he learned from the guerrilla experience. But he also attributes crucial importance to the locus of that experience, the Chinese countryside and the world of the peasants who inhabit it.

The dialectics of development

The point has often been made that the Chinese revolution diverges from the Soviet model by the nature and importance of the role played in it by the peasants and the countryside, and that this difference is reflected in the theoretical formulations put forward by Mao Tse-tung. This is unquestionably a central and seminal issue in understanding the Chinese experience, but the dialectic between cities and countryside should be viewed in the broader context of the network of contradictions which goes to make up Mao's dialectical vision of society and of the universe.

In his enormously important speech of April 1956 'On the

Ten Great Relationships' (Text 1), Mao singled out, as the title implies, ten crucial pairs of opposites, or contradictions, which serve to characterize the Chinese economy and polity. This list, while it includes many of the most significant points, does not cover all aspects of China's pattern of economic development and social change. An important complement is to be found in Mao's speech of 20 March 1958 at Chengtu, in which he mentioned on the one hand the relation between traditional labour-intensive ways of getting things done and mechanized or semi-mechanized techniques, and on the other hand the tension between 'deliberation' and 'haste' in fixing the tempo of socialist transformation (Text 4b, pp. 103–13).

For Mao, contradictions are not merely, as for Hegel and Marx, the motor of change; they are the very stuff of life and reality. In April 1956, he declared: 'Contradictions are everywhere in the world. Without contradictions, there would be no world' (Text 1, p. 62). At Chengtu, he put it more strongly still: 'If there were no contradictions and no struggle, there would be no world, no progress, no life, there would be nothing at all' (Text 4b, p. 108).

This is not the place for an extended and systematic discussion of Mao's philosophical views in general, and of his theory of contradictions in particular, to which many studies have already been devoted. Nevertheless, although this volume seeks to document primarily Mao's thinking about political, economic and cultural questions, it is not possible to neglect his philosophy altogether, especially as he himself regards a correct philosophical standpoint, and above all a correct understanding of the problem of contradictions, as a necessary precondition to correct political analysis. Just how intimate, in Mao's own view, is the link between abstract concepts and concrete policy, is illustrated by the fact that one of the most detailed and interesting discussions of broad philosophical issues to be found in this entire volume is contained in Mao's speech of 20 March 1958 at Chengtu, which was delivered before a meeting concerned to hammer out guidelines for the forthcoming Great Leap Forward, and which began with a discussion of something as down-to-earth as the reform of agricultural implements, before taking off into reflections on the future of man and the universe (Text 4b). Conversely, the talk of August 1964 on questions of philosophy (Text 11) is largely taken up with illustrations drawn from the history of the Chinese revolution.

The core of Mao's interpretation of contradictions lies in his characterization of the phenomenon as the unity and struggle of opposites which transform themselves into one another. This view, which is expounded in Paragraph 5 of 'On Contradiction', and is touched on repeatedly in the speeches included in this volume, is in conformity with the letter of Lenin's dicta on the subject, which are explicitly quoted by Mao as authority for his own statements.* And yet, as Mao suggested with some bitterness in his speech of 20 March 1958, there were some professional philosophers, in China and the Soviet Union, who did not regard his views as altogether orthodox. They apparently felt that the Chairman's understanding of contradictions was inspired not so much by Marxism as by the old Chinese dialectic of waxing and waning, decline and renewal, the *yin* and the *yang*. The importance of these influences in shaping Mao's thinking has been noted by most of those who have written on the subject, and it is suggestive that Mao should have stressed, in his philosophical conversations of 1964, that neither Buddhism nor Taoism should be left out of account (in favour of an exclusive concentration on the largely non-dialectical Confucian tradition) in studying the history of Chinese thought. In the same conversations, he utterly rejected the principle of the negation of the negation as an axiom of dialectics, on the grounds that every historical phenomenon was simultaneously or successively affirmation and negation (Text 11, pp. 230, 226). This remark, too, indicates a certain affinity with the traditional view of history as flux and reflux, rather than purposeful forward movement.

I do not mean to suggest, of course, that this Chinese component in Mao's understanding of dialectics is more important than the Marxist component. To the extent that it is present, however, it undoubtedly explains in part the Olympian detachment with which he looks forward not only to the ultimate

* 'On Contradiction', *Selected Works*, Vol. I, pp. 337, 341–2.

supersession of communism itself by a higher social form, but to the extinction of the human race, and/or to the advent of creatures evolved from horses, cows, sheep or insects. 'When the theologians talk about doomsday,' he declared, 'they are pessimistic and terrify people. We say the end of mankind is something which will produce something more advanced than mankind' (Text 4b, p. 110, and Text 11, pp. 220–21, 228). Such reflections as these are not, perhaps, strictly incompatible with Marx's own ideas, but they go against the grain of the Marxist tradition, with its optimistic faith in the transition to socialism and communism as a definitive breakthrough from pre-history to history.

More directly relevant to the main content of this volume, and to the themes of this introduction, are the implications of Mao's para-traditional dialectics for policy and leadership style. Characteristically, Mao gives as an example of the transformation of opposites into one another the fact that 'elements of spring and summer are contained in autumn and winter' (Text 4b. p. 108). The dialectics of Taoism are, in large part, the dialectics of the rhythm of nature, and Mao in fact explicitly puts forward as an aim, in discussing the application of dialectics to economic development, the achievement of the correct *rhythm* of production, through the unity of the opposites 'fast' and 'slow'. Harking back, as he so often does, to the experience of the civil war, he declared in March 1958 that there was 'a rhythm in warfare, too', which found its expression in the unity of the opposites 'hard fighting' and 'rest and consolidation'. This feeling, rooted in his peasant inheritance, for the importance of rhythm, and for the need to allow time for things to come to fruition, is perhaps the deepest source of the remarkable balance and sense of what is possible at a given time which Mao has nearly always displayed in his approach to political and economic problems, and which is expressed most strikingly in his speech of 20 March 1958. On that occasion, even as the Great Leap Forward was gathering momentum, he declared: 'Right now there is a gust of wind, amounting to a force 10 typhoon. We must not impede this publicly, but within our own ranks we must speak clearly, and damp down the atmosphere a little.' More broadly still, he called for the union of 'realism' and 'romanticism', of 'toil' and 'dreams' (Text 4b, pp. 106–7).

This sense of timing, this insistence on combining the two opposites 'haste' and 'moderation', is only one element of Mao's overall vision of the dialectics of development, as it can be apprehended from the documents in this volume. Another and vitally important aspect of the problem is, as already suggested, that of the relations between the two closely linked pairs of opposites, the cities and the countryside, and modern and traditional technologies.

The difference in pattern between the Chinese revolution and the Russian revolution, analysed by so many Western observers, was long ago pointed out by Mao Tse-tung himself. 'In Russia', he recalled in 1956, 'the revolution developed from the cities to the countryside, while in our country it developed from the countryside to the cities' (Text 2, p. 84). Having achieved power, Mao declared in March 1949 that henceforth this relation would be reversed, and the cities would lead the villages.* And yet, he remained strongly marked by the populist mentality inculcated into him by Li Ta-chao, from whom he first learned about revolution in Peking in 1918.

That Mao still bears the imprint of such ideas regarding the moral superiority of the countryside is eloquently demonstrated by his remarks on this theme at the First Plenum of the Ninth Central Committee, in April 1969:

> For years we did not have any such thing as salaries . . . We had only a fixed amount of food, three mace† of oil and five of salt. If we got 1½ catties‡ of millet, that was great. As for vegetables, how could we get vegetables everywhere the army went? Now we have entered the cities. This is a good thing. If we hadn't entered the cities, Chiang Kai-shek would be occupying them. But it is also a bad thing because it caused our Party to deteriorate [Text 25, p. 288].

Statements such as these should not be over-interpreted to

---

* *Selected Works*, Vol. IV, p. 363.
† One tenth of a Chinese ounce.
‡ The Chinese pound, approximately 1⅓ lb. avoirdupois.

make of Mao a backward-looking admirer of pastoral inno-
cence. He is not opposed to progress and economic development, but concerned lest they produce, in China, the negative
effects engendered elsewhere by urbanization and industrialization. Moreover, his overwhelming emphasis on the importance of the countryside is not inspired by mere moralism; it
also reflects the realities of the Chinese situation, both before
and after the conquest of power. Not only was the countryside
the theatre of revolutionary warfare before 1949; it is in the
countryside that the vast majority of China's population con-
tinues to reside, and it is there that the greatest economic, social
and cultural changes must take place if the revolution is to
continue to move forward. Hence Mao's constant insistence that
the younger generation should experience not merely reality,
but *rural* reality.

During the crucial months preceding the outbreak of the Cultural Revolution, Mao Tse-tung returned repeatedly to this
theme. 'I said to my own child,' he declared at Hangchow in
December 1965, 'You go down to the countryside and tell the
poor and lower-middle peasants: "My dad says that after studying a few years we become more and more stupid. Please,
uncles and aunts, brothers and sisters, be my teachers ..."'
(Text 14, p. 236). And in the spring of 1966, he instructed his
nephew Mao Yüan-hsin to tell his political commissar 'that I
said from now on you should go to the countryside once each
year. There are great advantages in this!' (Text 15, p. 252.) To
be sure, he added, at Hangchow, that 'only to go to the countryside' was not enough, and that students should also go to factories, shops, and army companies (Text 14, p. 237). But the
emphasis during the early years of the Cultural Revolution was
on learning from the peasants, rather than from the workers.
This clearly reflects Mao's resolve to struggle not only against
the Confucian prejudice regarding the superiority of mental
over manual workers, but also against the Marxist prejudice
regarding the superiority of the worker over the peasant.

It can fairly be argued that Mao has never completely accepted the Marxist postulate of a sharp qualitative difference
between the political attitudes and capacities of the urban

workers on the one hand, and the peasants, sunk in 'rural idiocy', on the other. Indeed, he went so far in 1926 as to assert that the peasants were more uncompromisingly revolutionary than the workers.* Despite this momentary aberration, he is, of course, a disciple of Marx and Lenin who recognizes, in principle, the necessity for 'proletarian' leadership over the revolution. His conception of the modalities of the relationship between the workers and the peasantry, as it applies both to the political struggle and to the process of modernization and economic development, is, however, vastly different from the notions of strict hierarchical subordination which characterize Leninist thinking and Soviet practice.

To the extent that Mao Tse-tung, as he states repeatedly in these speeches, attaches a high priority to industrialization and economic development, he does attribute a certain primacy to the cities, which are in the last analysis the source of the modern technology indispensable to this process. He does not believe, however, that progress is possible by concentrating on the development of heavy industry in the cities, while largely neglecting the countryside, as has been done in a certain number of Asian countries. In his view, the level of technical knowledge must be raised throughout the whole of society, and above all among the peasant masses, who have hitherto remained largely untouched by such modern influences. Therefore, as he put it in 1949, on the eve of the conquest of power: 'The serious problem is the education of the peasantry.'† But Mao does not see this education, as did Lenin and Stalin, simply in terms of enlightened workers and technicians from the cities ministering to the ignorant and passive inhabitants of the countryside. On the one hand, his whole approach to political work, discussed in the first section of this introduction, makes him see education, and

---

*See his article 'The National Revolution and the Peasant Movement' Chinese text in *Collected Writings of Mao Tse-tung* (Tokyo: Hokubosha, 1972), Vol. I, pp. 175–9. For a discussion of this article and its implications, see my essay 'Mao Zedong and the role of the various classes in the Chinese revolution, 1923–1927', in *The Polity and Economy of China* (Tokyo: Toyo Keizai Shinposha Publishing Company, 1974).
† *Selected Works*, Vol. IV, p. 419.

more broadly the spread of modern knowledge in society, as a reciprocal process requiring the active participation of the learners as well as of the teachers.* On the other hand, he regards the traditional skills of the peasantry as a valuable resource which must also be mobilized, side by side with modern techniques, in an overall economic strategy of 'walking on two legs', or, as he put it more concretely in March 1958, of combining machines and carrying-poles:

> The mass movement for the improvement of agricultural implements must be extended to every single locality. Its significance is very great, it is a sprout of the technical revolution, it is a great revolutionary movement. Several hundreds of millions of peasants are striving mightily to negate the negative aspect of carrying things on a pole over the shoulder. Whenever they succeed in doing this, they reduce the labour force required to a fraction of what it was before; the economies resulting from the replacement of carrying-poles by mechanization greatly increase labour efficiency, and this permits in turn a further step forward in mechanization [Text 4b, pp. 103–4].

Thus, in Mao's view, economic development is a spiral process in which successive increments in material and human resources combine and reinforce one another to produce a continual forward movement. The canvas on which he views economic problems is exceedingly broad, and includes, as already suggested, political mobilization and cultural change as the conditions and concomitants of industrialization. The pairs of opposites which enter into the dialectics of development as he understands it include not only those relating to the pattern and tempo of economic activity, but others, such as the Centre and the regions, or the state and the units of production, which serve to define the degree of grass-roots participation and enthusiasm, as compared to centralized control and discipline, in the overall social effort. Mao included the two points just mentioned

* For a discussion of the patterns by which modern knowledge is spread throughout the Chinese countryside through participation in productive activity, see Jon Sigurdson, 'Rural Industry and the Internal Transfer of Technology', in *Authority, Participation and Cultural Change in China*, pp. 199–232.

among the 'Ten Great Relationships' in April 1956, and characterized them in March 1958 as among the five most important of these relationships (Text 1, p. 62; Text 4a, p. 101). Finally, the picture should be enlarged to include the relation not merely between Chinese and Western technology, but between Chinese and Western ideas and traditions.

If, in the complex interplay of many factors which go to make up the process of development as a whole, Mao refuses to accept the notion that the impetus to progress must always rest primarily with the cities, this attitude is intimately linked to his firm belief that the Chinese need not regard themselves as inferior to foreigners. Here lies the nub of his rebellion not only against Soviet domination, but against the whole Europe-centred logic of Marxism. For Marx, the only salvation for the backward and stagnant societies of Asia lay in what he called 'Europeanization'.* Similar premises have informed the thinking of the Russian communists about the Orient, from Lenin to the present day. This does not mean, of course, that Marx and Lenin were racists – their view that Europeans must show Asians 'how it is done' was based partly on the fact that only Europe (and its extension in North America) possessed a working class which could lead the revolution, and partly on the conviction that only European culture could supply the Promethean thrust that would enable non-European countries to develop their economies and thereby acquire a proletariat of their own. Hence the conclusion that the world revolution must be led from Europe – which has meant, since 1917, from Moscow. Unfortunately, it is only a step from this interim practical conclusion to a belief in the ingrained inferiority of Asia to Europe – a step which Mao, at least, is persuaded that Lenin's successors have already taken. The Russians, he said to Edgar Snow in December 1970, 'looked down on the Chinese and also looked down on the people of many other countries'.† Needless

---

* For a discussion of Marx's ideas regarding Asian society, and some of the essential texts, see H. Carrère d'Encausse and S. Schram, *Marxism and Asia* (Allen Lane, 1969), pp. 7–16 and 115–33. The reference to 'Europeanization' occurs on p. 116.
† *The Long Revolution*, p. 175.

to say, he does not accept either the premise about the inferiority of Asian culture, or the practical conclusions which flow from it.

Mao is by no means unaware of China's economic backwardness, and of the enormous problems involved in changing this condition. 'Whenever we talk about it,' he declared in January 1958, 'we say that our country has such an enormous population, it has such a vast territory, abundant resources, so many people, four thousand years of history and culture . . . We have bragged so much about this, yet we cannot compare with a country like Belgium.'

And yet he is persuaded that the drive and talent of the Chinese people are such that these weaknesses can be overcome. 'Ours is an ardent nation, now swept by a burning tide,' he continued in 1958. 'There is a good metaphor for this: our nation is like an atom . . . When this atom's nucleus is smashed the thermal energy released will have really tremendous power. We shall be able to do things which we could not do before . . . We shall produce forty million tons of steel annually . . .' (Text 3, pp. 92–3).

It is, of course, not merely a matter of raising China's economic level – though this is important to Mao. It is equally a question of affirming China's national dignity, particularly in the face of the Soviets. This is one point on which Mao's stance has never varied, however much he may have changed his position on questions of tactics.

In March 1958, while stressing that China should be on friendly terms with the Soviet Union, and with the communist parties and working classes of all countries, and should 'learn from the good points of the Soviet Union and other foreign countries', he added: 'There are two methods of learning: one is merely to imitate, and the other is to apply the creative spirit. Learning should be combined with creativity. To import Soviet codes and conventions inflexibly is to lack the creative spirit' (Text 4a, p. 96).

By January 1962 he was proposing to overtake the most advanced capitalist countries, not in fifteen years as he had said in 1958, but in fifty or a hundred years (Text 8, p. 175). Precisely in such a context of retreat from overly ambitious objectives, he insisted overwhelmingly not only on the correctness of the basic policies followed since the Great Leap of 1958, but on the originality of the Chinese road to socialism. In the early years of the Chinese People's Republic, he declared,

the situation was such that, since we had no experience in economic construction, we had no alternative but to copy the Soviet Union . . . At that time it was absolutely necessary to act thus, but at the same time it was also a weakness – a lack of creativity and a lack of ability to stand on our own feet. Naturally this could not be our long-term strategy [Text 8, p. 178].

The same point regarding the need to 'smash conventions' rather than 'crawling step by step behind others' and thus show that China is the equal of the West is made in a brief but eloquent statement of 1964 (Text 12).

Despite some passing aberrations in the early stages of the Cultural Revolution, the assertion of China's originality does not, for Mao, imply either xenophobia or isolation. Repeatedly, throughout the texts translated here, he insists on the importance of learning from foreign countries, and of not adopting a parochial attitude. Foreign things must, however, be transformed in such a way as to fit Chinese conditions and serve Chinese needs, and this could be done only if the Chinese divested themselves of the inferiority complex which was the obverse of the traditional attitude of arrogant superiority. (See Text 1, pp. 82–3).

Though this general position has remained constant in the course of the past two decades, and is consistent with that adopted earlier by Mao at the Yenan Forum on Art and Literature of 1942 and elsewhere, there has been a shift of emphasis clearly reflected in this anthology. Perhaps the most striking expression of this is to be found in the contrasting treatment of the so-called 't'i-yung rationalization' in the 1950s and in the 1960s. This formula, first put forward at the end of the nineteenth century by the conservative modernizer Chang Chihtung, implied that borrowing from the West should be limited to techniques, while the Chinese 'essence' should be safeguarded. Quoting it in August 1956, in a talk to music workers, Mao said:

> Some people advocate 'Chinese learning as the substance, Western learning for practical application'. Is this idea right or wrong? It is wrong. The word 'learning' in fact refers to fundamental theory ... Marxism is a fundamental theory which was produced in the West. How then can we make a distinction between what is Chinese and what is Western in this respect? [Text 2, pp. 85–6].

This statement should not be interpreted too starkly as a plea for the wholesale and uncritical importing of Marxist theory as elaborated in the West or in the Soviet Union. As early as 1938, Mao Tse-tung had called for the 'Sinification of Marxism', and the speeches contained in this book are studded, as already noted, with denunciations of copy-book imitation of Soviet ideas and methods. Moreover, in his talk to music workers Mao went on to denounce 'complete Westernization' as unacceptable to the common people of China, and to declare that the reason for learning foreign things was 'to study and develop Chinese things'. Nevertheless, it was implied in the passage quoted above that the universal essence of Marxism somehow transcended its adaptation to the conditions and culture of each nation.

In the 1960s, in the context of the widening Sino–Soviet split and of the emergence of a distinctive 'Chinese road to socialism', the Chinese, and Mao in particular, came to adopt a more positive attitude towards many aspects of their traditional culture. Perhaps the most striking illustration of this in the present volume is to be found in the critical, but in many respects sympathetic, view of Confucius taken by Mao in remarks of February and August 1964. He is described as of poor peasant origins, and as having been originally close to the masses; and though the judgement on his philosophy is mixed, Mao suggests that there were many democratic elements in it, especially in the context of the times, and that many of the vices of the Confucian tradition are the result of the use to which Confucius' writings were subsequently put (Text 10, pp. 208, 210; Text 11, p. 214).

Thus, when Mao came to refer once more, in his Hangchow speech of December 1965, to the '*t'i-yung* formula', he stood his view of 1956 exactly on its head:

At the end of the Ch'ing Dynasty some people advocated 'Chinese learning for the substance, Western learning for practical application'. The substance was like our General Line, which cannot be changed. We cannot adopt Western learning as the substance, nor can we use the substance of the democratic republic. We cannot use 'the natural rights of man' nor 'the theory of evolution'. We can only use Western technology [Text 14, pp. 234–5].

This volte-face reflects, of course, a change in Mao's evaluation of that particular form of Western learning known as Marxism. By 1965, this no longer constituted a universal and immutable 'fundamental theory', but merely one more contribution from the West which must be digested critically and made to serve China.

Foreign relations: opposing imperialism and
social-imperialism

These speeches offer new and vivid insights into Mao's thinking on various aspects of foreign policy during the period 1956–69. The most crucial single problem in this domain is no doubt that of relations with the Soviet Union, since Mao's conception of the 'socialist camp' was a major element in his view of the international situation as a whole. Here the change was dramatic indeed during these thirteen years. In April 1956, while warning against copying foreign experience mechanically, Mao took pains to stress that victory in the Chinese revolution had come more than thirty years after the October Revolution, so that China was backward as compared to the Soviet Union, though ahead of 'some colonial countries' (Text 1, pp. 82–3). In April 1969, in his address to the First Plenum of the new Central Committee, he dismissed the Soviet Union in one contemptuous paragraph, concluding: '. . . they label us a "party of the petit-bourgeoisie". We . . . say that they are a bourgeois dictatorship, and are restoring the dictatorship of the bourgeoisie' (Text 25, p. 282).

The evolution of Sino–Soviet relations between these two dates is far too complex a phenomenon to be analysed here in its entirety, and is not fully documented in the texts contained in this volume. These Mao speeches do, however, cast some extremely revealing light on the problem. It is worth pointing out, first of all, that as late as March 1958 Mao hailed Khrushchev as an exemplar of those vigorous elements from the provinces who emerge from time to time to strengthen the leadership at the Centre (Text 4c, p. 114). While too much weight should not be given to this passing reference, it does tend to confirm that Mao's real disillusion with his Soviet comrades dates only from the middle of 1958, and not from de-Stalinization in 1956, though he undoubtedly had reservations about the way that operation was carried out.

Mao himself has indicated, in the speeches published here, the ambiguity of the Chinese reaction to Khrushchev's initiative at the Twentieth Congress. The most explicit statement on this theme is contained in his speech of 10 March 1958, in which he said:

When Stalin was criticized in 1956, we were on the one hand happy, but on the other hand apprehensive. It was completely necessary to remove the lid, to break down blind faith, to release the pressure, and to emancipate thought. But we did not agree with demolishing him at one blow [Text 4a, p. 101].

Mao was happy at the downgrading of Stalin, both because the Chinese revolution had suffered from the Soviet leader's errors of judgement, and because he himself had been obliged to bow to Stalin's dictates, and had been slighted in comparison to him. Stalin, Mao complains repeatedly, tried to prevent the Chinese from carrying the revolution forward in 1945, and regarded their revolution as a 'fake' and Mao as a potential Tito when it did succeed. (Speech of 10 March 1958, Text 4a, p. 103; speech of September 1962, Text 9, p. 191.) Even in China moreover, Stalin loomed symbolically larger than Mao:

Buddhas are made several times life-size in order to frighten people. When heroes and warriors appear on the stage they are made to look quite unlike ordinary people. Stalin was that kind of person. The Chinese people had got so used to being slaves that they seemed to want to go on. When Chinese artists painted pictures of me together with Stalin, they always made me a little bit shorter, thus blindly knuckling under to the moral pressure exerted by the Soviet Union at that time [Text 4a, p. 99].

In a lighter vein, Mao protested that he 'couldn't have eggs or chicken soup for three years because an article appeared in the Soviet Union which said that one shouldn't eat them', though later they said one could. 'It didn't matter whether the article was correct or not, the Chinese listened all the same and respectfully obeyed' (Text 4a, p. 98). Despite his resentment at Soviet political, economic, and cultural domination in the early years of the Chinese People's Republic, Mao was 'apprehensive' when Khrushchev 'demolished Stalin at one blow', not only because of the implications of this gesture for the re-evaluation of other leaders (himself included), but because he feared that the attack on the abuses of Stalinism might open the door to the repudiation of aspects of the Soviet past which he regarded as worthy of respect and emulation. He said in March 1958:

There are two kinds of cult of the individual. One is correct, such as that of Marx, Engels, Lenin, and the correct side of Stalin. These we ought to revere and continue to revere for ever . . . As they held the truth in their hands, why should we not revere them? . . . A squad should revere its squad leader; it would be quite wrong not to. Then there is the incorrect kind of cult of the individual in which there is no analysis, simply blind obedience. This is not right [Text 4a, p. 99].

Though he did not altogether approve of de-Stalinization, Mao Tse-tung took advantage of the blow which Khrushchev had thus struck against the ideological infallibility of the Soviet leadership to assert more and more strongly the pre-eminence of his own thought within the world communist movement. As early as the meeting of the Military Affairs Committee in June and July 1958, Mao, echoed by Lin Piao, stressed the superiority of Chinese military experience and of Chinese military theory over that of the Soviets (Text 5, pp. 128–30). By the summer of

1959, during and immediately after the Lushan Plenum, he was denouncing Soviet meddling in the internal affairs of the Chinese Communist Party, particularly their criticism of the people's communes and their support for P'eng Te-huai's opposition to the policies of the 'Great Leap Forward'.* By January 1962, in his 7,000 cadres speech, Mao was ready to state explicitly (though not for open publication) that the Party and state leadership of the Soviet Union had been 'usurped by revisionists', and by implication to call on the people of the Soviet Union to rise up and overthrow these renegades.†

Not only had the solidarity between 'fraternal parties' thus come to an end, but even state-to-state relations had little appeal for Mao. The Soviets, he said in February 1964, wanted to expand commercial relations between the two countries. 'We can do a little business,' he commented, 'but we can't do too much, for Soviet products are heavy, crude, high-priced, and they always keep something back' – in other words, they failed to reveal to the Chinese all the technical secrets of their equipment, in order to keep them in the state of tutelage to the experts from Moscow which Mao had come so deeply to resent. It was therefore better, Mao concluded, to deal with the French bourgeoisie, 'who still have some notion of business ethics' (Text 10, pp. 198–9).

As for France, Mao believed that de Gaulle's decision to establish diplomatic relations with China, and more generally his 'opposition to the United States', had been dictated by the French capitalists (Text 10, p. 198).

There is a great deal less in these speeches about relations with the imperialists, and in particular with the American imperialists, than there is concerning the Soviet Union – not surprisingly, in view of the virtual immobility of Sino–American relations during the period covered. Nevertheless, it is possible

---

*This volume includes only two of Mao's speeches at this time (Texts 6 and 7); the Soviet Union is referred to on pp. 145 and 151. For a much more extensive documentary record of this episode see *The Case of Peng Teh-huai 1959–1968* (Hong Kong: Union Research Institute, 1968).

† This paragraph (Text 8, p. 181) was officially published in November 1967; see *Peking Review*, No. 46 (1967), p. 16.

to discern the outlines of Mao's position, which is naturally the converse of his attitude towards Moscow. In April 1956, Mao called on the Chinese to develop 'the spirit of looking with contempt on the [American] imperialists' which had been manifested in the Korean War (Text 1, p. 82). By April 1969, as already noted, his contempt was directed rather against the Soviets. In June 1958, speaking to the Military Affairs Committee, he continued to refer to America, possibly supported by Japan, as China's principal enemy (Text 5, p. 128). In September 1959, addressing the same body, he showed himself more concerned at Soviet meddling in Chinese affairs (Text 7, pp. 151–2). In September 1962, at the Tenth Plenum, he still saw imperialism as the main enemy, but significantly defined the contradiction between 'the people of the whole world and imperialism' as the primary one. The contradiction 'between socialism and imperialism' came only at the end of a long list, well after 'the contradictions between the people of all countries and revisionism' (Text 9, p. 192). In his 7,000 cadres speech of January 1962, Mao had reaffirmed that 'whenever possible' China wanted to establish diplomatic relations with 'the anti-communist, anti-popular imperialists and reactionaries of various countries', and 'strive to have peaceful coexistence with them on the basis of the five principles', though these matters were 'in a different category' from that of 'uniting with the people of all countries' (Text 8, p. 182).

Thus, by 1962, Mao had already begun the transition from the view of a world polarized into two blocs, with China as a member of the 'socialist camp', to one in which the peoples of the world, including the Chinese people, were confronted with the twin dangers of imperialism and 'social-imperialism'. The latter term did not come into use until after the invasion of Czechoslovakia and the proclamation of the Brezhnev Doctrine in 1968, and in 1966 Mao listed the 'American imperialists' before the 'Soviet revisionists' as opponents of the Cultural Revolution (Text 16, pp. 253–4). Nevertheless, by 1962 the trend was clear.

The new perspective in which Mao had by then come to envisage foreign affairs also comes through most eloquently in his remarks at the Tenth Plenum about the situation in other non-European countries. He had, he acknowledged, been pessimistic on this score in 1949, but events had proved him wrong. On the contrary, 'since the Second World War thriving national liberation struggles have developed in Asia, Africa and Latin America year by year'. Needless to say, Mao hailed the 'very good struggle' in Vietnam, and the victory of armed struggle in other countries such as Algeria. His main concern, however, was not so much with the revolutionary character of a given régime as with its attitude towards imperialism. Egypt and Iraq, he said, 'are to the right of centre, but both oppose imperialism' (Text 9, pp. 191–2). This criterion would, of course, be replaced today by that of opposition to 'imperialism and social-imperialism' – in other words, of opposition to great-power intervention in the affairs of smaller countries.

Of fundamental significance, finally, is the clear-cut affirmation, in April 1969, that China's policy is a defensive one. 'Others may come and attack us, but we shall not fight outside our borders ... I say we will not be provoked. Even if you invite us to come out we will not come out, but if you should come and attack us we will deal with you.' (Text 25, pp. 285–6.) This statement, wholly in harmony with what Mao had told Edgar Snow in January 1965,* specifically in the context of the escalation of the Vietnam War, clearly corresponds to the practice of Chinese diplomacy in recent years, and confirms that it was Mao, rather than Liu Shao-ch'i, who adopted a prudent stance in Indochina.

Continuity and change, 1956–71

The speeches in this volume can, as suggested earlier, be read not only as an addition to the corpus of Mao Tse-tung's theoretical writings, but as a running commentary on events in China and the world, from de-Stalinization to the fall of Lin Piao, as seen by Mao. It is, of course, only in this context that ideological formulations, such as those singled out above, can be properly understood.

* *The Long Revolution*, pp. 215–16.

The texts included here do not add up to a connected account of the history of the period 1956–71, but they do reflect the shift from year to year in Mao's main concerns. The speeches of 1956 and of early 1958 are dominated by cultural and economic problems. The first item, the speech of April 1956 'On the Ten Great Relationships' (Text 1), states some of Mao's most basic convictions in both these domains. The paragraph on the seventh relationship, that between Party and non-Party people, contains a call for the 'long-term coexistence and mutual supervision' which was one of the slogans of the 'Hundred Flowers' policy initiated in the spring of 1956. Mao is known to have made another speech, on 2 May 1956, specifically on this theme, of which the text has never become available abroad; the definitive statement of his ideas as to how criticism of Party policy and the advocacy of heterodox ideas should be encouraged and at the same time kept within reasonable limits was given the following February in his speech 'On the Correct Handling of Contradictions among People'.* As for economic policy, most of the main themes of the 'Great Leap Forward' which Mao promoted in 1958 are to be found in his speech of 1956 'On the Ten Great Relationships'. Mao himself characterized this, in March 1958, as his first attempt at proposing a line for building socialism distinct from that of the Soviet Union (Text 4a, p. 101). It should be read in conjunction with his speech of July 1955 on the formation of cooperatives,† and with the directive of January 1958 already mentioned,‡ as well as with the speeches of 1958 included here.

By 1959, as the Great Leap began to run into difficulties, Mao's utterances on economic problems took on a more defensive tone. Whereas in January 1958 (Text 3) he had boldly and confidently sketched out a programme and called for its

---

* For the text as published in June 1957, with revisions dictated by the snow-balling of criticism during the ensuing months, see *Selected Readings from the Works of Mao Tse-tung* (Peking: Foreign Languages Press, 1967), pp. 350–87. The full original text as presented on 27 February 1957 is not available, though summaries have appeared.

† *Selected Readings*, pp. 316–40.

‡ *Current Background*, No. 892 (21 October 1969), pp. 1–14, or Jerome Ch'en, *Mao Papers* (Oxford University Press, 1968), pp. 57–76.

rapid implementation, his speech of July 1959 at Lushan (Text 6) appears rather as an attempt to vindicate his approach to development against criticisms by comrades, and against his own doubts. At roughly the same time, summing up after the confrontation at Lushan had ended in the disgrace of his bluntest critic, P'eng Te-huai, Mao sharply condemned Soviet meddling in the internal affairs of the Chinese Communist Party (Text 7). These two themes of resisting Soviet pressure and upholding the basic correctness of his economic philosophy, while admitting errors in its application, clearly remained constantly in his mind during the next few years. Both found their culmination in the 7,000 cadres speech of January 1962. (They were, of course, intimately related, since the harshest attacks on Mao's unorthodox methods for building socialism had come from the Soviets.)

In the sphere of Sino–Soviet relations, the 7,000 cadres speech was the occasion, as already noted, on which Mao first called in effect for the overthrow of the 'revisionist' leadership in Moscow. In discussing China's internal affairs, Mao went to great lengths in his self-criticism, saying that 'any mistakes the Centre had made' ought to be his responsibility (Text 8, p. 167). But at the same time he held to the view that the path taken in 1958, with its emphasis on the importance of small-scale industry and of creative initiatives at the grass roots, was basically correct and should be pursued. It was at the 7,000 cadres conference that the conflict between Mao Tse-tung and Liu Shao-ch'i first began to come to a head, though in Mao's view it did not become irreconcilable until three years later.* During this crucial period, Liu, while paying lip-service to the correctness of the 'Great Leap' line, in fact took the lead in moving China closer to a more orthodox pattern of socialist development, based on centralized planning, priority to heavy industry, and material incentives. Mao, for his part, shifted his attention to a certain extent from economic affairs as such to the political and cultural problems of combating bureaucracy and bringing up revolutionary successors by suitable educational

*For a sketch of the emergence of these differences, see *Authority, Participation and Cultural Change in China*, pp. 61–85.

methods (Texts 10–15). He objected to the substance of the economic policies promoted by Liu and the Party bureaucrats, such as the weakening of collective control over agricultural production in the communes, accounting on the basis of the individual household, and increased scope for the profit motive,* but he was even more deeply concerned about what he saw as a deterioration of the moral and political climate of Chinese society. Corruption, he complained in August 1964, had attained such proportions that 'you can buy a Party branch secretary for a few packs of cigarettes, not to mention marrying a daughter to him' (Text 11, p. 217).

The reason for the proliferation of such undesirable tendencies lay, in Mao's view, in the failure to recognize the continuing importance of class struggle in a socialist society. The philosophical theories of Yang Hsien-chen, to the effect that 'two combine into one', appeared to Mao as the ideological expression of the prevailing political climate of class compromise; hence the bitterness of his references to these doctrines, to which he opposed the view that 'one divides into two', i.e. that reactionary and erroneous tendencies constantly emerge within society and within the Party, and must be combated (Text 11, pp. 217, 224–5). Mao's effort to reassert the importance of class struggle, launched at the Tenth Plenum in September 1962 (Text 9), took the form of the 'Socialist Education Movement' of 1963–5; the principal political force on which he relied to promote this policy, despite the reluctance of the Party bureaucracy, was the People's Liberation Army.

There is little in this volume (and relatively little in any of the available materials) about Mao's involvement in Lin Piao's effort, beginning in 1960, to turn the People's Liberation Army

---

*Virtually the only reference in this volume to Mao's views on the organization of the economy in the 1960s is contained in his talks on philosophy of August 1964 (Text 11, p. 216). The large collection of materials which only became available to scholars outside China in the summer of 1973, and which is described in detail in the 'Note on the Texts' which follows this introduction, does contain items on Mao's economic views at this time. See, in particular, his talk of 28 December 1964 at a central work conference (*Wan-sui* (1969), pp. 598–602), as well as his detailed comments on a Soviet manual of political economy (ibid., pp. 319–99).

into a 'great school of Mao Tse-tung's thought'.* The most extended comments on the campaign of 1964 to learn from the army are contained in Mao's talks with his nephew Mao Yüan-hsin, in which he also deals most bluntly and explicitly with the problem of bringing up successors to the revolutionary cause, and with his doubts about the younger generation (Text 15).

Even with the beginning of the Cultural Revolution, the number of references to the military in Mao's speeches does not increase in proportion to the PLA's real importance in these events. Mao was, of course, more aware than anyone that he had only been able to maintain control of the situation thanks to the support of Lin Piao and the army, but he professed to be quite unperturbed by the charge that as a result a fundamental change had occurred in the character of the Chinese régime. Indeed, at the First Plenum of the Ninth Central Committee, in April 1969, he treated the matter in a humorous vein:

> The Soviet revisionists . . . say it is a military–bureaucratic system . . . When they see that there are many military men in our lists of personnel they call us 'military'. As for the 'bureaucratic' part, I suppose they mean the batch of 'bureaucrats' comprising me, [Chou] En-lai, K'ang Sheng and Ch'en Po-ta. In a word, those of you who are not military are all supposed to belong to a bureaucratic network, and we are collectively called a 'military–bureaucratic dictatorship' [Text 25, p. 282].

According to a letter from Mao Tse-tung to Chiang Ch'ing, dated 8 July 1966 and circulated within the Chinese Communist Party in 1972, in the context of the effort to explain the origins of the conflict between Mao and Lin Piao, he had been suspicious, from the very beginning of the Cultural Revolution, of the methods and intentions of his chosen successor, and had failed to speak out on the subject only because he needed Lin's

---

*See, however, the resolution of 20 October 1960, now criticized for its vulgarization and distortion of Mao's thought, but described at the time as having been revised and approved by Mao. *The Politics of the Chinese Red Army*: a translation of the *Bulletin of Activities* of the People's Liberation Army (Stanford: Hoover Institution, 1966), pp. 65–94. The fact that Mao had revised the draft is stated on p. 33 of the same volume.

support against Liu Shao-ch'i and his adversaries in the Party.*
In any case, a little over a year after he had dismissed as a joke
the notion of military predominance within the Chinese Communist Party, at the Second Plenum of the Ninth Central Committee in the autumn of 1970, the tensions between Mao and
Lin culminated in a sharp, though muted, confrontation. A year
later, Lin Piao was dead, and shortly thereafter the man who
had been acclaimed at the Ninth Party Congress of April 1969
as Mao Tse-tung's 'closest comrade-in-arms' was denounced as
his would-be assassin.

The official Chinese account of these events has now been
made public in the wake of the Tenth Congress of the Chinese
Communist Party.† It closely parallels the version which had
been given privately to foreign visitors by Mao himself and
other authorized spokesmen since mid-1972, and which was
known to be circulating within the Party. The last item in this
anthology (Text 26) contains a summary of the explanation
which Mao gave of divergences within the Party in August and
September 1971, a few weeks prior to Lin Piao's demise. I do
not have access to any information which would enable me to
determine whether this document contains the truth, or the
whole truth, regarding Mao's relations with Lin Piao and with
his former close literary collaborator Ch'en Po-ta. I have included it here so that the reader can compare it with the speeches
at the Tenth Party Congress, and draw his own conclusions. It is
also of considerable interest because it contains Mao's most
recent discussion of the conflicts of line which have arisen in the
Chinese Communist Party since its foundation in 1921, as well
as a passage deprecating Lin Piao's praise of the Chairman as a
'genius' which complements Mao's discussion, in his last interview with Edgar Snow, of the uses and misuses of his own
cult.‡

Is there anything constant in the man who stood, and stands,

*Chinese text in *Hsing-tao jih-pao* (Hong Kong), 4 November 1972. English
translation in *Issues and Studies*, IX (4), pp. 94–6.
†See, in particular, the speech of Chou En-lai, together with the other
materials in *Peking Review*, No. 35–36 (1973).
‡*The Long Revolution*, pp. 168-70.

at the centre of this shifting scene, apart from a forceful character and a genius for earthy metaphor? I have tried, in the course of this introduction, to suggest that there is. Perhaps the essential points can be summed up at the end in two contradictions. On the one hand, there is the tension between Mao's genuine concern for mass participation, and his strong feeling for the importance of organization, reinforced at times by the conviction that he alone is right. Secondly there is the contradiction between Mao's pride in China's past, and his resolve to re-shape Chinese society and culture into new, revolutionary patterns. Calling on his fellow-countrymen to 'look on the mighty with contempt', as during the Korean War, he cited Mencius as his authority (Text 1). Democracy and centralism, Marxism and the Chinese heritage – which, as Mao would put it, is the 'principal aspect' of these contradictions? It must be for the reader to judge. The texts making up this anthology do not provide any tidy answers, but they will perhaps help to combat false and oversimplified notions of whatever nature, by highlighting some new facets in the personality of the man who incarnates these contradictions.

STUART SCHRAM

Note on the texts

This book, as indicated in the Introduction, is composed of speeches and writings which have not been officially published in China, but are available in so-called 'Red Guard publications'*, or in other sources which reproduce materials circulating within the Chinese Communist Party. Details regarding the source or sources used for each text, and regarding other available translations, are given below. First, however, it is necessary to say a word about the problem of authenticity, which is in reality a dual problem: Are the documents employed authentic materials disseminated in China? Even if they are, can the texts of Mao's utterances they contain be regarded as necessarily accurate?

The former question is the easier to answer. 'Red Guard' newspapers and other such materials *were* forged, in Hong Kong and elsewhere, in the course of the Cultural Revolution, but such spurious documents are relatively few in number, and on the whole easily recognized. The overwhelming majority of the 'Red Guard' materials now available in libraries and research centres outside China were indeed produced, in the years 1966–9, within the Chinese People's Republic. I am convinced that the materials translated here are, in this sense, authentic. This judgement rests partly on points of style and presentation that stamp the books and periodicals containing these Mao speeches

*For simplicity's sake, the term 'Red Guard publications' is used here to designate documents printed and distributed without official sanction not only by the Red Guards properly so called, but also by other 'rebel' organizations, in the course of the Cultural Revolution.

as genuine, and partly on evidence internal to the Mao texts themselves.

It should be stressed that 'genuine' does not necessarily mean wholly accurate. Even in the case of pre-Cultural Revolution speeches, of which there apparently exists a single official record, generally based on a tape recording, to which the Red Guard editors obtained access, there are small variants presumably resulting from typographical or copyists' errors in successive reproductions. Moreover, some such texts contain a note stating that they have not been checked by the speaker. (See, for example, Text 2 in this anthology.) For speeches made during the Cultural Revolution, the situation is even less satisfactory, since there are often several different records extant, made by members of the audience who were not trained stenographers, and who sometimes mistook one homonym for another. Nevertheless, the judgement that these texts are substantially accurate is borne out in at least three ways: by consistency among independently edited versions in several different collections of materials, by the publication in the official press of brief extracts from the speeches translated here, and by the testimony, in certain cases, of persons who read or heard the speeches in China. On all of these grounds, I believe the authenticity of these materials to be adequately established. There is, finally, another argument, which will perhaps not appear altogether frivolous to the reader once he has savoured some of these speeches: in their scope, pungency, and verve, they are beyond the powers of any forger to invent.

The foregoing comments regarding the substance of these speeches and writings by Mao Tse-tung apply to all the texts included in this volume. There are, however, two of the sources employed which, by their form and/or provenance, require a further word of explanation. The first twenty-three texts were originally taken from xerox copies of 'Red Guard' publications, and it was therefore possible to form the kind of judgement regarding the presentation of the document as a whole to which I referred above. The remaining three have been taken from a periodical devoted to Chinese communist affairs published in Taipei. This might appear to render them suspect, but in fact the organizations on Taiwan involved in research on these problems, while free in their speculations regarding events in China, have been exceedingly prudent in reproducing documents, and those they have made available have often been subsequently proved to be authentic. Moreover, the style of these three speeches of 1969 and 1971 gives us every reason to believe that they are genuine, and the substance of Mao's account of his relations with Lin Piao in Text 26 is corroborated to a considerable extent by his statements to Western diplomats, and by the official interpretation of these events put forward in August 1973 at the Tenth Congress of the Chinese Communist Party. I therefore have no hesitation about including them.

The other source different from those originally used in compiling this volume likewise comes from Taiwan, but is considerably more remarkable in character. It is a printed book, reproduced by photo-offset from a volume ostensibly published in the Chinese People's Republic, with a preface dated August 1969. The fact that this source was available in Taiwan first became known when the Institute of International Affairs in Taipei began translating items from it, in the spring of 1973, in its English-language periodical *Issues and Studies*. Subsequently, the Institute of International Affairs has made copies of this book, and of another, smaller volume dated 1967, both bearing the title *Mao Tse-tung ssu-hsiang wan-sui!* (*Long Live Mao Tse-tung Thought!*), to libraries and individuals in the West. The surprise that might be occasioned by their taking the trouble to reproduce the books, not by xeroxing but in actual printed form, is largely pushed into the background by surprise at the scope of the collection. The present anthology, as originally planned, included approximately 60,000 words of Mao's speeches, in English translation, amounting to a substantial fraction – probably over half – of all the texts, from all known 'Red Guard' sources, available for the period since the mid-1950s. These two collections total (or would total, in translation) approximately half a million words, or four to five times the amount of material hitherto not officially published which is available from all other sources combined.

Their sudden appearance, at a time when the manuscript of

this book was already in the hands of the printer, raised two obvious problems. The first was the recurrent issue of authenticity. Amazing as it seemed to be confronted with such a mass of additional documentation, an examination of the volumes creates a strong presumption that the contents are genuine. To begin with, they contain a significant number of items (including several in this book) which *are* available from other sources, and in nearly all such cases the text proves to be either substantially identical with that to be found elsewhere, or more complete and accurate. Secondly, a great many of the new items project an image of Mao which must be regarded as generally favourable, and it seems absurd to assume that forgers would have been hired by the Nationalists to work for several years to produce a result which would redound to the credit of their adversary. Finally, the sheer size of the volumes is a strong argument in favour of their authenticity, for even if their contents might, in some way, be seen in Taipei as discreditable or embarrassing to Mao, there would have been no need to go to the trouble of producing a document of this length in order to make the point – 100,000 words of new material would have been quite sufficient.

Assuming that these new materials were genuine, it remained to be decided what to do about it. Not only was the manuscript of this book already with the printer, but I had quoted extensively from the materials included here in the introduction to a volume scheduled for publication in September 1973 (*Authority, Participation and Cultural Change in China*. Essays by a European Study Group, Cambridge University Press). Under the circumstances, the best solution appeared to lie in a compromise. Fuller versions of items already included in this anthology (Texts 10, 11 and 15), and additional speeches before the same forum (Text 4, speeches of 10 and 20 March 1958 at the Chengtu Conference, which now precede the speech of 22 March) have been drawn from the volume reprinted in Taiwan, but no wholly new items have been included, and the numbering of texts has not been changed.* Thus the character of the

---

*There is one small exception: because of a change in the dating of two items, Mao's philosophical conversations with K'ang Sheng and Ch'en Po-ta

book as a relatively brief, readable anthology has not been changed, but approximately 20,000 words of new material, shedding further light on some aspects of Mao Tse-tung's thinking, have been added.

Below is a list of sources and available translations for each of the items included in this volume. In each case, the source on which we have principally relied is given first, followed by other versions. The titles of five collections of Mao's writings frequently cited, and of five important series of translations, have been abbreviated as follows:

TITLE AND PUBLICATION DATA	ABBREVIATION
(a) Chinese sources:	
Mao Tse-tung s su-hsiang wan-sui! (n.p., April 1967)	*Wan-sui !*
Untitled collection, appended to the previous item in the only known copy	*Wan-sui* (suppt.)
Mao Tse-tung ssu-hsiang wan-sui! (n.p., preface dated August 1969) (i.e. principal Taiwan reprint discussed above)	*Wan-sui* (1969)
Mao Tse-tung ssu-hsiang wan-sui! (n.p., 1967) (Taiwan reprint)	*Wan-sui* (1967)
Mao Chu-hsi wen-hsüan (n.p., n.d.)	*Wen-hsüan*
Mao Chu-hsi tui P'eng, Huang, Chang, Chou fan-tang chi-t'uan ti p'i-p'an	*Tui P'eng*
(b) Collections of translations:	
Current Background (US Consulate General, Hong Kong)	CB, followed by issue no.
Joint Publications Research Service (Washington, D.C.) sub-series *Translations on Communist China*	JPRS, followed by issue no.
Jerome Ch'en, *Mao* (Englewood Cliffs, N.J.: Prentice Hall, 1969)	Ch'en, *Mao*
Jerome Ch'en, *Mao Papers*. Anthology and Bibliography (Oxford University Press, 1970)	Ch'en, *Mao Papers*
Chinese Law and Government (White Plains, New York)	CLG, followed by volume and issue no.

---

have now become Text 11, instead of Text 14; Texts 12 and 13, cited as such in my other book just published, have become respectively 13 and 14 and the original Text 11 has become Text 12.

SELECTIVE LIST OF SOURCES AND TRANSLATIONS

Text no.	Principal source	Other sources	Translations
1	*Wan-sui* (suppt.), pp. 19–28	*Wan-sui* (1969), pp. 40–59	Ch'en, *Mao*, pp. 65–85 CB 892, pp. 21–34
2	*Mao Tse-tung ti ko-ming wen-i lu-hsien sheng-li wan-sui!* (Peking, July 1967)		none
3	*Tui P'eng*, pp. 1–3		CLG I (4), pp. 10–14
4	*Wan-sui* (1969), pp. 159–80	*Wen-hsüan*, pp. 78–83 (third speech only)	JPRS 90, pp. 45–52 (third speech only)
5	*Tui P'eng*, pp. 3–5		CLG I (4), pp. 15–21
6	*Tui P'eng*, pp. 6–11	*Wan-sui* (1969), pp. 294–304 and *Wan-sui* (1967), pp. 67–71, 270–76	CLG I (4), pp. 27–43
7	*Tui P'eng*, pp. 22–4, followed by *Wan-sui* (1967), pp. 97–101	*Wan-sui* (1969), pp. 312–15	CLG I (4), pp. 79–84
8	*Wen-hsüan*, pp. 64–78	*Wan-sui* (1969), pp. 399–423	JPRS 109, pp. 39–58
9	*Tui P'eng*, pp. 24–7	*Wan-sui* (1969), pp. 430–36	CLG I (4), pp. 85–93
10	*Wan-sui* (1969), pp. 455–65	*Wan-sui*, pp. 26–8	CB 891, pp. 42–4 Ch'en, *Mao Papers*, pp. 93–7
11	*Tui P'eng*, p. 27		CLG I (4), pp. 94–5
12	*Wan-sui* (1969), pp. 548–61	*Wen-hsüan*, pp. 40–42	JPRS 90, pp. 26–8
13	*Wan-sui* (suppt.), p. 9	*Wan-sui* (1969), pp. 615–16	JPRS 90, p. 24
14	*Wan-sui*, pp. 31–4	*Wan-sui* (1969), pp. 624–9 *Wen-hsüan*, pp. 36–40	CB 891, pp. 51–5 Ch'en, *Mao*, pp. 103–11

15	Wan-sui (1969), pp. 465–71 (for the first talk) Wen-hsüan, pp. 42–3 (for the second and third talks)	Wan-sui (1969), pp. 631–2 (for second talk only)	JPRS 90, pp. 29–30 (second and third talks only)
16	Wan-sui, pp. 36–7	Wan-sui (1969), pp. 648–50 Wen-hsüan, pp. 44–5	CB 891, pp. 58–9 Ch'en, Mao Papers, pp. 24–6
17	Wan-sui, pp. 43–4	Wan-sui (1969), pp. 646–8	CB 891, pp. 60–62 Ch'en, Mao Papers, pp. 26–34
18	Wan-sui, pp. 35–6		CB 891, p. 63
19	Wan-sui, pp. 37–8	Wen-hsüan, p. 49	CB 891, p. 64 Ch'en, Mao Papers, pp. 34–5
20	Wan-sui, pp. 44–6	Wan-sui (1969), pp. 653–7 Wen-hsüan, pp. 50–53	CB 891, pp. 75–7 Ch'en, Mao, pp. 91–6
21	Wan-sui, pp. 40–42	Wan-sui (1969), pp. 657–61 Wen-hsüan, pp. 53–5	CB 891, pp. 75–7 Ch'en, Mao, pp. 96–7, plus Mao Papers, pp. 42–5
22	Wan-sui (suppt.)	Wan-sui (1969), pp. 662–3 Wen-hsüan, pp. 57–8	CB 892, pp. 47–8 JPRS 90, pp. 38–9 Ch'en, Mao Papers, pp. 45–7
23	Wen-hsüan, pp. 61–3		JPRS 90, pp. 44–5
24	Chung-kung yen-chiu IV (3), pp. 118–19		Issues and Studies IV (6), pp. 92–3
25	Ibid., pp. 120–26		Ibid., pp. 94–8
26	Ibid., VI (9), pp. 85–97		CLG V (3–4), pp. 33–42

Since this book has been conceived as an anthology to be read for pleasure, rather than a rigorously critical edition even of those speeches included, I have not indicated in the notes all the points where the various available Chinese texts disagree. In most cases, it is fairly obvious which text is generally most accurate, and/or makes best sense of the passage in question. Where there is room for serious doubt as to which reading should be preferred, I have followed my own judgement; whenever the point at issue involved an important matter of substance, I have called the reader's attention to this fact by a note, and have indicated the alternative readings.

It will soon be noticed by the reader that a great many names in the texts are missing, and have been replaced by either XX or XXX. This results, of course, from the work of the Red Guard editors, who have eliminated the names for one of two reasons: either because the person in question had been criticized in the course of the Cultural Revolution, and should therefore not be mentioned in a favourable context; or because Mao makes critical, or insufficiently flattering, comments on a person who, in the view of the editors, ought to appear in a positive light. In most cases, it appears that each X is meant to stand for one Chinese character. XXX therefore represents the full name (including the surname) of a person with a two-character given name or *ming*: e.g., Liu Shao-ch'i, Teng Hsiao-p'ing. XX represents either the given name alone, or the full name of a person with a single-character *ming*: e.g., Chu Te, Lin Piao, P'eng Chen. Because of the probable significance of the Xs, we have left the double and triple Xs as they stand, rather than replacing them uniformly by a dash or a single X, so that the reader can speculate as to their meaning. Whenever one of the texts includes a name which is replaced by Xs in the other Chinese sources, I have assumed that they had good reason for doing so, and have inserted the actual name in the translation. In a few instances, the Chinese editors have beaten about the bush and included part of a name, while omitting the rest. (For example, in Text 6, p. 133, we read that 'Lin X' is still not fat, even after eating a catty of meat a day for ten years; this presumably stands for Lin Piao.) In these cases too, we have followed the Chinese text.

From time to time, Mao Tse-tung addresses or refers to his comrades by their given names only – usually with the prefix 'Comrade', but occasionally, at least in the case of Chou En-lai, without any prefix. Since this may be taken as an index of the degree of intimacy or informality which prevails in his relations with these people, I have left Mao's own usage in every case. When the names concerned might not be immediately recognized by the average reader, I have inserted the surname (*hsing*) in square brackets; in the case of 'Comrade Shao-ch'i', 'Comrade Hsiao-p'ing', and 'Comrade En-lai' (or simply En-lai), I have dispensed with this.

The numbered notes, which appear at the end of the volume, contain my own comments and explanations. All asterisked footnotes appearing on the page contain annotations by the editors of the Chinese originals (or conceivably by the Chairman himself), which appear in the Chinese texts either as footnotes or in brackets.

Brief interruptions or comments by members of the audience in the course of Mao's speeches are distinguished from the Chairman's own words by being set in italics. In other cases, such as in Texts 10 and 15, when there is an extended dialogue made up of alternate paragraphs by two or more speakers, this procedure has not been adopted. Text 26, which has been compiled by the Chinese editors from Mao's remarks on several different occasions, contains from time to time the words 'Chairman Mao said,' apparently for the purpose of showing where a new bit begins. We have chosen to indicate these divisions by asterisks instead. In all other respects, the translations which follow constitute as faithful and accurate a reproduction as possible of the Chinese originals.

Chairman Mao Talks to the People

Talks and Letters: 1956–1971

1 On the Ten Great Relationships

25 April 1956

During the past two months the Politburo has individually heard and accepted the work reports of thirty-four economic and financial departments of the Centre.[1] It has exchanged views with these departments on a number of issues, and after further discussions has made a synthesis containing ten problems, ten contradictions.

Raising these problems has but one aim: to mobilize all positive elements and all available forces in order to build socialism more, faster, better and more economically.

It has always been our policy to mobilize all positive elements and all available forces. In the past we followed this policy in order to win victory in the People's Democratic Revolution, and to put an end to the rule of feudalism and bureaucratic capitalism. Now we follow it in a new revolution, the Socialist Revolution, and in the building of the socialist state. No matter whether it is for revolution or construction, this policy should always be followed. Everybody is clear about this. But there are some problems which are still worth discussion, among them some points which are new. Our work still has its defects and shortcomings. If we discuss these problems and consider them and handle these contradictions correctly, then we can avoid some detours.

Let me read out the ten problems:

(1) The relationship between industry and agriculture, and between heavy industry and light industry.

(2) The relationship between industry in the coastal regions and industry in the interior.

(3) The relationship between economic construction and defence construction.

(4) The relationship between the state, the units of production and the individual producers.

(5) The relationship between the Centre and the regions.

(6) The relationship between the Han nationality and the national minorities.

(7) The relationship between Party and non-Party.

(8) The relationship between revolutionary and counter-revolutionary.

(9) The relationship between right and wrong.

(10) The relationship between China and other countries.

These relationships are all contradictions. Contradictions are everywhere in the world. Without contradictions there would be no world.

I will now discuss the above ten contradictions.

(1) *The relationship between industry and agriculture, heavy industry and light industry*

Everyone is agreed that heavy industry is the key sector which must be given priority. In dealing with the relationship between heavy industry and light industry and between industry and agriculture, we have not committed mistakes of principle. We have not committed the mistakes of some socialist countries which put undue emphasis on heavy industry and neglected light industry and agriculture. As a result they have not enough goods on the market, daily necessities are in short supply, and their currency is unstable. We put comparatively more emphasis on light industry and agriculture. Our market is comparatively well supplied with goods. This differs from the state of the market in some countries after their revolutions. While it would not be true to say that we have a superabundance, we have fairly good supplies of articles in daily use by the people. Also our prices are stable and the People's Currency is stable. That is not to say that there are no more problems. There are still problems. We must make appropriate adjustments to the proportion of investment between heavy industry and light industry, and between light industry and agriculture. We must make appropriate increases in the proportion of investment in light industry and agriculture which is contained in the total industrial and agricultural investment.

Does this mean that heavy industry is no longer the leading sector? No, it is still the leading sector. Are we no longer to emphasize heavy industry? If the question is posed in this way, the reply is that the emphasis in investment is still to be on heavy industry.

In future we must put more investment into light industry and agriculture so that the proportion of investment they receive is increased. When we increase this proportion, does this mean that we have changed the key sector? No, the key sector has not been changed. It is still heavy industry, but more emphasis will now be put on light industry and agriculture.

What will be the outcome of this increase in emphasis? The outcome will be to bring greater and faster development to heavy industry, greater and faster development to the production of the means of production.

The development of heavy industry demands capital accumulation. Where will this accumulation come from? It can come from heavy industry itself. It can also come from light industry and agriculture. But light industry and agriculture can provide the greater and faster accumulation.

Here a question arises. Is it really your desire to develop heavy industry? Either you have a strong [literally, a fierce] desire to do so, or you are not so very keen. If you don't desire to do so at all, then you will attack light industry and attack agriculture. If you are not very keen, then you will not put so much investment into light industry and agriculture. But if you have a strong desire to develop heavy industry, then you will pay attention to the development of light industry and agriculture. This will result in more daily necessities, which in turn will mean more accumulation, and after a few years still more funds will be invested in heavy industry. So this is a question of whether your desire to develop heavy industry is genuine or only a pretence.

Of course this question of whether one's desire to develop heavy industry is genuine or not does not apply to us. Who does not genuinely desire to? With us, it's merely a question of whether our desire is strong or weak. If your desire is really strong then you should put more investment into light industry. Otherwise your desire is not one hundred per cent genuine, only ninety per cent genuine. It is not strong. That is to say, you do not wholeheartedly stress heavy industry. If you whole-heartedly stressed it, then you would pay attention to the development of light industry, because in the first place it can satisfy the needs of the people, and secondly it can provide greater and faster accumulation.

On the question of agriculture the experience of some socialist countries proves that even where agriculture is collectivized, where collectivization is mismanaged it is still not possible to increase production. The root cause of the failure to increase agricultural production in some countries is that the state's policy towards the peasants is questionable. The peasants' burden of taxation is too heavy while the price of agricultural products is very low, and that of industrial goods very high. While developing industry, especially heavy industry, we must at the same time give agriculture a certain status by adopting correct policies for agricultural taxation, and for pricing industrial and agricultural products.

The importance of agriculture for the national economy as a whole is very clear from our own experience. The practice of the years since Liberation proves that whenever there is a good harvest, life is better all around during the corresponding year. This is a general law.

Our conclusion is as follows: one way of developing heavy industry is to develop light industry and agriculture somewhat less. There is another way, which consists in developing light industry and agriculture somewhat more. The result of the first method, i.e. of one-sidedly developing heavy industry without paying attention to the people's livelihood, will be to make the people dissatisfied, so that even heavy industry cannot really be run well. In a long-term perspective, this method will lead to somewhat slower and inferior development of heavy industry. When the overall account is added up a few decades hence, it won't be favourable. The second method, i.e. developing heavy industry on a foundation of satisfying the needs of the people's livelihood, will provide a more solid foundation for the development of heavy industry, and the result will be to develop it more and better.

(2) *The relationship between coastal industry and industry in the interior*

It is correct to develop industry in the interior. This is of primary importance. But it is necessary to look after the coastal regions.

On this question we have not made big or fundamental mistakes, yet we have a few weaknesses. In the past few years we have not laid enough stress on industry in the coastal regions. I think we should make some changes.

How much of the industry, heavy and light, which we had at the outset, was in the coastal regions, these being taken to include Liaoning, Hopei, Peking, Eastern Honan, Shantung, Anhwei, Kiangsu, Shanghai, Chekiang, Fukien, Kwangtung, Kwangsi? Seventy per cent of all our industry is in these coastal regions, and seventy per cent of our heavy industry. Only thirty per cent is in the interior. It would be quite wrong not to take account of this fact, not to give proper weight to coastal industry, and not to utilize its productive power to the full.

We must do our utmost and use all our available time to enable the industry of the coastal regions to develop. I am not saying that all our new factories should be built in the coastal regions. More than ninety per cent of them should be built in the interior. But some can be built in the coastal regions. For example, the Anshan steel mills and the Fushun coal mines are in the coastal regions; Dairen has its shipbuilding, T'angshan has its iron and steel and building-material industries, T'angku has its chemical industry, Tientsin its iron and steel and machine industries. Shanghai has its machine and shipbuilding industries, Nanking has its chemical industry, and there is industry in many other places. Now we are planning to produce synthetic petroleum at Maoming in Kwangtung Province, where there is oil-shale. This is also heavy industry.

In future the greater part of heavy industry – ninety per cent or perhaps still more – should be set up in the interior so that industry may become evenly distributed and rationally sited over the whole country. There is no doubt at all about that. But a proportion of heavy industry must still be constructed or expanded in the coastal regions.

Our old industrial base is mainly in the coastal regions. If we do not pay attention to industry in the coastal regions this will be to our detriment. On the other hand, if we make full use of the capacity both in plant and technology of coastal industry and develop it properly, then we shall have all the more strength to develop and maintain industry in the interior. It is wrong to adopt a negative attitude towards coastal industry. This will not only hinder the full utilization of coastal industry, it will also hinder the rapid development of industry in the interior.

We all desire to develop industry in the interior. The question is only whether your desire is genuine or not. If your desire is genuine and you are not just pretending, then you must make more use of the industry of the coastal regions, and build more industry in the coastal regions, especially light industry.

In the light of available information, industrial plant can be constructed very quickly in some light industries. After going into production and developing their productive capacity they can recoup their capital outlay within one year. Hence within five years they can build three or four new factories in addition to the original one. In some cases they will be able to build two or three new factories, in other cases one new factory. At the very least they can build half a new factory. This provides further demonstration of the importance of utilizing coastal industry.

In our long-term plans we have a shortage of 400,000 technical cadres. These can be provided by training workers and technicians from the coastal industries. Technical cadres do not need to come from literary families. Gorki only had two years of elementary schooling. Lu Hsün was not a university graduate. In the old society he could only be a lecturer, not a professor. Comrade Hsiao Ch'u-nü never went to school at all.[2] You must realize that skilled workers have learned through practical experience and can make very good technical cadres.

The technical level of coastal industry is high, the quality of its products good, its costs low, and it produces many new products. Its development has a stimulating effect on the technical level and quality of national industry as a whole. We must be fully aware of the importance of this question.

In short if we do not develop light industry we cannot develop heavy industry. If we do not utilize the industry of the coastal regions we cannot establish industry in the interior. We must not simply maintain coastal industry. We must also develop it where appropriate.

(3) *The relationship between economic construction and defence construction*

We cannot do without defence. Would it be a good idea to demobilize all our troops? No, it would not, because we still have enemies. These enemies are 'containing' us. Haven't they got us encircled?

We already have quite considerable defence forces. After the war to resist America and support Korea, our armies grew even stronger. Our defence industry is in process of being built up. Since P'an Ku separated heaven and earth,[3] we have never been able to manufacture automobiles or aeroplanes. Now we are beginning to be able to do both. Our motor industry started with the manufacture of lorries, not cars. So each day we have to come to our meetings in foreign cars. We want to be patriotic, but have to be patient. Roll on the day when we can come to meetings in our own cars!

We still do not have atomic bombs, but in the past we didn't have aeroplanes or big guns either. We defeated the Japanese invaders and Chiang Kai-shek with millet and rifles. We are already pretty strong and will be still stronger in future. A reliable way of ensuring this is to lay down appropriate ratios for military expenditure, so that it is reduced step by step to about twenty per cent of the state budget, while expenditure on economic construction is increased so that it can develop more and faster. On such a basis defence construction can make still greater progress, and in the not-too-distant future we shall have not only many aeroplanes and guns, but also our own atomic bombs.

Do you genuinely want atomic bombs? If you do, you must decrease the proportion of military expenditure and increase economic construction. Or do you only pretend to want them? In that case you will not decrease the proportion of military expenditure, but decrease economic construction. Which is the better plan? Will everybody please study this question: it is a question of strategic policy.

In 1950 at the Third Plenum of the Seventh Central Committee, the question of streamlining the state organs and decreasing military expenditure was raised. Moreover it was considered as one of the three preconditions for achieving a fundamental turn for the better in our financial and economic situation. But during the period of the first five-year plan, military expenditure made up thirty-two per cent of the state's expenditure. That is to say, one third of the expenditure was for non-productive purposes. This proportion is too high. In the second five-year plan, we must find a means of reducing this proportion in order to make more funds available for economic and cultural construction.

(4) *The relationship between the state, the units of production and the individual producers*

In our recent discussions with comrades from the various provinces, they had quite a lot to say on this question. As regards the workers, the productivity of their labour has gone up, the value they produce per working day has also gone up, therefore their wages should be adjusted accordingly. It would be wrong to neglect this point.

Since Liberation there has been a great improvement in the standard of living of the workers. This everyone knows. In the past some families had not a single employed member. Now these families have employed members. Some families had only one member in employment. Now they have two or three. I have come across families which in the past had no employed members. Subsequently, both husband and wife and one daughter were employed. If their wages are added up, then of course their standard of living will be good. Generally speaking our wage levels are not high, but we have a high rate of employment. Since prices are both low and stable, and life is secure, it follows that standards are incomparably better than before Liberation. The mass of the workers has maintained a high level of enthusiasm.

I mean we should pay attention to arousing the initiative and enthusiasm of the workers. The factory as a complete unit of production also has a problem of initiative and enthusiasm.

Everything has both unity with other things and its own independence. Everything also has features in common with other things as well as its own distinctive features. Things cannot only possess unity and common features, without also having independence and distinctive features. For instance, this meeting is an example of unity. After the meeting is over comes independence. Some of us will go for a walk, some will study, some eat. Each has his own independence. It would never do to keep the meeting going on and on without a break. That would be the death of us. So each unit of production, each individual has to have initiative and a certain degree of independence. All must have an independence which is linked with unity.

Would giving to the individual producers their due rewards, and to the units of production a certain amount of initiative, be of benefit to the industrialization of the whole country? It ought to result in some improvements. If it makes things worse then it should not be done. If everything is centralized, if the factories' depreciation funds are taken from them, then the units of production would no longer have any initiative; this would not be beneficial. On this question we do not have much experience. I think that the comrades here present also have little experience. We are studying it. We have so many factories, and in future we shall have still more. If we could arouse their enthusiasm to the full, this would certainly be of very great benefit to our country's industrialization.

As for the peasants, our relations with them have always been good. But we have made a mistake on the question of grain. In 1954 floods caused a loss of production throughout the country, and yet we purchased 7,000 million more catties of grain. This contrast between reduced production and increased state purchase led to criticism by the peasants. We cannot claim that we never make mistakes. We purchased 7,000 million catties too much because we had no experience and did not have a proper understanding of the problem. This was a mistake. In 1955, having discovered this mistake, we purchased 7,000 million catties less and put the 'three stabilizations'[4] into operation. That year there was a bumper crop. Thus an increase in production coincided with a decrease in purchasing, so that the peasants had 20,000 million extra catties of grain on their hands. All those peasants who had criticized us in the past now no longer criticized us. They all said, 'The Communist Party is fine.' The whole Party should remember this lesson.

The peasants' collective economic organizations are just like factories. They are also units of production. Within these collective economic units the relationship between the collective and the individual must be properly regulated and properly managed. If we do not manage this relationship properly and do not pay attention to the peasants' welfare, then the collective economy cannot be properly run. Some socialist countries may have committed mistakes in this respect. Some of their collective economic organizations are generally well run, others are not so well run. In those which are not well run, agricultural production is not so developed. The collective needs accumulation, but we must be careful not to make too great demands on the peasants. We should not give them too hard a time. Except where we meet with unavoidable natural disasters, we should enable the peasants' income to increase year by year on the basis of increased agricultural production.

We have discussed the questions of distribution of the

summer and autumn harvests with the comrades from the various provinces. By problems of distribution we mean: (1) how much is taken by the state, (2) how much is taken by the collective, and (3) how much is taken by individual peasants and in what form they take it. The state takes it in the form of taxes, the collective economic organizations in accumulation and management expenses, and the individual peasants in their shares of grain and money.

Everything in the collective economy is for the service of the peasants. Not only production expenses, which goes without saying, but management expenses are also necessary. The accumulation fund is for the purpose of expanding production, while the welfare fund is for the peasants' welfare. On all of these we should work out appropriate ratios together with the peasants.

The state must have accumulation and so must the collective, but neither should be too high. State accumulation comes mainly through taxation and not through pricing. In the exchange of industrial and agricultural products we adopt in our country a policy of reducing the 'scissors' gap, a policy of the exchange of equal or near-equal values, a policy of low profit and high sales in industrial products, and a policy of stable prices.

In short, the relationships between state and factory, state and worker, factory and worker, state and collective economic organization, state and peasant, collective economic organization and peasant must all be seen from both sides and not from one side only. There are some new points here. This is a big problem which concerns 600 million people, and which demands the attention of the whole Party.

(5) *The relationship between the Centre and the regions*

The relationship between the Centre and the regions is also a contradiction. In order to resolve this contradiction, what we now need to consider is how to arouse the enthusiasm of the regions by allowing them to run more projects under the unified plan of the Centre.

As things look now, I think that we need a further extension of regional power. At present it is too limited and this is not favourable to building socialism. It is laid down in our Constitution that the regions do not have legislative powers, and that these are concentrated in the hands of the National People's Congress. But where the situation and the work demand it, the regions should also make rules and regulations, provided they do not conflict with the policies of the Centre, and that they fall within the limits sanctioned by the law. The Constitution does not prohibit this.

If heavy and light industries are to develop, then markets and raw materials are needed, and to achieve these you must arouse the enthusiasm of the regions. If we are to consolidate the leadership of the Centre, then we must attend to the interests of the regions.

At present there are dozens of hands meddling in regional affairs, making them difficult to manage. Every day various ministries issue orders to the offices of provincial and municipal governments. These orders are supposed to come from the Centre, even though the Centre knows nothing about them and neither does the State Council. They put a great strain on the regions. Statistics and reports come rushing in like a torrent. This must be changed. We must discuss ways of correcting it.

There are two kinds of departments at the Centre dealing with local affairs. The first kind extend their leadership right down to enterprises. The management organs and enterprises which they set up in the regions are locally supervised by the regions. The other kind have the task of laying down guidelines and work plans, which are put into operation by the regions, with the regions in charge of the work.

We advocate a consultative mode of operation with the regions. Whenever the Central Committee of the Party does anything, it always consults the regions. It has never issued blind commands without doing so. We hope that the various ministries at the Centre will take note of this and consult with the regions on all matters affecting them, and not issue any orders until after consultation has taken place.

We want unity together with individuality. If local enthusiasm is really to be aroused, every place must have the individuality appropriate to its conditions. This individuality is not Kao Kang's kind of individuality, which amounted to striving for an independent kingdom; it is the individuality necessary in the interest of the whole country and to strengthen national unity.

The provinces and municipalities have many opinions about the various departments of the Centre which ought to be expressed. It is possible that regions, counties, districts and townships also have many opinions about the provinces and municipalities. The provinces and municipalities should listen attentively so that they can arouse their enthusiasm.

There must be proper enthusiasm and proper independence. Provinces, municipalities, regions, counties, districts and townships should all possess both. Provinces and municipalities should not put regions, counties, districts and townships in a strait-jacket.

Naturally we must, at the same time, tell the comrades at the lower levels that they should not act wildly, that they must exercise caution. Where they can conform, they ought to conform. Where they ought to conform, they must conform. Where they cannot conform, where they ought not to conform, then conformity should not be sought at all costs.

Two enthusiasms are much better than just one. In our fight on the question of the regions, we do not take regionalism as our starting-point, nor the interests of individual units, but rather the interests of the whole state. We fight this fight wherever an opportunity arises.

The independence sanctioned by the Centre must be a proper degree of independence. It cannot be called 'separatism'.

In short, the regions should have an appropriate degree of power. This would be beneficial to the building of a strong socialist state. I consider that to restrict local powers too narrowly is not so beneficial. We still have little experience, and little maturity on the question of the state's handling of the relationship between the Centre and the regions. I hope that everyone will properly study and discuss it.

(6) *The relationship between the Han nationality and the national minorities*[5]

On this question our policy is stable. It has obtained the approval of the national minorities. Our emphasis lies on opposing Han chauvinism. Local nationalism exists, but this is not the crucial problem. The crucial problem is opposition to Han chauvinism. In respect to population, the Hans comprise the great majority. If they practised Han chauvinism and excluded the national minorities, that would be very bad. So we must conduct widespread education in proletarian nationalities policy among the Han nationality, and carry out an investigation into the relationship of the Hans and the national minorities. We made one such investigation two years ago. It is now time for another one. If there are cases where the relationship is abnormal, then it must be corrected. It is not sufficient merely to talk about it. There are plenty of people nowadays who say they do not want Han chauvinism. Their words are fine, but they do nothing about it in practice.

We need to make a proper study of what systems of economic management and finance would be appropriate to the national minority areas.

The national minority areas are extensive and rich in resources. While the Han nationality has a large population, the national minority areas have riches under the soil which are needed for building socialism. The Han nationality must actively assist the national minorities to carry out socialist economic and cultural construction, and, by improving relations between the nationalities, mobilize all elements, both human and material, which are beneficial to socialist construction.

(7) *The relationship between Party and non-Party*

By this is meant the relationship between the Chinese Communist Party and the democratic parties and non-party democrats. There is nothing new in this, but while we are on this subject, we should also include this relationship. Is it really better to have one party or several parties? As things are now, it would seem to be better to have several parties. Not only was this so in the past, it may very well be so in the future too, right up to the time when all parties wither away. Long-term coexistence and mutual supervision between the Communist Party and the various democratic parties has advantages.

Parties are the products of history. Of all the things in this world, there are none which are not the products of history. This is point number one. The second point is that everything which is produced by history will also be destroyed by history. The Communist Party was produced by history, and for that reason the day will inevitably come when it will be destroyed. The democratic parties have a similar destiny.

Proletarian political parties and the dictatorship of the proletariat will be destroyed in future. But at present they are indispensable. Without them we could not suppress counter-revolution, nor could we resist imperialism or build socialism. In order to carry out these tasks the proletarian dictatorship needs to have great coercive power. But it must oppose bureaucracy and it must not have an inflated establishment. I propose that the Party and government organs should be streamlined and that two thirds of their numbers should be axed.

This brings us back to the previous subject. If we are to streamline the Party and government organs, does this not mean that we can dispense with the democratic parties? In our country several democratic parties exist side by side.[6] Among them there are people who still have many criticisms of us. Towards these people we adopt a policy of unity combined with struggle, in order to mobilize them in the cause of socialism.

In China there is no formal opposition. All the democratic parties accept the leadership of the Communist Party. But within the democratic parties there are some people who in reality are in opposition. On 'Carry the revolution through to the end', on leaning to one side in foreign policy, the 'Resist America, Aid Korea' campaign, the land reform and other issues, they adopted an equivocal attitude of opposing us and yet not opposing us. They also criticized us about the suppression of counter-revolution. They said that the Common

Programme [of 1949] was a fine thing and that they didn't want a constitution. But when the Draft Constitution came out they all raised their hands in assent.[7] Things often move towards their opposites. The attitude of some people in the democratic parties towards many questions was like this. They are in opposition, and at the same time they are not in opposition. Because they want to be patriotic, they often move from being in opposition to not being in opposition.

The relationship between the Communist Party and the democratic parties has shown some improvement. We want to permit the people in the democratic parties to express their criticisms. We will accept any idea which makes good sense, no matter who puts it forward. This is advantageous to the Party, the state, the people and socialism.

I therefore hope that our comrades will grasp united-front work. Provincial Party secretaries should find the time to investigate the situation and put measures in hand to carry this work forward.

(8) *The relationship between revolutionary and counter-revolutionary*

What kind of element is a counter-revolutionary element? It is a negative element, a destructive element. It is not a positive element. It is a force opposed to positive elements.

Can a negative element turn into a positive element? Can a destructive element turn into a beneficial element? Can a counter-revolutionary change? This depends on social conditions. Completely stubborn, dyed-in-the-wool counter-revolutionaries undoubtedly exist. But where the majority of them are concerned, given our social conditions, the day may come when they do change. Of course, there are some who will not have time to change before they are summoned by the King of Hell. And, as for some others, who knows when they will change?

Because of the people's strength, and because of our correct policy towards counter-revolutionary elements of allowing them to reform themselves through labour and become new men, there have been many counter-revolutionaries who have given up being counter-revolutionary. They have taken part in agricultural and industrial labour; some of them have become very active and done useful work.

There are a number of points about the work of suppressing counter-revolution which need affirmation. For instance, should we have carried out the suppression of counter-revolution of 1951–2? It seems that some hold that we should not have carried this out. This view is wrong. It must be recognized that this campaign was necessary.

The methods of handling counter-revolutionaries are execution, imprisonment, probation and release. Everybody knows what execution is. Imprisonment means locking people up and allowing them to reform themselves through labour. Probation means placing them in society to be supervised and remoulded by the masses. Release means not arresting those who might or might not be arrested, or releasing those who behave well after arrest. It is altogether right that we give different kinds of counter-revolutionary elements different treatment according to circumstances. These methods all need to be explained carefully to the common people.

Whom have we executed? What sort of people? Elements for whom the masses had great hatred, and whose blood-debt was heavy. In a great revolution of 600 million people, if we did not kill some tyrants, or if we were too lenient to them, the masses would not agree. It is still of practical significance to affirm that it was correct to execute these people. Not to give that affirmation would be bad. This is the first point.

The second point needing affirmation is that counter-revolutionary elements still exist in society, though there are now far fewer of them. Our social discipline is very good, but we still should not relax our vigilance. To say that not one counter-revolutionary remains and then sit back and take things easy would be wrong. There is still a small number of counter-revolutionaries carrying out sabotage; for example, killing cattle, burning grain, wrecking factories, stealing information, peddling counter-revolutionary slogans, etc.

In future, in suppressing counter-revolution in our society

we must make fewer arrests and carry out fewer executions. We should hand the majority of counter-revolutionaries over to the agricultural cooperatives so that they may participate in productive work under supervision, and be transformed through labour. But we should not declare that we shall never execute anyone. We cannot abolish the death penalty. If a counter-revolutionary were to commit murder or to blow up a factory, do you think he should be executed? He most definitely should.

The third point which should be affirmed concerns the work of suppressing counter-revolutionaries in government offices, schools and the army. We must keep up the policy which we started in Yenan: 'No executions and few arrests.' There are some whom we do not execute, not because they have done nothing to deserve death, but because killing them would bring no advantage, whereas sparing their lives would. What harm is there in not executing people? Those amenable to labour reform should go and do labour reform, so that rubbish can be transformed into something useful. Besides, people's heads are not like leeks. When you cut them off, they will not grow again. If you cut off a head wrongly, there is no way of rectifying the mistake even if you want to.

If government departments were to adopt a policy of no executions in their work of suppressing counter-revolutionaries, this still would not prevent us from taking counter-revolution seriously. Moreover it would ensure that we would not make mistakes, or if we did they could be corrected. This would calm many people. If we do not execute people, we must feed them. So we should give all counter-revolutionaries a way out of their impasse. This will be helpful to the people's cause and to our image abroad.

The suppression of counter-revolution still requires a long period of hard work. None of us may relax our efforts.

(9) The relationship between right and wrong

Both inside and outside the Party we should clearly distinguish between right and wrong. How to treat people who have made mistakes is an important question. The correct attitude is to allow people to join the revolution. If people have committed mistakes, we must adopt a policy of 'punishing those who have erred in the past so as to provide a warning for the future, and curing the disease to save the patient,' thus helping them to reform.

The True Story of Ah Q[8] is a good piece of writing. I urge comrades who have read it to read it again, and those comrades who have not read it to read it carefully. In the story, Lu Hsün writes mainly about a backward and unenlightened peasant, and how he is afraid of being criticized. If someone criticizes him, he starts a fight with them. He has ringworm scars on his head which he never mentions, and he is terrified of others mentioning them. But the more he takes this attitude, the more others taunt him, so that he is pushed right on to the defensive. Lu Hsün wrote a special chapter in the story entitled 'Barred from the revolution', in which he tells how the fake foreign devil does not permit Ah Q to join the revolution. In fact, all Ah Q meant by revolution was stealing a few things, but even this kind of revolution was not permitted.

In the past we have made mistakes in the Party on this question. That was when the dogmatists headed by Wang Ming were in control. They were forever accusing people, who were not to their taste, of having committed such and such an error. They did not permit them to join the revolution. They attacked many people, causing the Party to suffer heavy losses. We must remember this lesson.

If we do not allow people in our society to join the revolution, that is a bad thing. It is also a bad thing if people who have joined the Party and committed mistakes are not allowed to correct those mistakes.

We should allow people to join the revolution. Some may say that in the case of people who have made mistakes, it depends on whether they have corrected them. That is correct, but it is only half the truth. There is another half, namely that work must be done on them to help them correct their mistakes. They must be given an opportunity to correct them.

People who have made mistakes we should first 'observe' and

then 'help'. They should be given work and assistance. We shouldn't gloat over them, refuse to help them, refuse them work. This is a sectarian way of doing things.

The more people who join the revolution the better. Of those who have committed mistakes, a small minority cling to their mistakes and keep repeating them, but the majority can be reformed. People who have had typhoid become immune to it afterwards. Similarly, people who have made mistakes, provided they are good at drawing lessons from their mistakes, will, if they take care, make fewer mistakes in future. We hope that all those who have made mistakes will acquire this immunity. It is those who have not made mistakes who are in danger and should be on their guard, because they do not have this immunity and so easily become over-confident.

We must realize that if we are excessive in our correction of those who have made mistakes, this will invariably rebound on us. It will be like lifting a rock and dropping it on our own feet. We will fall and be unable to rise. If we deal benevolently with those who have made mistakes, we can win their hearts. In dealing with those who have erred, do comrades take a hostile or a helpful attitude to them? This is the criterion for judging whether you wish them well or ill.

Right must be distinguished from wrong. Clarity on the relationship between right and wrong will enable us to educate people and unite the whole Party. Within the Party we have controversy, criticism, struggle. These are necessary. The use of an appropriate amount of criticism, or even struggle where circumstances warrant it, is a means of helping people to correct mistakes, and is helpful to them.

(10) *The relationship between China and other countries*

We have put forward the slogan of learning from other countries. I think that this slogan is correct. There is one kind of national leader who neither dares nor wishes to put forward this slogan. We must have the courage to reject such an upstage attitude.

We must learn the good points of all countries and all nationalities. Every nationality has its good points, otherwise how could it exist, how could it develop? To recognize that every nationality has its good points is not to deny that it has weaknesses and shortcomings. Strengths and weaknesses, good points and bad, it will have both. Our branch secretaries and company and platoon commanders all know – it is written in their little notebooks – that in summarizing experience there are always two points; one is the strengths, the other the weaknesses. Today's meeting is no exception to this. We all know that there are two sides to things. Why, then, should we only mention one side, the strengths, and omit the weaknesses? A state of affairs with only one side could not exist. For 10,000 years to come there will always be two sides. Each age has its two sides. The present age has its two sides. Each individual has two sides. In short, there are always two sides, not just one. If we say there is only one side, it means that we only know about one side and we are ignorant of the other.

We propose learning the good things of other countries, not the bad. In the past some of us were unclear about this and also learned the bad things. They were as pleased as Punch with what they had learned, but meanwhile the people from whom they had learned these useless things had already discarded them. So they came a cropper like Sun Wu-k'ung.[9]

Some people never analyse anything. They simply follow the prevailing wind. Today the north wind is blowing, so they join the north wind school. Tomorrow there is a west wind, so they join the west wind school. The day after tomorrow the north wind blows again, so they switch back to the north wind school. They haven't a single opinion of their own. They are absolutists, going from one extreme to another. We must not be like this, we must not copy things blindly, but we should learn analytically and critically. We should not become one-sided and copy everything which comes from abroad, and introduce it mechanistically.

We used to be sectarian on this question in the past, and we have conducted a long struggle against this sectarianism. But sectarianism is still to be found both in the academic world and in the economic world. We should continue our work of criticizing it.

We put the problem in this way: the study of universal truth must be combined with Chinese reality. Our theory is made up of the universal truth of Marxism–Leninism combined with the concrete reality of China. We must be able to think independently.

We openly put forward the slogan of learning from foreign countries, learning all their advanced and superior things, and continuing to learn them for ever. We openly acknowledge the weaknesses of our own nation, and the strengths of others.

If we are to learn from foreign countries, we must conscientiously learn foreign languages, if possible several.

I consider that China has two weaknesses, and at the same time, two strong points.

First, in the past we were a colony and semi-colony. We suffered the oppression of imperialism. Our industry was not developed and our scientific and technical level was low. Apart from our large territory, rich resources, large population and long history, we were inferior to others in many respects. So we were not prone to be stuck up or conceited. On the contrary, we had been slaves far too long and felt inferior to others in every respect – too much so. We could not hold up our heads in the presence of foreigners. We were like Chia Kuei in the opera *The Fa-men Temple*. When people asked him to sit down, he said he was used to standing and would not sit. Some real effort is needed on this problem, to raise the self-confidence of our people. We must do as Mencius says: 'When speaking to the mighty, look on them with contempt.'[10] We must develop the spirit which we had during the 'Resist America, Aid Korea' campaign, of looking with contempt on the imperialists. Our policy is that we should study all the good points of foreign countries, their politics, their economics, their science and technology, and their literature and art.

Second, our revolution came late. Although the 1911 Revolution, which overthrew the emperor, came before the Russian revolution, yet we then had no proletarian party and the revolution failed. The victory of the People's Revolution in 1949 came over thirty years later than the Soviet October Revolution. So it is not our place to be proud. And although our revolution is one step ahead of those of a number of colonial countries, we should resist the temptation to be proud of that too.

These two points are weaknesses, but also strong points too. As I have already said, we are very poor and have not much knowledge. We are first 'poor' and second 'blank'. By 'poor' I mean that we have not much industry and our agriculture is not so very advanced either. By 'blank' I mean that we are like a sheet of blank paper, since our cultural and scientific level is not high. Those who are poor want change; only they want to have a revolution, want to burst their bonds, and seek to become strong. A blank sheet of paper is good for writing on. I am, of course, speaking in general terms. The labouring people of our country are rich in wisdom, and we also have a pretty good bunch of scientists. I am not saying we have no knowledge at all.

Being first 'poor' and second 'blank' prevents us from being stuck up. Even if in future our industry and agriculture develop rapidly, and our scientific and cultural level is greatly raised, we must still preserve our modest and cautious attitude and not be stuck up. We must still learn from others. We must study for 10,000 years. What's wrong with that?

I have altogether discussed ten points. In sum, we must mobilize all positive factors – direct and indirect factors, direct and indirect positive factors – and strive to build a great socialist state. We must strive further to strengthen and consolidate the socialist camp, to win victory for the international communist movement!

2 Chairman Mao's Talk to Music Workers*
24 August 1956

The art of all the nations of the world is similar with respect to fundamental principles, but different with respect to form and style. The art of the various socialist countries each has socialism as its content, but each has its own national character. They have both similarities and differences, common features and individual characteristics. This is a natural law. All things are like this, no matter whether they belong to nature, society, or to the realm of the intellect. Take the leaves of a tree: at first sight they all look much the same, but when you examine them closely, each one is different; to find two absolutely identical leaves is impossible.

Class struggle, social revolution, the transition from capitalism to socialism have the same fundamental principles in all countries. But when it comes to some of the minor principles and manifestations which are dependent on the major principles, then each country is different. The October Revolution and the Chinese Revolution are like this. With respect to fundamental principles the two revolutions are similar, but with respect to the form in which these principles were manifested, the two revolutions have many differences. For example, in Russia the revolution developed from the cities to the countryside, while in our country it developed from the countryside to the cities. This is one of the many differences between the two revolutions.

*This is Chairman Mao's talk to responsible cadres of the National Association of Music Workers and some other comrades.

This item has not been read by the Chairman and is said still to need study and revision.

The art of the various nations of the world each has its own peculiar national form and national style. Some people do not understand this point. They reject their own national characteristics and blindly worship the West, thinking that the West is better in every respect. They even go so far as to advocate 'complete Westernization'. This is wrong. 'Complete Westernization' is impracticable; it will not be accepted by the common people of China. The arts and the natural sciences differ in this respect. For example, removing the appendix and taking aspirin have no national form. This is not the case with the arts: with them the question of national form does arise. This is because art is the manifestation of people's lives, thoughts and emotions, and it bears a very close relationship to a nation's customs and language. Historically the artistic heritage has grown up within the framework of the nation.

Chinese art, Chinese music, painting, drama, song and dance, and literature have each had their own historical development. In rejecting Chinese things, the people who advocate complete Westernization say that Chinese things do not have their own laws, and so they are unwilling to study or develop them. This is adopting an attitude of national nihilism towards Chinese art.

Every nation in the world has its own history and its own strengths and weaknesses. Since earliest times excellent things and rotten things have mingled together and accumulated over long periods. To sort them out and distinguish the essence from the dregs is a very difficult task, but we must not reject history because of this difficulty. It is no good cutting ourselves off from history and abandoning our heritage. The common people would not approve.

Of course this by no means implies that we do not need to learn from foreign countries. We must learn many things from foreign countries and master them. We must especially master fundamental theory. Some people advocate 'Chinese learning as the substance, Western learning for practical application'. Is this idea right or wrong? It is wrong. The word 'learning' in fact refers to fundamental theory. Fundamental theory should be the same in China as in foreign countries. There should be no distinction between Chinese and Western things in fundamental theory.

Marxism is a fundamental theory which was produced in the West. How then can we make a distinction between what is Chinese and what is Western in this respect? Are we to refuse to accept Marxism? The practice of the Chinese revolution proves that not to accept Marxism would be bad for us. It would be unreasonable not to accept it. In the past the Second International attempted to deny and revise the fundamental theories of Marxism and put forward some arguments for this, but they were completely refuted by Lenin. Marxism is a general truth which has universal application. We must accept it. But this general truth must be combined with the concrete practice of each nation's revolution. It was only because the Chinese people accepted Marxism and combined it with the practice of the Chinese revolution that they won victory in the Chinese revolution.

We learn foreign things because we want to study and develop Chinese things. In this respect natural and social science are similar. We must master all the good things from foreign countries and then apply them and, in the process, develop them. In the field of natural science we must do our own independent creative work, and use modern scientific knowledge and methods from abroad to sort out China's scientific heritage, until we can form our own schools of thought. Take, for example, Western medical science and other related modern sciences such as physiology, pathology, biochemistry, bacteriology and anatomy. Can you say we do not want to study them? We must study all these modern sciences. But some of those who have studied Western medicine should also study Chinese medicine, and use their modern scientific knowledge and method to put in order and study our ancient Chinese medical methods and materials. They should also combine Chinese and Western medicine and pharmacy to create new unified Chinese medical and pharmaceutical sciences.

If this applies to natural and social science, how much the more should it apply to the arts. We must learn from foreign countries and absorb the good things from foreign countries, but when we have learnt them we must use them to study and develop the arts of the various peoples of China, otherwise our work will benefit nobody. Our aim in studying foreign arts, studying their fundamental theories and techniques, is to create a new socialist art of the various peoples of China, which will possess its own individual national forms and styles.

We must acknowledge that in respect of modern culture the standards of the West are higher than ours. We have fallen behind. Is this the case in respect of art? In art we have our strengths and also our weaknesses. We must be good at absorbing the good things from foreign countries in order to make good our own shortcomings. If we stick to our old ways and do not study foreign literature, do not introduce it into China; if we do not know how to listen to foreign music or how to play it, this is not good. We must not be like the Empress Dowager Tz'u-hsi[1] who blindly rejected all foreign things. Blindly rejecting foreign things is like blindly worshipping them. Both are incorrect and harmful.

In learning from foreign countries we must oppose both conservatism and dogmatism. We have already suffered politically from dogmatism. Everything we copied from abroad was adopted rigidly, and this ended in a great defeat, with the Party organizations in the white areas losing one hundred per cent of their strength and the revolutionary bases and the Red Army losing ninety per cent of their strength, and the victory of the revolution being delayed for many years.[2] The reason is that there were some comrades who did not take reality as their starting-point, but dogmatism. They did not combine the fundamental theory of Marxism–Leninism with the concrete practice of the Chinese revolution. If we had not rejected this kind of dogmatism the Chinese revolution would not have won today's victory.

In the field of the arts we should also learn this lesson and take good care not to let dogmatism get the better of us. To study foreign things does not mean importing everything, lock, stock and barrel. We must accept things critically. We learn from the ancients in order to benefit the people of today, and we learn from foreigners in order to benefit the people of China.

We must learn good things from foreign countries and also learn good things from China. Half bottles of vinegar are no good: we must change two half bottles into two whole bottles.[3] We must master both Chinese and foreign things and combine them into an organic whole. Lu Hsün did this. He was very well versed in both Chinese and foreign works, but his brilliance was not primarily in his translations but rather in his creative work. His creative work was akin neither to foreign things nor to old-style Chinese things, but it is still Chinese. We should study Lu Hsün's spirit, master both Chinese and foreign things, absorb the good points of Chinese and foreign art, fuse them together and create a new art with a characteristic national form and style.

Of course it is not easy to make a successful combination of Chinese and foreign things. It is a process which takes time. There are some Chinese things into which it is possible to blend foreign things. For example, in writing novels, the language, characters and background must be Chinese, but they need not be written in the Chinese 'instalment' form.[4] You can produce some things which are neither Chinese nor Western. If what comes out is neither a donkey nor a horse but a mule, that would be not bad at all. When two things combine, their form is changed. It is not possible for them to remain completely unchanged. Chinese things will change. Politically, economically and culturally, the face of China is undergoing big changes. But however much they change, Chinese things will always have their own characteristics. Foreign things also change. After the October Revolution, the face of the world underwent a fundamental change. After the Second World War this change developed in a new direction. We must give our attention to the critical acceptance of foreign things, and especially to the introduction of things from the socialist world and from the progressive people of the capitalist world.

In short, art must have independent creative qualities; it must be distinctly imbued with the character of the times and also with the national character. China's art must not look more and more to the past, nor must it become more and more Westernized. It must increasingly reflect the characteristics of the times and of the nation. In trying to achieve this we should not shun experimentation. Especially in a country such as China, with a long history and a large population, it is even more necessary to carry out such experimentation as will serve the needs of the various nationalities the better. We do not want complete uniformity. Uniformity leads to writing to formulae.[5] No matter whether they are foreign or local formulae, both are lifeless and are not welcomed by the common people of China.

We have here the question of the treatment of bourgeois intellectuals who have received a Western education. If we do not tackle this question properly, it will have an adverse effect not only on art, but also on the whole revolutionary cause. The Chinese national bourgeoisie and its intellectuals consist of a few million people. Although their numbers are not great, they possess modern culture. We must unite with them, educate them and remould them. The comprador class has its own culture, which is a slave culture. The landlord class also has its culture – feudal culture. The Chinese workers and peasants, owing to their having been oppressed for a long time, still do not have much cultural knowledge. Until the tasks of the cultural and technical revolutions have been completed, the bourgeois intellectuals have comparatively more knowledge and skill. Provided our policy is correct and we educate and remould them, we can get them to serve the cause of socialism. Can we educate and remould them? We can. Many of the people here present were bourgeois intellectuals in the past who have crossed over from the bourgeoisie to the proletariat, so why should not they too cross over? In fact there are already many who have crossed over. We must not fail to unite with them, educate them and remould them. Only if we do this will they be of benefit to the revolutionary cause of the working class, to the socialist revolution, and to socialist construction.

You who are here present are all musicians. In studying Western music you have many important responsibilities. The ordering and development of Chinese music must depend on you who study Western-style music, just as the ordering and development of Chinese medicine depends on Western-style doctors. The Western things which you study are useful, but you should master both Western and Chinese things, and should not 'completely Westernize'. You should devote attention to Chinese things, do your utmost to study and develop them, with the aim of creating our own Chinese things with characteristic national form and style. If you grasp this basic policy your work will have a great future.

3 Speech at the Supreme State Conference
Excerpts. 28 January 1958

Today we shall talk about more general questions.

When I review the past seven or eight years, I see that this nation of ours has a great future. Especially in the past year you can see how the national spirit of our 600 million people has been raised to a level surpassing that of the past eight years. After the great airing of views, blooming and debating, our problems and tasks have been clarified: we shall catch up with Britain in about fifteen years; the publication of the Forty-Point Programme for Agricultural Development has given great encouragement to the masses. Many things which we could not do before we can do now, and we have the confidence to do them: for example the extermination of the four pests,[1] for which the masses have great enthusiasm. As for me, I may not be able to catch rats, but I can have a go at catching flies and mosquitoes!

Anyway isn't it generally the flies and mosquitoes which attack us? . . . In ancient times there actually was a man who wrote an essay advocating the extermination of rats. Now we are going to exterminate the four pests. For 4,000 years nobody – not even Confucius – made it their ambition to exterminate the four pests. Hangchow municipality is planning to exterminate the four pests in four years; some other places are planning to do it in two years, three years or five years. So there is great hope for the future development of our nation. There are no grounds for pessimism. Pessimism is wrong. When we criticize the pessimists we should not come to blows but reason with them. We must tell them that we really have great hope and not just a little hope. The stress here should be placed on the word 'great'. Or as the Japanese say [in speaking Chinese] we have 'great great hope' (*laughter*).[2]

Our nation is waking up, just like anybody waking from a night's sleep. We have overthrown the feudal system of many thousands of years and have awakened. We have changed the system of ownership; we have now gained victories in the Rectification Campaign as well as in the Anti-Rightist Campaign. Our country is both poor and blank. Those who are poor have nothing to call their own. Those who are blank are like a sheet of white paper. To be poor is fine because it makes you inclined to be revolutionary. With blank paper many things can be done. You can write on it or draw designs. Blank paper is best for writing on.

If we are to have drive, if we are to see to it that the Western world is left far behind, do we not have to rid ourselves of bourgeois ideology? If the West wanted to rid itself of bourgeois ideology, who knows how long it would take! If Dulles had the desire to get rid of bourgeois ways he would have to ask us to be his teachers (*laughter*).

Whenever we talk about it we say that our country has such an enormous population, it has such a vast territory, abundant resources, so many people, 4,000 years of history and culture ... we have bragged so much about this, yet we cannot compare with a country like Belgium. In short we are an outstanding people with a very long history, yet our steel output is so low. We only harvest 100+ catties of grain per *mu*[3] in the north and 300+ in the south; our literacy rate is so low. We cannot compare with Belgium on any of these counts. Yet we have great drive and we must catch up. We shall catch up with Britain within fifteen years.

These fifteen years depend on the first five. The first five depend on the first three, the first three on the first one, and the first year depends on the first month.

Now our enthusiasm has been aroused. Ours is an ardent nation, now swept by a burning tide. There is a good metaphor for this: our nation is like an atom ... When this atom's nucleus is smashed the thermal energy released will have really tremendous power. We shall be able to do things which we could not do before. When our nation has this great energy we shall catch up with Britain in fifteen years; we shall produce forty million tons of steel annually – now we produce only just over five million tons; we shall have a generating capacity of 450,000 million kWh. of electricity – at present we can generate only 40,000 million kWh., which means increasing our capacity ten times, for which we must increase hydro-electric production and not only thermo-electric. We still have ten years to carry out the Forty-Point Programme for Agricultural Development[4], but it looks as if we shall not need ten years. Some people say five years, others three. It would seem that we can complete it in eight.

To reach these targets in the present situation we must have great drive. When I was in Shanghai a professor discussed with me the *People's Daily* editorial, 'Ride on the Wind and Break through the Waves'. He said that we must summon up our energy to swim upstream. What he meant was to swim from Shanghai to Szechwan. This needs hard work; it's not like swimming downstream. He was quite right. I really appreciate this man. He is a good man with a sense of what is right. Some people[5] criticize others for 'craving greatness and success, being impatient for quick results, despising the past and putting blind faith in the future'. What sort of craving for greatness and success? Is it the craving for greatness and success of the revolutionaries or of the reactionaries? Is it a subjectivist, formalistic craving for greatness and success or is it a realistic one? When in olden times people used to talk about 'good fortune as wide as the Eastern Ocean, long life as extensive as the Southern Mountains', this was craving greatness and success, and what was wrong with that? Being impatient for quick results is not so bad either! ...

As for despising the past, this is not to say that there was nothing good in the past. There were indeed good things in the past. But always to put so much stress on the past, every day thinking of Yü, T'ang, Wen Wang, Wu Wang, the Duke of Chou and Confucius – I don't believe in this way of looking at history ... I consider that human history advances. One generation is not as good as another – people who went before are not as good as those who follow later . . .

As for blind faith in the future, our aims are concerned with the future. We believe that to put trust in the future is quite right, though our trust should not be blind . . .

There are two ways to give leadership. One is good, the other not so good. I do not mean that one is Dulles's way and one is ours, nor that one is the rightist way and the other ours. I mean that in building socialism there are two methods of leadership, two styles of work. On the question of cooperativization some people advocate more speed, others a more gradual approach. I believe that the former method is correct. It is better to strike while the iron is hot and to get it done in one go than to spin it out. For example, is it right to have a rectification campaign or not? It is right. To carry it out properly it is best to have a great airing of views and blooming . . .

I stand for the theory of permanent revolution. Do not mistake this for Trotsky's theory of permanent revolution. In making revolution one must strike while the iron is hot – one revolution must follow another, the revolution must continually advance. The Hunanese often say, 'Straw sandals have no pattern – they shape themselves in the making.' Trotsky believed that the socialist revolution should be launched even before the democratic revolution is complete. We are not like that. For example after the Liberation of 1949 came the Land Reform; as soon as this was completed there followed the mutual-aid teams, then the low-level cooperatives, then the high-level cooperatives. After seven years the cooperativization was completed and productive relationships were transformed; then came the Rectification. After Rectification was finished, before things had cooled down, then came the Technical Revolution. In the cases of Poland and Yugoslavia, democratic order had been established for seven or eight years, and then a rich peasantry emerged. It may not be necessary to establish a New Democratic government, but even so one must still unite all those forces which can be united.

It is possible to catch up with Britain in fifteen years.

We must summon up our strength and swim vigorously upstream ...

Our strength must be aroused and not dissipated. If we have shortcomings or make mistakes, they can be put right by the method of great airing of views and blooming. We must not pour cold water. We are criticized for craving greatness and success. Well then, should we seek pettiness and failure? Should we value the past and despise the future? We must crave greatness and success. The people who say so are good people. We must indeed keep up our fighting spirit.

'The revolution has not yet been completed. Comrades must still bend every effort.'[6]

4   Talks at the Chengtu Conference
March 1958

(a) Talk of 10 March

Codes and conventions consitute a problem, and I would like to use this problem as an example to discuss the question of ideological method – upholding principles while displaying the creative spirit.

Internationally we should be on friendly terms with the Soviet Union, all the people's democracies and the communist parties and working classes of all nations; we should pay proper attention to internationalism, and learn from the good points of the Soviet Union and other foreign countries. This is a principle. But there are two methods of learning: one is merely to imitate, and the other is to apply the creative spirit. Learning should be combined with creativity. To import Soviet codes and conventions inflexibly is to lack the creative spirit.

From its foundation up to the Northern Expedition (from 1921 to 1927) our Party was comparatively lively, even allowing for Ch'en Tu-hsiu's bourgeois ideology dressed up as Marxism.[1] We founded our Party in the third year following the victory of the October Revolution. Those who founded the Party were all young people who had participated in the May Fourth Movement and been influenced by it. After the October Revolution, while Lenin was still alive, while the class struggle was very acute and Stalin had still not come to power, they too were full of life. The origin of Ch'en Tu-hsiu-ism lay in foreign social democracy and our native bourgeoisie. During this period, though there occurred the mistakes of Ch'en Tu-hsiu-ism, generally speaking there was no dogmatism.

From the beginning of the Civil War period up to the Tsunyi

Conference (from 1927 to 1935) three separate 'leftist' lines arose in the Chinese Party, and the one from 1934 to 1935 was the worst.[2] At that time the Soviet Union had won victory over the Trotskyites, though on the theoretical plane they had only defeated the Deborin school.[3] The Chinese 'left' opportunists had nearly all been influenced while in the Soviet Union. Of course, this is not to say that all those who went to Moscow were dogmatists. Among the many who were in the Soviet Union at the time, some were dogmatists, others were not; some were in touch with reality, others had no contact with reality but saw only foreign conditions. What is more, Stalin's rule was beginning to be consolidated (it became firmly consolidated after the purge of counter-revolutionaries). The Comintern at that time was [run by] Bukharin, Pikov[4] and Zinoviev, while the head of the Eastern Bureau was Kuusinen and the head of the Far East Department was Mif. XXX[5] was a good comrade, humane, creative, but a bit too nice a chap. Mif's influence was the greater. These were the conditions which enabled dogmatism to develop, and some Chinese comrades were influenced by it too. Among young intellectuals there was also 'leftist deviation'. At that time Wang Ming[6] and others set themselves up as the so-called '28½ Bolsheviks'. When several hundred were studying in the Soviet Union, how was it that there were only 28½? It was because they were so terribly 'left' that they became self-restricting and isolated, thus reducing the Party's contacts.

Chinese dogmatism had its own Chinese characteristics. These were expressed in warfare and in the question of the rich peasants. Because the number of rich peasants was very small we decided in principle to leave them alone, and to make concessions to them. But the 'leftists' did not agree. They advocated 'giving the rich peasants bad land, and giving the landlords no land'. As a result the landlords had nothing to eat, and some of them fled to the mountains and formed bandit guerrilla bands. On the question of the bourgeoisie they advocated overthrowing them completely, destroying them not only politically but also economically, thereby confusing the democratic revolution with the socialist revolution. They made no analysis of imperialism, considering it all to be one uniform indivisible block supporting the Kuomintang.

In the period following the liberation of the whole country (from 1950 to 1957), dogmatism made its appearance both in economic and in cultural and educational work. A certain amount of dogmatism was imported in military work, but basic principles were upheld, and you still could not say that our military work was dogmatic. In economic work dogmatism primarily manifested itself in heavy industry, planning, banking and statistics, especially in heavy industry and planning. Since we didn't understand these things and had absolutely no experience, all we could do in our ignorance was to import foreign methods. Our statistical work was practically a copy of Soviet work; in the educational field copying was also pretty bad, for example, the system of a maximum mark of five in the schools, the uniform five years of primary school,[7] etc. We did not even study our own experience of education in the Liberated Areas. The same applied to our public health work, with the result that I couldn't have eggs or chicken soup for three years because an article appeared in the Soviet Union which said that one shouldn't eat them. Later they said one could eat them. It didn't matter whether the article was correct or not, the Chinese listened all the same and respectfully obeyed. In short, the Soviet Union was tops. In commerce it was less so, because there was more contact and exchange of documents with the Centre. There was also less dogmatism in light industry. The socialist revolution and the cooperativization of agriculture was not influenced by dogmatism because the Centre had a direct grasp of them. During the past few years the Centre has chiefly grasped the revolution and agriculture, and to a certain extent commerce.

Dogmatism appears under different sets of circumstances, which should be analysed and compared, and reasons for its appearance discovered.

1. We couldn't manage the planning, construction and assembly of heavy industrial plants. We had no experience, China had no experts, the minister was himself an outsider, so we had to copy from foreign countries, and having copied we were

unable to distinguish good from bad. Also we had to make use of Soviet experience and Soviet experts to break down the bourgeois ideology of China's old experts. The greater part of Soviet planning was correctly applied to China, but part of it was incorrect. It was imported uncritically.

2. We lacked understanding of the whole economic situation, and understood still less the economic differences between the Soviet Union and China. So all we could do was to follow blindly. Now the situation has changed. Generally speaking, we are now capable of undertaking the planning and construction of large enterprises. In another five years we shall be capable of manufacturing the equipment ourselves. We also have some understanding of Soviet and Chinese conditions.

3. Having cleared away blind faith, we no longer have any spiritual burdens. Buddhas are made several times life-size in order to frighten people. When heroes and warriors appear on the stage they are made to look quite unlike ordinary people. Stalin was that kind of a person. The Chinese people had got so used to being slaves that they seemed to want to go on. When Chinese artists painted pictures of me together with Stalin, they always made me a little bit shorter, thus blindly knuckling under to the moral pressure exerted by the Soviet Union at that time. Marxism–Leninism looks at everyone on equal terms, and all people should be treated as equals. Khrushchev's complete demolition of Stalin at one blow was also a kind of pressure, and the majority of people within the Chinese Party did not agree with it. Others wished to submit to this pressure and do away with the cult of the individual. There are two kinds of cult of the individual. One is correct, such as that of Marx, Engels, Lenin, and the correct side of Stalin. These we ought to revere and continue to revere for ever. It would not do not to revere them. As they held truth in their hands, why should we not revere them? We believe in truth; truth is the reflection of objective existence. A squad should revere its squad leader; it would be quite wrong not to. Then there is the incorrect kind of cult of the individual in which there is no analysis, simply blind obedience. This is not right. Opposition to the cult of the individual may also have one of two aims: one is opposition to

an incorrect cult, and the other is opposition to reverence for others and a desire for reverence for oneself. The question at issue is not whether or not there should be a cult of the individual, but rather whether or not the individual concerned represents the truth. If he does, then he should be revered. If truth is not present, even collective leadership will be no good. Throughout its history, our Party has stressed the combination of the role of the individual with collective leadership. When Stalin was demolished some people applauded for their own personal reasons, that is to say because they wanted others to revere them. Some people opposed Lenin, saying that he was a dictator. Lenin's reply was straightforward: better that I should be a dictator than you! Stalin was very fond of Kao Kang[8] and made him a special present of a motor car. Kao Kang sent Stalin a congratulatory telegram every 15 August. Every province now has examples of this. Is Chiang Hua a dictator, or is Sha Wen-han?[9] This sort of problem has arisen in Kwangtung, Inner Mongolia, Sinkiang, Chinghai, Kansu, Anhwei and Shantung. Don't run away with the idea that the world is at peace. The situation is unstable. You may think you are 'on firm ground', but it will not remain firm. One day the continents will sink, the Pacific Ocean will become dry land, and we'll have to move house. Small earthquakes are a frequent occurrence. The Kao–Jao affair[10] was an earthquake of the eighth degree of magnitude . . .

4. We have forgotten the lessons of historical experience, and do not understand the comparative method, nor the establishment of opposites. As I said yesterday, many of our comrades, when confronted by numerous codes and conventions, do not consider whether there might be alternative formulae, and that they should choose those which are more suited to Chinese conditions, and reject the others. They do not make any analysis, nor use their brains. They do not make comparisons. In the past when we were opposing dogmatism, their journal, the *Bolshevik*, indulged in self-adulation saying that they were one hundred per cent correct. Their method was to attack one point or a few points and not to mention the rest. Their journal

True Words attacked five big mistakes of the Central Soviet Area, without mentioning one single good point.[11]

In April 1956 I put forward the 'Ten Great Relationships', which made a start in proposing our own line for construction.[12] This was similar to that of the Soviet Union in principle, but had our own content. Among the 'Ten Great Relationships' five are primary: industry and agriculture; the coast and the interior; the Centre and the regions; the state, the collective and the individual; defence construction and economic construction. Expenditure on national defence should be small in peacetime. Administrative expenditure should be small at all times.

When Stalin was criticized in 1956, we were on the one hand happy, but on the other hand apprehensive. It was completely necessary to remove the lid, to break down blind faith, to release the pressure, and to emancipate thought. But we did not agree with demolishing him at one blow. They do not hang up his picture, but we do. In 1950 I argued with Stalin in Moscow for two months. On the questions of the Treaty of Mutual Assistance, the Chinese Eastern Railway, the joint-stock companies and the border[13] we adopted two attitudes: one was to argue when the other side made proposals we did not agree with, and the other was to accept their proposal if they absolutely insisted. This was out of consideration for the interests of socialism. Then there were the two 'colonies', that is the North-East and Sinkiang, where people of any third country were not allowed to reside.[14] Now this has been rescinded. After the criticism of Stalin, the victims of blind faith had their eyes opened a bit. In order that our comrades recognize that the old ancestor[15] also had his faults, we should apply analysis to him, and not have blind faith in him. We should accept everything good in Soviet experience, and reject what is bad. Now we are a bit more skilful in this, and understand the Soviet Union a bit better, and understand ourselves.

In 1957, in 'On the Correct Handling of Contradictions among the People', I raised the questions of the simultaneous development of industry and agriculture, of the road to industrialization, cooperativization, birth-control, etc. In that year a big thing happened, that was the nationwide Rectification Movement, the Anti-Rightist Movement, the mass criticism of our work. This was a great stimulus to the people's thinking.

In 1958 we have held three meetings at Hangchow, Nanning and Chengtu.[16] Everyone has expressed a lot of opinions at these meetings, we have done some hard thinking, and summarized our experience of the previous eight years. This was also a great stimulus to thought. A question which emerged at the Nanning Conference was the codes and conventions of the various departments of the State Council. They can be changed and they ought to be changed substantially. One way would be to meet the masses. Another way would be to promote big-character posters. Another question was that of devolution of power to the regions. We have begun to put this into effect. Now centralized power and devolved power exist simultaneously. It was decided at the Third Plenum last year that centralized power and devolved power should exist simultaneously, that power should be centralized where appropriate and devolved where that is appropriate. The devolution of power should, of course, not follow the pattern of bourgeois democracy. Before the advent of socialism bourgeois democracy is progressive, but once socialism has come it is reactionary. In the Soviet Union the Russian nationality comprises fifty per cent of the population, and the national minorities are fifty per cent, while in China the Han nationality is ninety-four per cent, while the national minorites are six per cent. So we cannot go in for a union of republics.

The Chinese revolution won victory by acting contrary to Stalin's will. The fake foreign devil [in Lu Hsün's *True Story of Ah Q*] 'did not allow people to make revolution'. But our Seventh Congress advocated going all out to mobilize the masses and to build up all available revolutionary forces in order to establish a new China.[17] During the quarrel with Wang Ming from 1937 to August 1938, we put forward ten great policies, while Wang Ming produced sixty policies.[18] If we had followed Wang Ming's, or in other words Stalin's, methods the Chinese revolution couldn't have succeeded. When our revolution succeeded, Stalin said it was a fake. We did not argue with him, and as soon as we fought the war to resist America and aid Korea, our revolution became a genuine one [in his eyes]. But when we brought out 'On the Correct Handling of Contradictions among the People' we talked about this question but they didn't, and what's more they said we were going in for liberalism, so it seemed that we were not genuine again. When this report of ours was published, the *New York Times* printed it complete, and also carried an article which claimed that China was being 'liberalized'. It is quite natural for the bourgeoisie to clutch at straws when drowning. But bourgeois politicians are not altogether without discernment. For example when Dulles heard about our report he said he wanted to see it. Within a couple of weeks he had come up with a conclusion: China was bad through and through; the Soviet Union was a little better.[19] But the Soviet Union couldn't see it, and sent us a memorandum because they feared we were moving to the right. When the Anti-Rightest Movement started, naturally our 'liberalization' vanished.

In short, our basic line is universal truth, but details differ. This applies to each country and to each province. There is unity and there are also contradictions. The Soviet Union stresses unity, and doesn't talk about contradictions, especially the contradiction between the leaders and the led.

(b) Talk of 20 March

I am going to talk about four problems:

1. The mass movement for the improvement of agricultural implements must be extended to every single locality.[20] Its significance is very great, it is a sprout of the technical revolution, it is a great revolutionary movement. Several hundreds of millions of peasants are striving mightily to negate the negative aspect of carrying things on a pole over the shoulder.[21] Whenever they succeed in doing this, they reduce the labour force required to a fraction of what it was before; the economies resulting from the replacement of carrying-poles by

mechanization greatly increase labour efficiency, and this, in turn, permits a further step forward in mechanization. This great country of China cannot be completely mechanized; there will always be some corners where mechanization is impracticable. In 1,000 years, 500 years, 100 years, 50 years, there will always be some things which are only partly mechanized – for example, making wooden boats. There are also some handicrafts which may yet survive hundreds of millions of years hence, such as the preparation of food, which will eternally remain a handicraft. Such activities constitute a unity of opposites with mechanization: their natures are different, but they must be combined.

2. Honan has put forward the slogan of carrying out the [grain-production targets of] four [hundred], five [hundred], and eight [hundred catties per *mu*][22], irrigation, the elimination of the four pests, and the abolition of illiteracy – all in the space of one year. It is possible that some of these things can be achieved, but even if all of them can be achieved, we should not say so in published reports. We should not even print reports saying that it can all be done in two years, though such reports can be circulated for internal use. It is like land reform: in the beginning, we did not publish reports, but published them only when we could announce that the reform had been partly implemented. If everyone is trying to surpass everyone else, the country may be thrown into confusion [*kao-te t'ien-hsia ta luan*] as a result. The thing is to go ahead and carry it out energetically. Every province should not follow the same wind, as though when they say it can be done in one year in Honan, everyone should do it in one year, and when they say Honan is number one, every other province should strive to be first. That would not be good. There must always be a number one: 'Every three years, there is a *chuang-yüan*; a beauty is scarcely found once in a thousand years.'[23] Let Honan try it for a year, and if Honan achieves miracles, next year every province can launch another drive for a great leap forward – wouldn't that be better?

If, in the space of one year, they carry out the four, five, and eight, and abolish illiteracy, naturally there may be very great shortcomings. At the very least, the work will be crude, and the masses will be overly tense. We should do our work boldly and joyfully, not hesitantly and coldly.

All that is necessary is that the line should be correct – going all out and aiming high to achieve greater, faster, better, and more economical [results][24] (or an even more popular formulation of these phrases) – and then, within the next year, two years, or three to five years, we will carry out the Forty Articles. In that case, we certainly can't be regarded as not having any face, it can't be considered as dishonourable, and perhaps it could even be said to be a bit better than that. As for comparisons, they should be made four times a year. Cooperativization made Chou Hsiao-chou extremely tense.[25] In the transition to higher-stage cooperatives in Szechuan, X X X[26] took it easy and didn't hurry things, so that it was finished only in 1957, and conditions there weren't at all bad. What does it matter if it takes a year longer? It may even be a bit better. On the other hand, it isn't correct either to say that it will certainly take four or five years to complete [these tasks]. The problem is to see what the conditions are, and whether the level of consciousness of the masses has been raised or not. How many years are required will depend on objectively existing circumstances. There are two lines for building socialism: is it better to go about it coldly and deliberately, or boldly and joyfully? If we carry out the Forty Articles in eight or ten years, building socialism will not involve excluding [anyone] from the Party. In forty years, the Soviet Union has been able to produce only such a little bit of food and other stuff. If, in eighteen years, we can equal what they have done in the past forty years, it will naturally be all right, and we should do precisely that. For there are more of us, and the political conditions are different, too: we are livelier, and there is more Leninism here. They, on the other hand, have let part of Leninism go by the boards, they are lifeless and without vitality. Lenin's writings of the revolutionary period attacked people very fiercely, but his attacks were justified, he was in tune with the mood of the masses, he had given his heart to the masses.

The speed of construction is a thing that exists objectively.

Everything which, objectively and subjectively, is capable of achievement, we must endeavour to achieve by going all out, aiming high, and producing greater, faster, better, and more economical results. But that which cannot be achieved, we should not try to force ourselves to do. Right now there is a gust of wind, amounting to a force 10 typhoon. We must not impede this publicly, but within our own ranks [nei-pu] we must speak clearly, and damp down the atmosphere a little. We must get rid of the empty reports and foolish boasting, we must not compete for reputation, but serve reality. Some of the targets are high, and no measures have been taken to implement them; that is not good. In a word, we must have concrete measures, we must deal in reality. We must deal in abstractions, too – revolutionary romanticism is a good thing – but it is not good if there are no measures [for giving it practical effect].

3. Every two months, each province, city, and autonomous region must hold a meeting to make an investigation and sum up the results, a small meeting of from several people to a dozen or so. Coordinated regions[27] must also hold a meeting every two or three months. The changes in the course of the movement are very great, there must be exchange of information. The aim of the meetings is to coordinate the rhythm of production. While one wave has not yet fallen, another rises in turn; this is the unity of the opposites, fast and slow. Under the general line of going all out and aiming high to achieve greater, faster, better and more economical results, a wave-like form of progress is the unity of the opposites, deliberation and haste, the unity of the opposites, toil and dreams. If we have only haste and toil, that is one-sided. To be concerned only with the intensity of labour – that won't do, will it? In all of our work, we must use both deliberation and haste. (For example, the Party secretary in Wuchang hsien did not take account of the peasants' sentiments, and wanted them to go on working on the reservoirs on the twenty-ninth day of the twelfth [lunar] month, so half of the civilian workers just took off.) This means also the unity of hard fighting with rest and consolidation. In the past, when we waged war, there had to be an interval between two campaigns for rest and consolidation, bringing our forces up to

strength and training the soldiers. We could not keep fighting one battle after another – there is a rhythm in warfare, too. The one hundred per cent 'Bolshevization' carried out in the Central Soviet Area was opposed to rest and consolidation, and advocated: 'Be audacious and resolute, follow up victories and pursue the foe immediately, crush Nanchang.' How could that work?[28] The unity of the opposites, hard fighting, and rest and consolidation, is a law; moreover, they are transformed into one another. There is nothing which does not undergo such transformation. 'Haste' is transformed into 'deliberation', and 'deliberation' is transformed into 'haste'. 'Toil' is transformed into 'dreams', and 'dreams' are transformed into 'toil'. It is the same with rest and consolidation, and hard fighting. Toil and dreams, deliberation and haste, also have [an element of] identity; rest and consolidation and hard fighting also have an element of identity. Going to bed and getting up is also a unity of opposites. I ask you, for example, who can guarantee that after getting up he will not go to bed? On the contrary: 'He who has been lying down for a long time thinks of getting up.' Going to bed is transformed into getting up, and getting up is transformed into going to bed. Convening a meeting moves towards its opposite, and is transformed into dismissing a meeting. As soon as a meeting is called, it bears within itself factors leading to its own dismissal. We can't meet for 10,000 years here in Chengtu. Wang Hsi-feng says, 'However grandiose the banquet, it must always come to an end.'[29] This is the truth. A statement cannot be rejected because of the speaker; our judgement must be based on whether it is true or not. After a meeting is dismissed, problems accumulate again, until there is once more a transformation into convening a meeting. We unite, and then after we have carried out our work for a while, ideas diverge, and this is transformed into struggle; divergencies arise, and once more there are splits. We can't go on uniting day after day and year after year. As soon as we talk about unity, there is disunity; disunity is unconditional. At the very time we talk of unity, there still remains disunity – this is why we have work to do. To talk all the time about monolithic unity, and not to talk about struggle, is not Marxist–Leninist. Unity passes through struggle, only thus can unity be achieved. It is the same within the Party, as regards classes, and among the people. Unity is tranformed into struggle, and then there is unity again. We cannot talk of monolithic unity alone, and not talk about struggle, about contradictions. The Soviet Union does not talk about the contradictions between the leaders and the led. If there were no contradictions and no struggle, there would be no world, no progress, no life, there would be nothing at all. To talk all the time about unity is 'a pool of stagnant water'; it can lead to coldness. We must destroy the old basis for unity, pass through a struggle, and unite on a new basis. Which is better – a stagnant pool, or 'the inexhaustible Yangtse comes roaring past'?[30] It's like this with the Party, and it's like this, too, with classes and the people. Unity–struggle–unity: this means we have done our work. Production is transformed into consumption, consumption is transformed into production. Production is carried out for the sake of consumption; production is carried out not merely for the sake of other toilers – the producers themselves are also consumers. If a person doesn't eat, he has no energy at all, and he can't produce. If he easts hot meals, he can do more work. Marx says: production also includes consumption. Production and consumption, construction and destruction, are unities of opposites, they are transformed into one another. The production of the Anshan Iron and Steel Works is done for the sake of consumption; in a few decades, the installations will be replaced. Sowing is transformed into reaping, reaping is transformed into sowing. Sowing consists in consuming seeds; after the seeds are sown, they move towards their opposite, and are not called seeds, but rice plants, crops; after the crops are harvested, new seeds are once more obtained.

We must cite abundant examples, put forward several dozen or a hundred examples in order to explain the concepts of the unity of opposites and their transformation into one another. Only thus can we correct our ideology and raise our level of understanding. Spring, summer, autumn and winter are also transformed into one another. Elements of spring and summer are contained in autumn and winter. Birth and death are also transformed into one another. Living is tranformed into dying, lifeless matter is transformed into living beings. I propose that when people over the age of fifty die, a party should be held to celebrate, for it is inevitable that men should die, this is a natural law.[31] Grain is an annual plant, every year it is born once, and dies once; moreover, the more that dies, the more that is born. To take [another] example, if pigs were not slaughtered, there would be fewer of them all the time; who would feed them?

The *Concise Philosophical Dictionary* makes a specialty of opposing me. It says the transformation of birth into death is metaphysical, and the transformation of war into peace is wrong.[32] In the last analysis, who is right? Let me ask: if living beings do not result from the transformation of inanimate matter, where do they come from? In the beginning, there was nothing but inorganic matter on earth; organic matter appeared only subsequently. All living substances result from changes in twelve elements such as nitrogen and hydrogen.[33] All living beings result from the transformation of inanimate matter.

Sons are transformed into fathers, fathers are transformed into sons; women are transformed into men, men are transformed into women. Such transformations cannot take place directly, but, after marriage, sons and daughters are born; is this not transformation?

The oppressors and the oppressed are transformed into one another, as in the relations between bourgeoisie and landlords on the one hand, and workers and peasants on the other. Naturally, when we talk about these oppressors, we are referring to the old ruling classes, it is a matter of class dictatorship and not of individual oppressors.

War is transformed into peace, peace is the opposite of war. When there had been no fighting, that was peace; as soon as the 38th Parallel was crossed, that was war, and as soon as the armistice was concluded, that was peace again. Military affairs are politics under particular circumstances, they are the continuation of politics; politics is also a kind of war.

To sum up, quantitative changes are transformed into qualitative changes, and qualitative changes are transformed into quantitative changes. Europe is heavily infested with dogmatism, and the Soviet Union has some shortcomings, but all of this is bound to change, and if we don't do our work well, we can become rigid again. If, at such a time, our industry has become number one in the world, we might grow cocky, and then our thinking might ossify.

The finite is transformed into the infinite, the infinite is transformed into the finite. The dialectics of ancient times was transformed into the metaphysics of the Middle Ages, and the metaphysics of the Middle Ages was transformed into the dialectics of modern times. The universe, too, undergoes transformation, it is not eternal. Capitalism leads to socialism, socialism leads to communism, and communist society must still be transformed, it will also have a beginning and an end, it will certainly be divided into stages[34], or they will give it another name, it cannot remain constant. If there were only quantitative changes and no qualitative changes, that would go against dialectics. There is nothing in the world that does not arise, develop, and disappear. Monkeys turned into men, mankind arose; in the end, the whole human race will disappear, it may turn into something else, at that time the earth itself will also cease to exist. The earth must certainly be extinguished, the sun too will grow cold – it is already much cooler than it was in ancient times. During the ice age, there was one change in two million years. When the ice came, a large part of all living creatures perished. Beneath the South Pole there is a great deal of coal, so you can see that in ancient times it was very warm there. In Yen-ch'ang *hsien* they have discovered petrified bamboo. (An author of the Sung dynasty said that bamboo grew in Yen-ch'ang in ancient times, but now it can't.)

All things must have a beginning and an end. Only two things are infinite: time and space. The infinite is made up of the finite. All things of whatever kind develop and change step by step.

I have talked about all this in order to extend and enliven our thinking. Whenever the mind becomes rigid, it is very dangerous. We must educate our cadres. The Central, provincial, regional, and *hsien*-level cadres are very important. Including all the various systems,[35] there are several hundred thousand of them. In a word, we must do more thinking, we must not have constantly in mind the classic writings,[36] but we must make use of our brains and enliven our thinking.

4. The line for building socialism is still being created, but we already have the basic ideas. Of the 600 million people of the whole country, and the 12 million Party members, only a minority – only a few millions, I fear – feels that this line is correct. It may be that a great many people still have doubts, or are not aware. For example, when the peasants carried out irrigation, you couldn't say they were doubtful, but when it comes to the line, they are not aware. Or, to take another example, the number of those who really have faith in the campaign to get rid of the four pests has now gradually increased. I myself used to have doubts, and whenever I ran into someone, I would ask: 'Is it really possible or not to get rid of the four pests?' It was the same with cooperativization; so long as we had not demonstrated [its feasibility] there were bound to be doubts. There was also a part of the people who basically mistrusted it, amounting perhaps to a few tens of millions – landlords, rich peasants, bourgeois, intellectuals, democratic personages, and even including some from within the labouring people, and a part of our cadres. At present, we have already induced a minority of people to feel that this line is correct. As for ourselves, we recognize that this line is correct, in theory and as demonstrated in practice in some of our work – for example, there is a substantial increase in production, we have had quite a few successes in our work, and the majority of the people feel at ease. Nevertheless, the Forty Articles, and overtaking England in fifteen years, are in the domain of theory. The four, five and eight have, for the most part, not yet been carried out, the industrialization of the whole country has not yet been carried out, overtaking England in fifteen years is still a slogan, the 156 key projects[37] have not yet all been built. There remains a question in my mind about producing, in the course of the second five-year plan, 20 million tons of steel. Is this a good thing, or will it throw everything into confusion? I'm not sure at present, so I want to hold meetings. We'll meet four times a year, and if there are problems,

we will make adjustments. The situation after construction has been carried out must be one of the following: excellent, fairly good, not too good, bad, or great disorder [*ta luan*]. It looks as though, if disorder results, it won't be all that great, there will be just a spell of disorder, and then things may well move towards 'order' [*chih*]. The appearance of disorder contains within it some favourable elements, we should not fear disorder. In the course of building up industry in Hungary, disorders occurred, but now things are all right again.

The line has already begun to take shape, it reflects the creations of the masses in their struggles. This is a law. The leading organs have put forward some directives which reflect these creations. So many things we did not foresee. Laws exist objectively, they cannot be diverted by man's will. For example, in 1955, when the high tide of cooperativization was seething, we did not foresee the emergence of the question of Stalin, of the Hungarian affair, and of the slogan 'Oppose adventurism'.[38] How will it be next year? What else is likely to happen? What 'ism' will they oppose? Who can predict this? Concrete affairs cannot be foretold.[39]

At present the reciprocal relations between people are determined by the relationship between three big classes:

The first is [composed of] imperialism, feudalism, bureaucratic capitalism, the rightists and their agents. If we do not carry out a revolution aimed at these, our productive forces will be fettered. The rightists make up two per cent of the bourgeoisie. The great majority of these can in future be changed and transformed –but that's another question.

The second is the national bourgeoisie, by which I mean all [the members of this class] except for the rightists. They are of a divided mind about the new China. They are drawn to us in spite of themselves, and at the same time they want to engage in capitalism. Now that they have passed through rectification, there have been some changes; we may perhaps have the support of two thirds of them. Incidentally, the democratic parties and groups in Peking have called a big meeting for self-criticism, reform, and oath-taking;[40] such meetings should be held in the whole country.

The third is the left, that is to say the labouring people, the workers, the peasants. (In reality there are four classes – the peasants are a separate class.)

The line has already begun to take shape, but it has yet to be perfected and verified in practice, so we cannot say that it is finally complete. The workers put on airs of extravagance *vis-à-vis* the peasants, and some cadres strive for fame and position – all this is bourgeois thinking. If we do not resolve these problems, we will not do well in production; if we do not sort out these reciprocal relations, how can we do our work well? In the past, we put far too little thought into construction; most of our energy was devoted to making revolution. Mistakes will inevitably be committed. It is impossible not to commit them. The commission of mistakes is a necessary condition for the formation of a correct line. The correct line is formulated with reference to the erroneous line, the two constitute a unity of opposites. The correct line is formed in the struggle with the incorrect line. To say that mistakes can all be avoided, [so that] there are only correct things, and no mistakes, is an anti-Marxist proposition. The problem lies in committing fewer mistakes, and less serious ones. The correct and the erroneous are a unity of opposites, the theory of inevitability is correct. That there should be only correct things, and nothing erroneous, as without precedent in history, it amounts to denying the law of the unity of opposites. It is metaphysical. If there were only men and no women, if women were negated, what would we do then? It is possible to strive for a situation in which very few mistakes are committed. The number of mistakes [should be like] the relation between a giant and a dwarf. It is possible to commit few errors, and we must achieve this. Marx and Lenin achieved it.

(c) *Talk of 22 March*

'People do not go to a Buddist temple for no reason,'[41] and I have a number of problems on which I would like to exchange views with you.

In the play *The Story of the Western Chamber*[42] there is an episode involving the two characters Chang Sheng and Hui Ming. Tiger Sun has surrounded the P'u Chiu Monastery and the scholar Chang Sheng wants to get a message through to his friend, the White Horse General, to bring him to the rescue. There is nobody to carry the message and so they hold a mass meeting at which Hui Ming steps forward and volunteers to go. Hui Ming is depicted as a courageous, bold and resolute fellow. I hope that China will have more Hui Mings to develop a movement of 'great airing of views, great blooming and big-character posters'[43] among the hundreds of thousands of people at county [*hsien*] committee level and above, in order to criticize the leadership. This will make for a proletarian atmosphere, a communist atmosphere. When the masses give you a good telling-off to vent their feelings, this does not mean that they are going to cut off your head or take away your job. It just means that they are in a lively militant mood, that they have a very good communist style. The way that the masses are now carrying out these struggles is excellent, and we comrades should also promote such a style among ourselves.

Ch'en Po-ta[44] has just written to me. Before this nothing would induce him to run a journal. Now he has made a 180-degree turn and agreed to start one this year. This is fine. Our Party used to have several journals – *Guide, Struggle, Truth,* etc. Although we now have the *People's Daily* we have no theoretical magazine. We originally made plans for the Centre and Shanghai to publish one each, in order to bring about a direct confrontation of competing views, but now it is proposed that each province should start a separate one. This is very good. In this way our theoretical level can be raised and our thinking enlivened. Each provincial journal should have its own individual characteristics, and whilst each one should base its discussion mainly on the situation in its own province, they may also talk about China as a whole, or about the whole world, the universe – even the sun and the Milky Way.

Comrades working in the provinces will sooner or later come to the Centre. Comrades at the Centre will sooner or later either die or leave the scene. Khrushchev came from a local area. At the local level the class struggle is more acute, closer to natural struggle, closer to the masses. This gives the local comrades an advantage over those at the Centre. Ch'in was a kingdom before it proclaimed itself an empire.

We must improve our style of work, speak with sincerity, take a firm hold of ourselves and possess the spirit to sweep all before us and climb to the highest peak. To do this we must have a thorough understanding of Marxist theory and of the basic contradictions in our work. But at present our comrades have no ambition to be invincible, rather they have a lethargic air about them. This is no good. It exemplifies a slave mentality, like that of Chia Kuei, who had become so used to standing up that he was afraid to sit down. We must respect the classics but we must not follow them blindly. Marxism was itself created, not copied or lifted straight from books. On this point Stalin was relatively good. The *History of the Communist Party of the Soviet Union* says in its conclusion: 'Particular points of Marxist principle which are not in accord with reason[45] may be changed, such as the principle that one country cannot be victorious*.' Confucian scholars worshipped Confucius so blindly that they dared not use his name K'ung Ch'iu. Li Ho of the T'ang dynasty was, however, quite different. He referred to Emperor Wu of Han by his name Liu Ch'e, or Master Liu, and to the Empress as Mistress Wei.[46]

Once we give in to blind faith our minds become cramped and our thought cannot burst out of its confinement. Unless you have a conquering spirit it is very dangerous to study Marxism–Leninism. Stalin could be said to have had this spirit, though it became somewhat tarnished. The Leninist foundation of his writing on linguistics and economics was relatively correct – basically correct. But there are some issues worth studying, for example the role of the theory of value in the socialist stage. Should we take the amount of time expended in preparing people for labour as a criterion for fixing wages? Under socialism private property still exists, the small group still exists, the family still exists. The family, which emerged in the last period of primitive communism, will in future be abolished. It

*i.e., that socialism cannot first be victorious in one country alone.

had a beginning and will come to an end. K'ang Yu-wei perceived this in his book *Universal Harmony*.[47] Historically, the family was a production unit, a consumption unit, a unit for the procreation of the labour force of the next generation, and a unit for the education of children. Nowadays the workers do not regard the family as a unit of production; the peasants in the cooperatives have also largely changed, and peasant families are generally not units of production. They only engage in a certain amount of subsidiary production. As for the families of government workers and members of the armed forces, they produce even less; they have become merely units of consumption, and units for rearing and bringing up labour reserves, while the chief unit of education is the school. In short, the family may in future become something which is unfavourable to the development of production. Under the present system of distribution of 'to each according to his work', the family is still of use. When we reach the stage of the communist relationship of distribution of 'to each according to his need', many of our concepts will change. After maybe a few thousand years, or at the very least several hundred years, the family will disappear. Many of our comrades do not dare to think about these things. They are very narrow-minded. But problems such as the disappearance of classes and parties have already been discussed in the classics. This shows that the approach of Marx and Lenin was lofty, while ours is low.

Professors – we have been afraid of them ever since we came into the towns. We did not despise them, we were terrified of them. When confronted by people with piles of learning we felt that we were good for nothing. For Marxists to fear bourgeois intellectuals, to fear professors while not fearing imperialism, is strange indeed. I believe this attitude is another example of the slave mentality, a relic from the time of 'gratitude for His Majesty's favours'. We must not tolerate it any longer. Naturally we cannot go out tomorrow and beat them up. We have to make contact with them, educate them and make friends with them. They may have studied more natural science than we have, but they do not necessarily know more social science. They may have studied more Marxism–Leninism but they are incapable of entering into the spirit of it, or really understanding it. Wu Ching-ch'ao[48] read a great deal, but opposed Marxism at every opportunity.

We should not feel ashamed of ourselves. Bernstein, Kautsky, Plekhanov in his late period, all studied Marxism–Leninism much more than we have, yet they were not much good. They transformed the Second International into the servant of the bourgeoisie.

Now the situation has changed, as indicated by Comrade Ch'en Po-ta's speech 'Stress the Present, not the Past', his letter 'To the Chairman', and his communication 'Be prepared to explain to the lower levels'. All of these are very forceful. Yet there are many comrades who are indifferent to the struggle on the ideological front, such as the criticism of Hu Feng, Liang Shu-ming, *The Life of Wu Hsün*, the *Dream of the Red Chamber*, and Ting Ling, [49] etc. Our basic views on the elimination of the bourgeoisie were stated in the resolution of the Second Plenum of the Seventh Central Committee. During the democratic revolution we used to say that the revolution had two stages, and that the first stage was a preparation for the second.[50] We believe in permanent revolution, yet many comrades gave no thought to the timing of the socialist revolution or to what should be done after land reform. They closed their eyes to sprouts[51] of socialism even after such forms had appeared. The mutual-aid teams in Jui-chin[52] and in the anti-Japanese bases were such sprouts.

Wang Ming and Ch'en Tu-hsiu were of the same ilk. Ch'en Tu-hsiu considered that after the bourgeois revolution had succeeded, the bourgeoisie should hold political power, and the socialist revolution should not be launched until the proletariat had been consolidated and enlarged. Hence Ch'en Tu-hsiu was not a Marxist–Leninist but a bourgeois-democratic revolutionary radical. Yet thirty years later there are still people like him. Bad people like Ting Ling and Feng Hsüeh-feng and good people like XXX are nothing but bourgeois democrats. They proclaim the 'four great freedoms',[53] assert that peasants are afraid of showing off, thus sharply opposing us. The rich middle peasants in Honan did not want the cadres to see their valuables and feigned poverty. They bought cloth from pedlars when nobody was looking. This was excellent. It meant that the poor and lower-middle peasants were so strong that the rich middle peasants were afraid to show off. It meant that socialism has a great future. But some people did not like it and felt that this fear should be removed. They issued announcements proclaiming the 'four great freedoms', while failing to ask for instructions or even to consult others. Clearly this was defiance of the policies laid down by the Second Plenum. They were not spiritually prepared for socialism, though now they have become convinced and have become activized.

From ancient times the people who have created new schools of thought have always been young people without great learning. Confucius started at the age of twenty-three; and how much learning did Jesus have? Sakyamuni founded Buddhism at the age of nineteen; his learning was only acquired gradually later on. What learning did Sun Yat-sen have in his youth? He only went through higher middle school. Marx was also very young when he first created Dialectical Materialism. His learning was also acquired later on. He was about thirty when he wrote the *Communist Manifesto*, by which time his school of thought was already established. When he started to write books he was only in his twenties. The people whom he criticized were all learned bourgeois scholars of the time like Ricardo, Adam Smith, Hegel, etc. In history it is always those with little learning who overthrow those with much learning. The things Chang T'ai-yen[54] wrote in his youth were lively and full of the spirit of the democratic revolution. His aim was to overthrow the Manchus. K'ang Yu-wei was the same. Liu Shih-p'ei[55] made his name when he was only twenty and was only thirty when he died. Wang Pi[56] was in his teens when he annotated Lao-tzu and died from mental strain when still in his twenties. Yen Yüan[57] (a sage of the second rank) was only thirty-two when he died. Li Shih-min[58] was in his teens when he rebelled and became commander-in-chief. At twenty-four he ascended the imperial throne. He was neither particularly old nor learned. The question is whether your direction is right or not. Ch'in Shu-pao[59] was also very young. When young people grasp a truth they are invincible and old people cannot compete with them. Lo Ch'eng and Wang Po-tang[60] were only in their twenties. When Liang Ch'i-ch'ao[16] was young, he too was invincible, yet when we are faced by professors we become feeble and afraid that their scholarship will show us up.

Once our journals are published, provided that their direction is correct, they will do fine. Lei Hai-tsung had studied Marxism–Leninism, but he was not as good as us because while we believed in it, the more he read the more right-wing he became. Now we want to run journals and to prevail over the bourgeois intellectuals; we only need to read a dozen or so books and we can beat them. Once we start to run our journals we shall be forced to study the classics, to think about problems, and turn our hands to writing. All this will raise our ideological level. Now a whole pile of publications has come to our attention. If we do not produce our publications people will not be reading books: they will only be discussing abstract matters and not talk about how to be 'red'.

Each province can run a journal and thus set up a kind of confrontation. They can also be responsible for sending articles to the central publication. Six articles a year from each province would be sufficient. Anyway, there should be less than ten. You people go and organize this. This is the way to produce heroes.

Ever since ancient times the people who founded new schools of thought were all young people without too much learning. They had the ability to recognize new things at a glance and, having grasped them, they opened fire on the old fogeys. The old fogeys with learning always opposed them. When Martin Luther founded the Reformation, and Darwin's theories appeared, many people opposed them. The inventor of sleeping-pills was not even a doctor, let alone a famous doctor; he was only a pharmacist. At first the Germans did not take him seriously, but the French welcomed him. That was how sleeping-pills started. I am told that penicillin was invented by a man who worked as a laundryman in a dyers and cleaners. Franklin of America, who discovered electricity, began as a newspaper boy. Later he became biographer, politician and scientist. Gorki only had two years of elementary schooling. Of course some things can be learnt at school; I don't propose to close all the schools. What I mean is that it is not absolutely necessary to attend school. The main thing is whether your direction is correct or not and whether you come to grips with your studies. Learning has to be grasped. As soon as they had grasped the truth the young founders of new schools embarked on discoveries, scorning the old fogeys. Then those with learning oppressed them. Isn't that what history is like? When we started to make revolution, we were mere twenty-year-old boys, while the rulers of that time, like Yüan Shih-k'ai and Tuan Ch'i-jui[62] were old and experienced. They had more learning, but we had more truth.

I am glad to see how spirited the big-character posters have been recently. Their sharp criticism and lively style have blown away the stale atmosphere. Yet we always walk sedately with measured tread. 'Meeting people we only say three tenths of what we mean, afraid to lay bare our whole heart.' We don't speak sincerely.

Wang He-shou's second article dares to criticize dogmatism. P'eng T'ao's article is also good.[63] It has persuasive power, although it is not sharp enough. It is 'attacking others and elevating oneself', though not in an individualistic way. Rather it attacks incorrect ideas and elevates correct ideas, which is absolutely necessary. (Of course the errors also include his own.) T'eng Tai-yüan's article is also good, but he is deficient in persuasive power. He should explain the reasons for building so many railways, otherwise people will be frightened off. Chang Hsi-jo[64] criticized us for 'craving greatness and success, being impatient for quick results, scorning the past and putting blind faith in the future'.

This is just what the proletariat is like! Any class 'craves greatness and success'. Should we rather 'crave pettiness and failure'? King Yü valued every moment of time. We too must treasure every minute. Confucius said: 'Three days without seeing my lord makes me worried.' He also said: 'I never sit long enough to warm my mat.' Mo-tzu's 'stove was not used long enough to be blackened'. They were both men who were hungry for success and quick results. We too follow this rule.

Irrigation, rectification, anti-rightism, 600 million people engaged in a great movement. Isn't this 'craving for greatness and success'? In setting average advanced norms for workers, aren't we 'being impatient for quick results'? Unless we despise the old system and the old reactionary productive relationships, what do we think we are doing? If we do not have faith in socialism and communism, what do we think we are doing?

We have made mistakes and we have been subjectivist, but it is correct to 'crave greatness and success, to be impatient for quick results, to despise the past and put blind faith in the future'. Although they oppose me, the spirit of the letters from Tientsin and Nanking is praiseworthy. I think they are good. The one from Tientsin is the better, the one from Nanking being insipid and weak. As for Ch'en Ch'i-t'ung and the other three,[65] apart from Ch'en I who is a rightist, their courage in speaking out is praiseworthy. It is very bad to whisper behind people's backs and not to speak out to their faces. We should have general agreement – at least in principle. We should be able to speak either more sharply or more tactfully, but we must speak out. Sometimes we must be sharp and clear-cut. But in any case, if we take our desire for unity as our starting-point and adopt a helpful attitude, then sharp criticism cannot split the Party; it can only unite the Party. It is very dangerous to leave unsaid things which you want to say. Of course, we must choose our time to speak, and it does not do to ignore strategy. Take, for example, the three big cases of the Ming dynasty. Those who opposed Wei Chung-hsien paid too little attention to strategy and were themselves eliminated.[66] Among those who fell into disfavour with the emperor at that time, there was a Szechwanese, Yang Shen,[67] who was exiled to Yünnan. Those who spoke the truth in history, such as Pi Kan,[68] Ch'ü Yüan,[69] Chu Yün[70] and Chia I,[71] all failed in their purpose but they fought for a principle. Those who are afraid to speak out are afraid of being called opportunists, afraid of getting the sack, afraid of being expelled from the Party, afraid of being divorced by their wives (and thus losing face), afraid of being confined to the guardroom, afraid of having their heads chopped off. I feel that as long as you are prepared for these eventualities and are able to see through the vanities of this world, you need be afraid of nothing. If you make no psychological preparation, you will not dare to speak. But should fear of martyrdom seal our lips? We must create an environment in which people will dare to speak out and reveal what is in their hearts. The Report to the Nineteenth Congress of the Communist Party of the Soviet Union said: We must create an environment. From the masses' point of view this is correct, and advanced elements should not be afraid of this sort of thing. They should have the spirit of Wang Hsi-feng who said: 'He who is not afraid of the death by a thousand cuts dares to unhorse the emperor.'

We ought to be leading the masses, yet the masses nowadays are more advanced than us. They have the courage to put up big-character posters criticizing us. Of course this is different from Ch'u An-p'ing.[72] In his case it was the enemy cursing us. Today it is criticism among comrades. Some of our comrades' style of work is not good. There are some things they don't dare to say. They only say three tenths. This is first because they are afraid of being unpopular, second because they are afraid of losing votes. This is a vulgar working style which must be changed, and now we have the possibility of changing it.

In 1956 three things were blown away: the general line of achieving greater, faster, better and more economical results, the promoters of progress, and the Forty Articles. There were three kinds of people with three kinds of reaction: distress, indifference, and delight. A millstone had dropped from their neck and there would be peace in the world. Of those exhibiting these three attitudes the ones in the middle were numerous, while the two extremes were small. In 1956 there were the same three attitudes towards many problems. They were comparatively unanimous on the question of opposing Japan and Chiang Kai-shek and on land reform. But on the question of cooperativization there were these three attitudes. Is this a correct assessment?

This conference has solved a number of questions and reached agreement, and prepared some documents for the Politburo. Its weakness is that there has been relatively little discussion of ideology. Should we devote two or three days to talking about ideology, and say what is on our minds? The comrades say that this conference is a rectification conference. But we do not talk about ideology or fulfil our pledges. Isn't there a contradiction here? We have neither been carrying out struggles nor identifying rightists, but talking in gentle tones like light breezes and sweet showers, so that everyone can say what is on his mind. My purpose is to get people to dare to speak out with vigour and invincible force, like Marx or Lu Hsün, freeing themselves from inhibitions. We should make a breakthrough at the level of the local Party secretariat, within groups of about three people. This would create a new atmosphere. When he was eighteen or nineteen, Tsou Jung wrote a book entitled *The Revolutionary Army* which directly denounced the emperor.[73] When Chang T'ai-yen wrote his article refuting K'ang Yu-wei he too was still full of spirit. The older you get the less useful you are. You must not underestimate yourself, but mobilize all your energies. Of course we still need old people: they must also take the helm. Liu Pei of the Three Kingdoms period was no good; this too was a case of an old man taking command. We must break out of the dull atmosphere in the Party.

All the poems which have been published are relics of the past. Why not produce some folk poems? Will every comrade on his return please be responsible for collecting folk poems. Each social stratum, as well as the young people and children, have many folk poems. We should have a go at this. Everyone can be issued with a few sheets of paper to write folk poems on. Those among the labouring people who cannot write can ask others to write for them. We can set a time limit of ten days. We can collect large numbers of old folk songs, and next time publish a collection.

The future of Chinese poetry is folk songs first and the classics second. On this basis we can produce a new poetry. In form it should be in the folk-song style, while in content it should combine the two opposites, realism and romanticism. If you are too realistic you can't write poetry. The new poetry of today is formless. Nobody reads it. Anyway I wouldn't read it, not unless you gave me a hundred dollars. In the field of collecting folk poetry, Peking University has done a lot of work. If we do this job it is possible that we may discover millions and millions of folk poems. This will not involve much work, and they will be much easier to read than the poems of Tu Fu and Li Po.[74]

5 Speech at the Group Leaders' Forum of the Enlarged Meeting of the Military Affairs Committee

Excerpts. 28 June 1958

This has been a good conference. Some comrades' speeches were very good.* Comrade Chang Tsung-hsün's speech was very good. I agree with it. He wrote it under pressure from the fourth-grade cadres conference of the Military Training Headquarters. This proves that when you compel people, they can write good stuff. There is just one point I don't agree with. Chang Tsung-hsün says that the reason he made mistakes was that he had not studied Mao Tse-tung's writings properly. This is not correct. He should have said that it was primarily because his Marxist–Leninist level was not high enough. Comrade Ya-lou's speech is also pretty good. This illustrates the point that the army comrades' level is high and that they can write. The best thing would be to organize some of the comrades at army and divisional level to speak and write because they are the people who do the practical work, and they have contact with the lower echelons. The stuff they write can achieve unity of theory and practice. The content of conferences should be rich and varied and should introduce advanced experience in the work. In our articles and speeches we should not criticize the Soviet Union. Dogmatism is a problem in our own study; it is not just a question of whether the Soviet Union is advanced or not.

From the beginning there has existed in our army a struggle between two lines in military construction. We had a struggle at

*XX asked the Chairman especially to read the speeches of nine comrades. The Chairman read the speeches of Comrades Chang Tsung-hsün and Liu Ya-lou[1].

the Kut'ien Conference,[2] but we were unable to convince the comrades who held incorrect ideas. Some comrades still adhere to their incorrect line right up to today. Comrade Hsiao K'e[3] was not only guilty of dogmatism, but had a warlord mentality marked by bourgeois ideology, dogmatism and feudal ideology.

In wartime it will not do to implement orders according to Soviet army regulations. It is better for us to have our own regulations. I don't know how much Marxism–Leninism there is in the Military Academy and the Military Training Command. Marxism–Leninism should be a guide for action, yet they use it as a dogma for recitation. If Marx and Lenin were still alive, they would certainly criticize these comrades as being dogmatic. Today the dogmatists advocate copying the Soviet Union. Whom, I would like to know, did the Soviet Union copy in the past? In the resolutions of the Eighth Congress there is a passage dealing with the problem of technological reform. From the point of view of present conditions this is inappropriate because it over-emphasizes Soviet aid. It is very necessary to win Soviet aid, but the most important thing is self-reliance. If we over-emphasize Soviet aid, the question I would like to ask is, on whom did the Soviet Union depend for aid in the past?

The Great Leap Forward in industry and agriculture has destroyed blind faith. We can catch up with Britain in — years, and in from — to — years catch up with America. Next year our steel output will reach from — to — tens of thousands of tons. It is reported that the north-east will produce — tens of thousands of tons by 1962. This is all the result of rectification. The Nanning Conference and the Chengtu Conference broke down blind faith, liberated our thinking and resulted in the Great Leap Forward in industry. Yet we have been training armies for over eight years and have not produced even one book of combat regulations. Now we must gather together some comrades who have rich experience in work and combat to produce a book of combat regulations of our own. Some people mentioned that when the Soviet comrade advisers saw that we were not copying theirs, they made adverse comments and were displeased. We might ask these Soviet comrades: Do you copy

Chinese regulations? If they say they don't, then we will say: If you don't copy ours, we won't copy yours.

Why is it that XX hasn't performed well since the victory of the revolution? Apart from the fact that he has not made a sufficiently deep appraisal of his experience in the former period and learned the historical lessons, the reasons are: first, he has blindly accepted old things and old dogmas; second, he has put blind faith in foreign dogmas and in the Soviet Union; third, he has blind faith in himself. He has been very active, hard-working and conscientious, but his direction was haywire and he was not strong enough on politics. The main aim of this conference is to overthrow the slave mentality and to bury dogmatism; also to use the methods of rectification, with a great airing of views and great blooming, to break down blind faith, raise our ideological level, absorb the lessons of experience and, above all, to educate the whole Party and whole army and to unite the whole Party and whole army. Therefore during the conference we can criticize people by name. But I would suggest that when we are formulating resolutions, we only need to distinguish between right and wrong and clarify problems. We do not have to put in the names of those comrades who have made mistakes. After all, in the resolutions of the Kut'ien Conference no names were mentioned.

With X it is mainly a case of blind faith in foreigners. He has an inferiority complex. He hasn't been able to rid himself of this blind faith. He doesn't regard our own experience as of primary importance. Nowadays even a cooperative has to summarize its experience, otherwise it would lag behind. The five cooperatives of Hsinchou in Hupei Province did pretty well, Mach'eng was not so good. But Hsinchou paid no attention to summarizing its experience. Mach'eng sent people round to Hsinchou to study their experience so that they could summarize and extend their own work. In the end the work in Mach'eng went into the lead. When the army went into battle in the past, did it not summarize the experience of its various units, re-train them, and then go into battle again? In all our work we must pay attention to the summing up of our good experience in order to publicize it.

The Soviet Union defeated the intervention of fourteen imperialist countries. That was a long time ago. The Soviet Union has had the experience of the Second World War. We defeated Chiang Kai-shek, Japanese imperialism, American imperialism. We have rich experience, more than the Soviet Union. We should not regard our own experience as worthless. This is wrong. (*Chief Lin*[4] *interjected: 'Our experience is very rich. We must not throw gold away as though it were yellow dust.'*) We must think of our experience as of primary importance, while studying other people's advanced experience. We must also study the conditions of enemy countries and of friendly countries. In the past we did study conditions in enemy and friendly countries as well as our own. We translated American and Japanese things. In future wars in the East, America won't get anywhere without depending on Japan, so we must make a thorough study of Japanese conditions. We must study the Soviet army's experience. Weapons technology is continually developing and evolving. Therefore in studying the Soviet army's technical experience, we must do so from the standpoint of development. In the past the Russians were very much afraid of Napoleon because he led his army to Moscow. In the end the Russians defeated him and so the Russians often boasted that they were more formidable than Napoleon. Nowadays the stuff produced by the Soviet military advisers (combat plans and ways of thinking) all deal with the offensive and are all concerned with victory. They have no defensive material and do not provide for defeat. This does not conform with real situations. Some people say that summing up the Resist America, Aid Korea War constitutes empiricism, but we know that the Korean War was a big war in which we defeated America and obtained valuable experience. This experience must be summed up. As for their calling us empiricists, well, we can say to them: Your stuff about the Soviet Union in the Second World War is also empiricism.

The errors committed by Comrade Hsiao K'e are serious ones. In the past we had no chance to convene such a big conference. Now that we have that chance we can dig out the roots of dogmatism.

As regards learning from the Soviet Union, for internal use we say 'study critically'. In speaking publicly, in order to avoid misunderstanding, it would be better to put it: 'Study the advanced experience of the Soviet Union analytically and selectively.' It is most important that in studying the advanced experience of the Soviet Union, we should combine it with our own independent creative achievements. The universal truth of Marxism must be combined with Chinese practice. We must not eat pre-cooked food. If we do we shall be defeated. We must clarify this point with our Soviet comrades. We have learned from the Soviet Union in the past, we are still learning today, and we shall learn in the future. Nevertheless our study must be combined with our own concrete conditions. We must say to them: We learn from you, from whom then did you learn? Why cannot we create something of our own? Moreover there have recently been changes among Soviet experts. Changes took place after the Twentieth Congress and the Zhukhov incident. (*Chief Ch'en* [*vice-premier Ch'en I*] *interjected: 'Soviet comrades who have returned home said that when they came, they brought their experiences with them; now they are returning they are taking our experiences back.'*) This shows that the situation of the Great Leap Forward inspired not only us in China, but also our Soviet comrades. (*Chief Lin said: 'In political matters, such as Party leadership and in political work, our army has a fine tradition of its own. Our Party's Marxist–Leninist level is very high, not to speak of the Chairman's. The Chairman has said that our editorials are at a higher level than those of* Pravda. *When it comes to the superstructure, in military science, in problems of strategy, we have our own fully developed system. Lenin died too early. He did not have time to attend to this question. Stalin had no developed system. We do not have to learn from the Soviet Union. As regards tactics, we can learn half and leave half. Their tactics are questionable both ideologically and as regards their attitude to the masses. The half we learn would consist of the use of naval and air forces and the coordination of the services. As for the half we don't learn, such as tactical thinking, we have Chairman Mao's so we don't need to learn theirs. We should study technology and science and also the organization of modern warfare, but we should use the methodology of the mass line to study it. We should take advantage of the fact that our generation is still alive to organize a group of cadres to put together our own system properly, and to pass it on.'*) That's the way.

Li Shih-min, Ts'ao Ts'ao[5] etc., all knew how to fight wars. China's past has quite a lot to offer. Comrade K'ai Feng[6] said that the *Sun-tzu ping-fa*[7] contained no Marxism, but when we asked him whether he had read it he could not answer. Obviously it is quite wrong to make categorical statements without having read it. (*Chief Lin interjected:* 'Sun-tzu ping-fa *does contain both materialism and dialectics. It is a collective work. The authors included Sun-tzu, Sun Pin, Ts'ao Ts'ao, Tu Yü, etc.'*)

The elimination of blind faith was brought up at the Chengtu Conference. It has progressed very rapidly in the last four months. Since the second session of the Eighth Congress it has further developed in every domain throughout the country. For example, Anshan, which originally planned to produce — tens of thousands of tons of steel, has now revised its target and next year will reach an output of from — to — tens of thousands of tons. They have also gone in for the combination of large, small and medium plants and of native and foreign methods. According to a letter from Comrade XXX in the north-east, in the second five-year plan the north-east can reach an output of — tens of thousands of tons. If we have steel and modernized industry, then we can easily develop a modernized defence industry. I am in favour of producing more light weapons so that we can arm a mass militia. (*Chief Lin interjected:* '*The militia is very important.*') In the past others have looked down on us. The main reason for this was that we were short of food, steel and machines. Now we have produced some things for all to see.

6 Speech at the Lushan Conference
23 July 1959

Now that you have said so much, let me say something will you? I have taken sleeping-pills three times, but I can't get to sleep.

These are the ideas I want to talk about. I have read the comrades' reports, speeches and documents, and talked to a certain number of them. I feel they have two tendencies and I want to say a few words about them here. One is the tendency to be touchy – with these people it's very much a case of: 'If you touch him he jumps.' Wu Chih-hui used to say that Sun Fo jumped if anyone touched him.[1] So some people feel the pressure; that is, they don't want others to say bad things about them. They don't want to hear bad things, only good things. I advise these comrades to listen. There are three kinds of words, and the mouth has two functions. A person has only one mouth and its duty is firstly, to eat, and secondly, to speak. Ears are for listening with. If someone wants to talk, what can you do about it? The trouble with some comrades is that they don't like listening to bad words. But good words and bad words are all words, and they should listen to both kinds. There are three kinds of words: one is correct, the second is basically correct, or not too correct, and the third is basically incorrect, or just plain incorrect. The two extremes are opposites: correct and incorrect are opposites.

We are under combined attack from within and outside the Party. The rightists say: Why was Ch'in Shih Huang overthrown? Because he built the Great Wall. Now that we have built the T'ien An Men[2] we shall collapse; this is what the rightists say. I have not entirely finished reading the criticisms from within the Party. They were expressed in their most concentrated form by the Kiangsi Party School, but they are to be found everywhere. All the speeches of the rightists have been published, and the Kiangsi Party School is their representative within the Party. Some of them are rightists and wavering elements. They do not see the whole picture. But if we do some work on them, they will come round. Some of them have had problems in the past and have been criticized. Moreover they think we are in a mess. An example of this is the material from the Kwangtung Military Region. These things were all expressed outside the conference. Now we shall combine things from within and without the conference. What a pity that the summit of Lushan is so small. We can't invite them all: the Kiangsi Party School, Lo Lung-chi, Ch'en Ming-shu, etc.[3] This is the responsibility of the Kiangsi people. This building is too small!

Whenever they speak they say we are in a mess. This is fine. The more they say we are in a mess the better, and the more we should listen. During the Rectification Movement we invented the phrase, 'Toughen our scalps and bear it.' This is what I have said to some of the comrades, 'Toughen your scalp and bear it.' But how long do we have to bear it? One month, three months, six months, one year, three years, five years, eight years, ten years? Some comrades talk of 'protracted war'. I quite agree. These comrades are in the majority.

Gentlemen, all of you have ears, so listen. They all say we are in a mess. Even if it is hard to listen to it, we must listen to it and welcome it. As soon as you think in this way, it ceases to be unpleasant to the ears. Why should we let the others talk? The reason is that China will not sink down, the sky will not fall. We have done some good things and our backbones are strong. The majority of comrades need to strengthen their backbones. Why are they not all strong? Just because for a time there were too few vegetables, too few hair-grips, no soap, a lack of balance in the economy and tension in the market, everyone became tense. People became psychologically tense. I did not see any reason for tension, but I was also tense nevertheless; it would be untrue to say I wasn't. In the first part of the night you might be tense, but once you take your sleeping-pills the tension will go away for the rest of the night.

People say that we have become isolated from the masses, yet the masses still support us. I think this was temporary, just for two or three months before and after the Spring Festival. I think that we and the masses are now combining well. There is a bit of petit-bourgeois fanaticism, but not all that much. I agree with the view of our comrades, the problem is that of the commune movement. I went to Suip'ing and discussed the matter in detail for more than two hours. The secretary of the Party Committee of the Cha-ya-shan Commune told me that on the average, during the three months of July, August, and September, 3,000 people a day came for a visit. That makes 30,000 in ten days and 300,000 in three months. I hear that there was an equally large number of visitors at Hsü-shui and Ch'i-li-ying.[4] They came from everywhere except Tibet to have a look. It was like the monk of the T'ang dynasty going in search of the scriptures.[5] These people were all *hsien*, commune, and brigade cadres; there were also provincial and local cadres. Their reasoning was: 'The people in Honan and Hopei have created the truth from experience, they have smashed Roosevelt's "freedom" from want.' How should we look upon such enthusiasm for communism? Shall we call it petit-bourgeois fanaticism? I don't think we can put it that way. It's a matter of wanting to do a bit more, it's nothing else but wanting to do a bit more, a bit faster. Is this analysis appropriate? In these three months, there were three times 300,000 people going to the mountains to burn incense.[6] We must not pour cold water on this kind of broad mass movement. We can only use persuasion and say to them: Comrades, your hearts are in the right place. When tasks are difficult, don't be impatient. Do things step-by-step. When you eat meat you have to do it one mouthful at a time; one bite won't make you a fatty. Lin X eats a catty of meat a day and he's still not fat, even after ten years of it. The ample figures of the Commander-in-Chief[7] and myself were not achieved in a day and a night.

Those cadres are leading several hundreds of millions of

people. At least thirty per cent of them are activists, thirty per cent are passive elements including landlords, rich peasants, reactionaries, undesirables, bureaucrats, middle peasants, and some poor peasants, and forty per cent follow the stream. How many people is thirty per cent? 150 million people. They are keen on running communes, communal canteens, large cooperative enterprises. They are very active, very keen to do these things. Do you think that this is petit-bourgeois fanaticism? They are not the petit bourgeoisie, they are poor peasants, lower-middle peasants, proletarians and semi-proletarians. Those who follow the stream are also prepared to do these things. There are just thirty per cent who won't. Now thirty per cent and forty per cent equals seventy per cent – so at one time there were 350 million fanatics. They wanted to do it.

Then during the two months before and after the Spring Festival they became dissatisfied and changed. When the cadres went into the countryside they would no longer talk to them; they gave them only sweet potato gruel to eat and their faces were unsmiling. This has been called 'blowing a communist wind'. We should make an analysis of this. Among these people there are some who are afflicted with petit-bourgeois fanaticism. Who are they? Those who 'blew a communist wind' were primarily *hsien-* and commune-level cadres, especially commune cadres who extorted things from production brigades and teams. This is bad. The masses disliked it. They were resolutely corrected and persuaded. It took about a month during March and April for the wind to be stilled. Those measures which had to be withdrawn were withdrawn, and the accounts between the communes and the brigades were cleared.

This period of over one month of settling accounts and education had its good effects. In a very short time they came to understand that egalitarianism was no good – 'First equalize, second adjust, third withdraw funds'[8] will not do. I hear that the majority have come round and only a minority still hanker after 'communism' and won't give it up. Where else can one find such a school, or intensive training course, which will enable a population of several hundreds of millions as well as several millions of cadres to be educated?

The things must be given back. You cannot say that what is yours is mine and just pick things up and walk off. No such rule has ever existed since ancient times. In another 10,000 years' time people will still not be able to pick things up and walk off. The Red and Green Gang[9] behaved like this, stealing and robbing away in broad daylight, expropriating the fruits of others' labour without recompense, and violating the principle of the exchange of equal values. Sung Chiang's government was called the Hall of Loyalty and Righteousness. He robbed the rich to help the poor and could take what he wanted since he had justice on his side. What they took belonged to the local despots and evil gentry, and so his code of behaviour was acceptable. What Sung Chiang took was 'a birthday tribute'. His action was like our attacks on the local despots. He took their ill-gotten property.[10] 'Ill-gotten gains can be taken with impunity.' What has been extorted from the peasants should be returned to the peasants. It is a long time since we attacked the local despots. When we attacked them, it was quite all right to divide their fields and return them to the people because they too were ill-gotten property. If we 'blow a communist wind' and seize the property of the production brigades and work teams, helping ourselves to their fat pigs and big white cabbages, this is quite wrong. Even when we deal with the assets of imperialist countries we have other methods: requisition, procurement and economic pressure. So how can we expropriate the working people's property? How did we succeed in suppressing this wind within a month? It proves that our Party is great, just and correct. If you don't believe it, I have historical material to prove it. In March, April and May, several million cadres and several hundred million peasants received an education. The situation was explained to them and they thought it out. It was mainly the cadres who had not understood that this kind of wealth was [not] ill-gotten.[11] They could not make the distinction between the two kinds. They had not properly studied political economy. They had not clearly understood the laws of value, exchange of equal values, and remuneration according to work done. In a few months they were convinced and stopped doing it.

There may not be anyone who understands all this completely. There are some who have understood some of it, perhaps seventy or eighty per cent. If they have not understood the textbooks, let them study them some more. If the top cadres in the communes do not understand a little political economy, this won't do. If people can't read, you can explain it to them and they will understand a certain amount. They do not have to read books; they can be educated by facts. Emperor Wu-ti of Liang had a prime minister called Ch'en Fa-chih. He could not read a single word. When he had to write poems, he recited them and got others to write them down, saying: 'You scholars are not as good as me, who learnt by ear.' Of course I am not opposing the campaign to get rid of illiteracy. Old K'o[12] said that everyone should attend university. I agree. But that would prolong the period of education to fifteen years.

In the Southern and Northen dynasties there was a general called Ts'ao* who wrote this poem after a battle:

> When I went to war,
> My children were sad.
> On my return
> I was greeted with horns and drums.
> I asked someone passing by,
> 'Knowest thou Huo Ch'ü-ping?'

There was also the *Song of Ch'i-lo* by Hu-lü-chin of the Northern dynasties:

> By the Ch'i-lo river, below the Yin mountains,
> The sky is like a great canopy,
> Spanning the plains.
> The sky is blue, the wilderness is vast.
> When the wind blows,
> The grass bends and cattle and sheep appear.

Neither of these poets could read a word.

If an illiterate can become a prime minister, why can't our commune cadres and peasants listen to some political economy? I think they can learn it. If it is explained to them, they can

*i.e., Ts'ao Ching-tsung of the Southern Liang dynasty.[13]

learn some political economy even if they can't read. Explain it to them and they will understand it. In fact they can understand things better than intellectuals. I myself have not read the text-books, and I have no right to discuss them until I have. We must squeeze out some time; the whole Party should run a study campaign.

Goodness knows how many inspections they have made. Since last year's Chengchow Conference they have gone in for them in a big way. A report had to be made even when a sixth-grade meeting affected a fifth-grade meeting. The people from Peking talked and talked, but made no impression on them. We made many reports, but you did not get to hear them. I would advise comrades: since people have mouths, let them speak. You must listen to the other person's point of view. I think that at this conference there are some problems which cannot be solved, and some people who will not give up their point of view, so they just procrastinate – one year, two years, three years, five years. It won't do if you can't listen to strange ideas. One should get into the habit of listening. I say we should toughen our scalps and listen. At the worst they will curse three generations of your ancestors. I know it's not easy. When I was a boy, and when I was in middle school, I used to get all steamed up whenever I heard unpleasant things [about myself]. If people don't attack me, I won't attack them. If people attack me, I will certainly attack them. They attack me first, I attack them later. This principle I have never abandoned down to the present time. Now I have learnt to listen, to toughen my scalp and listen for one or two weeks and then counter-attack. I would advise comrades to listen. Whether you agree or not is your business. If you don't agree and if I am wrong, then I will make a self-criticism.

Second, I advise some other comrades not to waver at this crucial time. I have observed that a proportion of comrades are wavering. They too say the Great Leap Forward, the General Line and the people's communes are correct. But when they speak we must note on whose side they stand as regards their ideological tendency, and what is the thrust of their words. This group is in the second category: those who are fundamentally correct, but partly incorrect and a bit unstable. Some people will waver in times of crisis and show a lack of resolution in the great storms of history. There were four lines in our history: the Li Li-san Line, the Wang Ming Line, the Kao–Jao Line, and now the General Line.[14] These people are not steady: they dance the Yang-ko dance[15] (the Kuomintang said that we are the Yang-ko dynasty). They are terribly anxious in their desire to make things better for their country. This is good. What is the class background of this? Is it bourgeois or petit bourgeois? I shall not discuss this now; I talked about it at the Nanning Conference, the Chengtu Conference and the Party Congress. As for the people who wavered in 1956–7, we did not put tall hats[16] on them; we regarded it as a question of ideological method. If we talk about the fanaticism of the petit bourgeoisie, then the opposite of this – the anti-adventurism of that period – is the sad and dismal flatness and pessimism of the bourgeoisie. We are not going to put tall hats on these comrades. They are different from rightists in that they are all engaged in building socialism. It is just that they lack experience. As soon as the wind starts blowing and the grass waves, they become unsteady on their pins and turn anti-adventurist. Yet those who were anti-adventurist at that time have now stood firm. An example is Comrade En-lai. He has a lot of energy. After this lesson I believe that Comrade Ch'en Yün will also stand firm. Strange that the people who criticized En-lai at that time, this time find themselves in his shoes. They are no longer adventurous; they even give the impression of being anti-adventurist. For instance, they say: 'While there is loss, there is also gain.' The fact that they put the word 'gain' second is the result of careful consideration. For example, when it comes to putting on tall hats, this is the wavering of the bourgeoisie; or to fall one step lower, the wavering of the petit bourgeoisie. For the nature of rightists is to be constantly influenced by the bourgeoisie. Under the pressure of the imperialists and the bourgeoisie they have moved to the right.

There are about 700,000 production brigades; if each brigade makes one error, and you wanted to publish all 700,000 errors within a year, how could it be done? Moreover some articles are long and some short; it would take at least a year to publish them all. What would the result be? Our state would collapse and even if the imperialists didn't come, the people would rise up and overthrow us. If the paper you publish prints bad news every day, people will have no heart for their work. It wouldn't take as long as a year; we would perish within a week. To print 700,000 items all about bad things is not proletarian. It is more like a bourgeois country or party, like the political planning department of Chang Po-chün.[17] Of course nobody present is in favour of this. I am exaggerating. But if we do ten things and nine are bad, and they are all published in the press, then we will certainly perish, and will deserve to perish. In that case, I will go to the countryside to lead the peasants to overthrow the government. If those of you in the Liberation Army won't follow me, then I will go and find a Red Army, and organize another Liberation Army. But I think the Liberation Army would follow me.

I would advise some comrades to pay attention to the tendency of what they say. The content of your speech may be basically correct, but parts are not apposite.

If you want others to stand firm, you must first stand firm yourselves. If you want other people not to waver, you must not waver yourself: this is another lesson. As I see it these comrades are not rightists but middle-of-the-roaders. They are not leftists (i.e. leftists without quotation marks). I am talking about tendencies because there are some people who have run into difficulties. They have suffered broken heads and they are anxious. They were unable to stand firm; they wobbled into the middle of the road. The question is whether they are more inclined to the right of the middle or to the left of the middle. We must analyse this. They have gone the same way as those comrades who made mistakes in the second half of 1956 and the first half of 1957. They are not rightists, but they are on the verge of becoming rightists. They are still thirty kilometres away from the rightists. The rightists very much welcomed the trend of what they had to say and it would be surprising if they didn't. These comrades' brinkmanship is rather dangerous. If you don't believe me, wait and see what happens. I am saying these things before a big audience. Some of what I say may hurt people. But if I remained silent now, this would not be in these comrades' interest.

To the subjects which I have raised might be added another one: the question of unity. But I will write a separate piece on it: 'Raise the banner of unity, unity of the people, the nation and the Party.' I am not saying whether this is good or bad for these comrades. Even if it is harmful I must still talk about it. Our Party is a Marxist political party. Those on one side must listen; so must those on the other side. Both sides should listen. Didn't I say I wanted to speak? One should not only speak, but also listen to others. I have not been in a hurry to speak: I have toughened my scalp to endure it. Why don't I go on doing so? I have done it for twenty days already and it's nearly time for the conference to adjourn. We may as well go on to the end of the month. Marshall came up to Lushan eight times.[18] Chou En-lai came up three times. Why shouldn't we come up once? We have every right to do so.

Now about the problem of canteens. Canteens are a good thing and should not be criticized too severely. I am in favour of their active and successful development on the basis of voluntary membership. Grain should go to individual households and any savings should be retained by individuals. If one third of the canteens in the whole country can be maintained, I will be quite content. As soon as I said this, Wu Chih-p'u[19] became quite tense. Don't be afraid. In Honan Province ninety per cent of the canteens are still running. We should try them and see how they go, not abolish them. I am talking on a nationwide scale. In dancing are there not four stages? 'Stand on one side; try it out; dance as hard as you can; do or die.' Does such a saying really exist? I am a rough fellow, not cultured at all. If one third of the peasants, amounting to 150 million, persevere, then this would be wonderful. My next hope is for a half of them to do so: 250 million. If we can gain experience from such examples as Honan, Szechwan, Hunan, Yünnan, Shanghai, we can do it and some of the canteens which have been disbanded can be reformed. We did not invent them; they were created by the masses. They had canteens in Hopei Province in 1956 before the establishment of the communes. In 1958 they were set up very rapidly.

Tseng Hsi-sheng[20] said that canteens liberate labour power. I think that there is another point, which is that they save materials. Without the latter benefit they would not last. Can we do it? We can. My proposal is that the Honan comrades should carry out some mechanization, such as laying on running water, so that the water does not have to be carried. In this way both labour and materials can be saved. It is a good thing that half of them have now been disbanded. Commander-in-chief, I approve of your way of putting it, but I also differ with you. We should not stop disbanding them altogether, but neither should we disband too many. I'm a middle-of-the-roader. Honan, Szechwan, Hupei are all leftists. But a right wing has emerged. The Ch'angli investigation committee of the Chinese Academy of Sciences say that the canteens have no merit at all, attacking them on one particular point and not mentioning any others. They imitate Teng T'u-tzu's 'Ode on Love of Sex'. Teng T'u-tzu attacked Sung Yü on three points: he was handsome, sex-mad, and eloquent.[21] Also he did not like his own wife and was very dangerous. Sung Yü retorted: 'My good looks I owe to my parents, my eloquence is due to my teachers, and it is not true that I am sex-mad. No other place has such beautiful women as the state of Ch'u. Among the beautiful women of Ch'u, the most beautiful are to be found in my own district. And the most beautiful woman of my district is the daughter of my neighbour on the East. If you increased her stature by one inch she would be too tall, and if you decreased it by one inch she would be too short.' ... Teng T'u-tzu was a *tai-fu* which is the equivalent of the head of a ministry today. His 'ministry' was a big one, like the Ministry of Metallurgy, the Ministry of the Coal Industry or the Ministry of Agriculture. The investigation group of the Academy of Sciences attacked only one point and ignored the rest. The way they attacked was to concentrate on such things as pork, hair-grips, etc. Everybody has faults. Even Confucius made mistakes. I have also seen Lenin's handwritten manuscripts which had been altered so much that they looked a real mess. If he had not made mistakes why did he have to correct them? We can have more canteens: after we have experimented with them for one or two years, I reckon that we can make a go of them.

Could the people's communes collapse? Up to now not one has collapsed. We were prepared for the collapse of half of them, and if seventy per cent collapsed there would still be thirty per cent left. If they must collapse, let them. If they are not well run they are sure to collapse. The Communist Party aims to run things well, to run the communes well, to run all enterprises well, to run agriculture, industry, commerce, communications, transport, and culture and education well.

Many things have happened which we could not possibly predict beforehand. Hasn't it been said that the Party does not concern itself with Party affairs? Now the planning organs do not concern themselves with planning: for some time they have not been concerning themselves with it. The planning organs are not confined to the Planning Commission; they also include other ministries as well as local governments. The local organs can be forgiven if for a time they did not concern themselves with the overall balance of the economy. But the Planning Commission and the central ministries have been in existence for ten years, and suddenly at Peitaiho they decided not to concern themselves with it. They called it a directive on planning, but it was tantamount to doing away with planning altogether. By doing away with planning I mean that they dispensed with overall balances and simply made no estimates of how much coal, iron and transport would be needed. Coal and iron cannot walk by themselves; they need vehicles to transport them. This I did not foresee. I and X X and the Premier did not concern ourselves with this point. You could say that we were ignorant of it. I ought not to make excuses, but I shall too, because I am not the head of the Planning Commission. Before August of last year my main energies were concentrated on revolution. I am a complete outsider when it comes to economic construction, and I understand nothing about industrial planning. At the West Tower* I said: 'Don't write about [my] wise leadership, I do not control a thing so

* In the Chung-nan-hai, Peking.

how can you talk about wisdom?' But comrades, in 1958 and 1959 the main responsibility was mine, and you should take me to task. In the past the responsibility was other people's – En-lai, XX – but now you should blame me because there are heaps of things I didn't attend to. Shall the person who invented burial puppets be deprived of descendants?[22] Shall I be deprived of descendants too (one son was killed, one went mad)?[23] Who was responsible for the idea of the mass smelting of steel? K'o Ch'ing-shih or me? I say it was me. I had a talk with K'o Ch'ing-shih and spoke of six million tons. Afterwards I sought out people to talk about it: XXX also said it was possible. In June I talked about 10,700,000 tons. Then we went ahead and did it. It was published in the Peitaiho communiqué; XX put forward some ideas and believed that it would be all right. With this, we rushed into a great catastrophe, and ninety million people went into battle. As I said, the person who invented burial puppets shoud have neither sons nor grandsons. Small native-type blast furnaces were built ... I read a lot of discussion reports; everyone said it could be done. Provided that we came to grips with the problem and worked really hard, we could raise the quality, reduce cost, lower the sulphur content, and produce really good iron. The Communist Party has a method which it calls 'coming to grips' with something. The Communist Party and Chiang Kai-shek have both got two hands. The Communist Party's hands are communist hands. When they grip things they pick them up. We must take a grip on steel and iron as well as staple crops, cotton, oil, hemp, silk, tea, sugar and vegetables; also tobacco, fruit and condiments. There are twelve items in agriculture, forestry, animal husbandry, subsidiary crops and fisheries, which must be grasped and which must achieve overall balance. Conditions vary in different localities. There cannot be a single model for every county. At Chiukungshan in Hupei they grow bamboo in the mountains. It would be very wrong for them only to tend the crops and neglect the bamboos. There are places where tea and sugar will not grow. Things must be grown according to local conditions. Didn't the Soviet Union make them grow pigs in Moslem areas? Ridiculous.

There is an article on industrial planning which is quite well written. As for the Party not concerning itself with Party affairs, the Planning Commission not looking after planning or drawing up overall balances, what have they been doing? They were not in the least worried about things. The Premier was worried, but they weren't. If someone is not worried and they have no energy or enthusiasm, they will not do anything properly. Some people in criticizing Comrade Li Fu-ch'un, head of the Planning Commission, say: 'His foot wants to move, but he hesitates; his mouth wants to speak, but he stammers.' But don't be like Li K'uei;[24] impetuosity is no good either. Lenin was full of enthusiasm, which the masses liked. If people want to speak but can only stammer, it is because they have a lot of worries. During the first half of the month people had a lot of worries. Now these worries have all come out into the open. If you have anything to say, say it and it will all be written down in the minutes. Spoken evidence has to be written down. If you have things to say, then say them. If you find faults in me, then you should correct me. Don't be afraid if your shoes pinch. I said at the Chengtu Conference that one should not fear the guardroom. One should not even be afraid of execution or expulsion from the Party. If a communist and senior cadre has so many inhibitions it is because he is afraid of saying the wrong thing and being corrected. This is what is called, 'The wise man looks after number one!' Disease enters through the mouth and trouble comes out through the mouth. If I cause trouble today, two kinds of people will not like it: one is the touchy ones and the other those whose direction is open to question. If you don't agree with me then argue back. I don't agree with the idea that the Chairman cannot be contradicted. Anyway the fact is that you have been contradicting me one after the other, though not by name. The ideas of the Kiangsi Party School and of the Intermediate Party School both contradict mine. When I said that the inventor of burial puppets should have no descendants, I was referring first to the target of smelting 10,700,00 tons of steel, which resulted in ninety million people going into battle and the expenditure of — dollars of People's Currency. 'The gain did not compensate for the loss.' This was my suggestion and my resolution. Next I was referring to the people's communes. I do not claim to have invented the people's communes, only to have proposed them. The Peitaiho Resolution was drafted according to my suggestion. At that time, it was as though I had found a treasure in the regulations of the Cha-ya-shan [Commune]. When I was in Shantung a reporter asked me: 'Are the people's communes good?' I said: 'They are good,' and he published it in a newspaper. There was a spot of petit-bourgeois fanaticism there, too. In future reporters should keep away.

I have committed two crimes, one of which is calling for 10,700,000 tons of steel and the mass smelting of steel. If you agreed with this, you should share some of the blame. But since I was the inventor of burial puppets, I cannot pass on the blame: the main responsibility is mine. As for the people's communes, the whole world opposed them; the Soviet Union opposed them. There is also the General Line. Whether it has any substance or not, you can share some of the responsibility for this. The proof is to be seen in its implementation in industry and agriculture. As for the other big guns, other people should also take some of the responsibility. Boss T'an[25], you have fired a lot of big shots, but your shooting was inaccurate, you had a rush of blood to the head and did not take enough care. You communized too quickly. It was talked about first in Honan, then accounts of it spread rapidly in Kiangsu and Chekiang. If you are careless in your speech, you will not keep control of things. You must be more cautious. Your strength is that you are energetic and willing to take responsibility; much better than those who are sad and dismal. But when you fire big guns on important questions, you should take care. I have also fired three big shots: the people's communes, the steel smelting, and the General Line. P'eng Te-huai said that he was a coarse fellow with no refinement. I am like Chang Fei who, though rough, had a certain delicacy.[26] About the people's communes, I said that they were a system of collective ownership. I said that for the transition to be completed from collective ownership to communist ownership by the whole people, two five-year plans was too short a period. Maybe it will take twenty five-year plans!

If you want to talk about haste, Marx also made many mistakes. Every day he hoped that a European revolution would arrive, but it did not arrive. There were many ups and downs and it had still not arrived when he died. It only arrived in Lenin's time. Wasn't this a case of impatience? Wasn't this petit-bourgeois fanaticism? (XX *interjected: 'Lenin said that conditions were ripe for world revolution, but it did not come.'*) Marx at first opposed the Paris Commune, while Zinoviev opposed the October Revolution. Zinoviev was put to death later. Should Marx also have been killed? When the Paris Commune rose up he supported it, although he reckoned that it would fail. When he realized that it was the first proletarian dictatorship, he thought it would be a good thing even if it only lasted three months. If we assess it from an economic point of view, it was not worth while. We also had our Canton Commune[27], but the Great Revolution failed. Will our present work also fail, like what happened in 1927? Or will it be like the 25,000 *li* Long March, when most of our bases were lost and the Soviet areas were reduced to one tenth of their former size? No, it will not be like these. Have we failed this time? All the comrades present say there have been gains; it is not a complete failure. Is it mainly a failure? No, it's only a partial failure. We have paid a high price. A lot of 'communist wind' has blown past, but the people of the whole country have learned a lesson.

I have spoken twice at Chengchow on the question of Stalin's *Economic Problems of Socialism*. But these were only speeches. Now we must study it in depth, otherwise we cannot develop and consolidate our cause.[28]

When talking of responsibility, XXX and XXX both have some responsibility, as does XXX of the Ministry of Agriculture. But the one with the most responsibility is me. Old K'o, does any responsibility rest on you for your invention? (*Old K'o said: 'Yes'.*) Was it lighter than mine? Yours is a question of ideology, mine of 10,700,000 tons and ninety million people going into battle. The chaos caused was on a grand scale and I take responsibility. Comrades, you must all analyse your own responsibility. If you have to shit, shit! If you have to fart, fart! You will feel much better for it.

7 Speech at the Enlarged Session of the
Military Affairs Committee and the
External Affairs Conference
11 September 1959

Comrades! This has been a very good meeting. I think that
people who bear malice in their hearts will move towards their
own opposites. Those who bear malice in their hearts towards
the world class, the world parties, the Party's cause, the class
cause and the people's cause will move towards their own opposites. That is to say, their aims cannot be achieved. For instance, when someone wants to reach a certain goal and this
goal finally cannot be reached, he suffers a moral defeat and
becomes isolated from the masses. There are, for example, a
number of comrades who in my view are not Marxists, and who
hitherto have never been Marxists. What are they? They are
fellow-travellers of Marxism. If we want to argue this point
further there is plenty of material. For example, a lot of material has been published recently – material from the period of
the anti-Japanese war, from the period of the Long March, for
example about activities tending to sow discord. The material
from the period of the war against Japan contained such things
as 'Liberty, Equality and Fraternity'; 'the anti-Japanese front
cannot be divided into left, centre and right'; 'it is incorrect to
make a division into left, centre and right'; 'what you do not
wish done to yourself, do not do to others'. Where class relationships prevail, where there is the proletariat and bourgeoisie, the oppressors and the oppressed, to put forward such
principles as this, to say things like 'when the prince commits a
crime the people are implicated' – such a viewpoint cannot be
called Marxist: it absolutely cannot be said to be a Marxist
viewpoint. It is an anti-Marxist viewpoint which deceives the

people, a bourgeois viewpoint. Later on the anti-Party views of Kao, Jao, P'eng, Huang[1] – such as their theory of an 'army party' – disrupted the proper relationships within the Party, holding that there was a domain here and a domain there. Their views and their behaviour were not those of Marxists. This time much material has come to light about their splitting activities many years before the Lushan Conference as well as about their Lushan Programme. In addition there is much material about the period of the Li Li-san Line. Most of this has been written down. What everybody has been bringing to light is what I have talked about just now. So if we want to argue the point of view which I have just talked about – that they have never been Marxists but only fellow-travellers and that they are merely bourgeois elements and opportunist elements who have infiltrated into our Party – if we are to prove this point and argue it to a conclusion there is plenty of material. I have no intention of doing so now because this would mean writing articles and could give a lot of comrades work to do. So I merely raise it. It is perfectly understandable that bourgeois revolutionaries should enter the Communist Party and that their bourgeois world outlook and standpoint should not have changed. They cannot avoid making mistakes. At crucial times it is impossible for such fellow-travellers not to make mistakes.

The Lushan Conference, this meeting, and the various levels of Party organization throughout the country have all discussed the resolutions of the Eighth Session of the Eighth Plenum and we have made use of this affair to educate the broad masses and enable them to raise their level and become more conscious. This has proved completely that the great majority of people, the great majority of the cadres of the whole Party, say ninety-five per cent, do not agree with them. It also proves that our Party is mature as demonstrated by the comrades' reaction to their attitude.

Bourgeois elements have infiltrated our Communist Party. Amidst our Party membership there are many bourgeois and petit-bourgeois elements. These should be analysed and divided into two groups. The great majority are good people. They can enter Communism because they are willing to accept Marxism. The minority are probably one, two, three, four or five per cent – this sort of figure – perhaps one per cent, perhaps two per cent, perhaps three per cent, perhaps four per cent, perhaps five per cent. During the past few weeks at provincial level conferences, quite a few high cadres have been exposed as right-opportunist elements and trouble-makers, whose one fear is that the world should be free of trouble. Whenever there is trouble they are happy. Their principle is: 'If the world is at peace, the four quarters are tranquil and work goes well: they are uncomfortable. As soon as the wind blows and the grass waves, they are happy.' For example if there is not enough pork, not enough vegetables, not enough soap, not enough women's hair-grips, they seize the opportunity to say, 'You have done things badly!' They say it is your affair and not theirs. When organizations hold meetings and reach decisions they don't utter a murmur. For instance at the Peitaiho Conference not a murmur, at the Chengchow Conference not a murmur, at the Wuch'ang Conference not a murmur. At the Shanghai Conference they did mumble something but we could not hear them. Then when things happened (when they thought things had happened) then, as you can see, it was all vegetables, pork, grain in a number of areas, soap and even umbrellas. For example there was a shortage of umbrellas in Chekiang and they called it a 'maladjustment of proportions', 'petit-bourgeois fanaticism', etc. It will be very difficult for this small minority of people to enter communism, to become real Marxists. When I say it will be difficult, I don't mean that it would be impossible. As Liu Po-ch'eng said: 'It is necessary to be completely reborn.' Those who were warlords were after all warlords, but what about those who were not warlords, such as Comrade XXX? How could he be counted as a warlord? He was a literary lord, an academic lord. If you are not completely reborn you cannot enter the door of communism.

Five times there have been mistakes of line: the [Li] Li-san Line, the first and second Wang Ming Lines,[2] the Kao–Jao Line and now this P'eng–Huang–Chang–Chou Line. Some people have made mistakes five times, some have not made mistakes five times. For example comrade XXX was not yet with us at the time of the Li-san Line. As for P'eng and Huang they were attacked at the time of the Li-san Line. This is no coincidence. Regarding the serious nature of the five erroneous lines, on the last two occasions – that is during the Kao–Jao and P'eng–Huang Lines – plots were hatched to split the Party. This contravenes Party discipline. A Marxist party must have discipline. They do not know that Lenin said that the party of the proletariat must have discipline, iron discipline. As for these comrades, what kind of discipline do they have? Iron discipline, steel discipline or metal, wood, water, fire and earth discipline, or wooden discipline, or is it bean-curd discipline? Water discipline means no discipline at all. In that case how can we talk of iron discipline? To carry out splitting activities is to break discipline, the purpose and result necessarily being to destroy the proletarian dictatorship and to establish another kind of dictatorship.

The banner of unity is exceedingly important. The Marxist slogan for unity is 'Proletarians of the world unite!' But not them! For them it would seem the fewer the better! They want to have their own clique and to do their own thing, acting against the wishes of the broad masses. At the Lushan Conference I said that they do not mention the slogan of unity because if this slogan were raised they would be unable to carry out their activities. This slogan is not in their interests so they do not dare to mention it. The unity in question even includes people who have made mistakes, who will be helped to correct their mistakes in order to unite with them once again, let alone those who have not made mistakes. But these people wish to destroy them. Their policy is a destructive policy, not a policy of unity. The banner which they wave is the banner of destruction – the destruction of those who hold opinions differing from their own. They consider that such people are bad. Yet these so-called bad people are really the great majority, more than ninety-five per cent.

If you want unity you must have discipline, in order that our whole nation may build a strong country within the space of a few five-year plans. The present task is for the people of the whole country, together with the whole Party, to build a strong country within the space of a few five-year plans. For this iron discipline is needed, it cannot be done without it, so we must unite. I ask you, how can we achieve this aim otherwise? Is it possible to build a great socialist country within the space of a few five-year plans? In the past we had to make revolution, now we must carry out construction. Is this possible or not? Without discipline nothing is possible. Unity requires discipline. As for the many documents about P'eng Te-huai in the T'aihang Mountains,[3] will comrades please compare Sun Yat-sen's Manifesto of the first National Congress of the Kuomintang with the views expressed by P'eng Te-huai in the T'aihang Mountains at the time of the anti-Japanese war. One was a Kuomintang member, the other a Communist Party member. As regards time, one was written in 1924, the other in 1938, '39 and '40. The communist had retrogressed in comparison with the Kuomintang member. The name of the Kuomintang member was Sun Yat-sen and he wanted to progress. Sun Yat-sen was influenced by the Communist Party. Why did he write that piece? Recently I found the text and had a look at it. Sun Yat-sen's Manifesto of the First National Congress of the Kuomintang contained the idea of class-analysis. How could he have the iron discipline of the communists? How could he be in agreement with proletarian discipline? Without speaking the language of the communists, without a common standpoint and common views, discipline cannot be established. I say that P'eng Te-huai is not the equal of Sun Yat-sen. As for Chang Wen-t'ien,[4] he is not Sun Yat-sen's equal either. Sun Yat-sen was revolutionary at that time; these comrades were retrogressing. They wanted to destroy the organization which had already been built up. The slogans which they raised were beneficial to the enemy and detrimental to the class and to the people. There were more views of this kind, for example . . .

It is absolutely impermissible to go behind the back of our fatherland to collude with a foreign country. Comrades have held meetings to criticize this affair because they are all in organizations of the Communist Party; they are all Marxists. We cannot allow one group to sabotage another. We cannot allow

Chinese Communist Party members to sabotage the party organizations of foreign countries and to provoke one group of people to oppose another group. At the same time we cannot allow people to entertain foreign provocation behind the back of the Centre.

Now I am going to admonish some comrades who have made mistakes. Prepare yourselves to listen to some off-hand remarks. In the past I have admonished others, for example Comrade Lo Ping-hui, who had committed mistakes during that period.[5] He got very angry, and afterwards I exhorted him further, saying 'Don't get angry. You have committed mistakes, so let people talk – let them talk until they have no more to say. The reason they won't have any more to say is that you will have corrected your errors. If you adopt a friendly attitude towards people, and if you display a spirit of self-criticism towards your own errors, why would others go on talking? They won't talk any more.' You comrades who have committed errors at present, I urge you to prepare to listen to some off-hand remarks. As soon as your errors are mentioned, you shouldn't be frightened out of your wits, as though people were going to talk about you for years on end. I can't go on all that long. It depends on how you go about correcting your errors. If you correct them quickly, people will stop talking about you within a few months. If you correct them more slowly, then they'll stop talking about you after a few years. The main thing is to correct your errors, whether it be fast or slowly. You must be sincere with people, and not dissemble. You must be honest, and speak honestly. I appeal to you comrades who have committed mistakes, you must place yourselves on the side of the overwhelming majority, you must cooperate with the overwhelming majority; you must not cooperate only with the minority who share your tastes. If only you can carry out these two points. First, you must be able to listen to remarks, you must prepare to listen, you must stiffen your scalps. When you spoke, I listened; I agreed that what you said was correct! I did indeed commit that error! This fellow Ah Q had some defects, which were manifested in the fact that his head wasn't all that pretty, it was covered with ringworm. Because he couldn't bear to speak of it, others insisted on talking about it, and as soon as they did he would fly into a rage. For example, even when his ringworm scars got bright red he wouldn't speak of it, and if others mentioned brightness, he flew into a rage. The author describes a naïve peasant who has not yet awakened to consciousness. Ah Q is a good man, he definitely didn't organize a faction, but he was a man who was not conscious, he couldn't bear to talk about shortcomings. He didn't take the initiative, and because he didn't take the initiative, others wanted to talk about it; as soon as they spoke of it, he flew into a rage, and as soon as he flew into a rage he got into a fight, and when he got into a fight he never won, and then he would say it was [like] a father being beaten by his son. People would say to him: 'Ah Q! If you don't want me to beat you, talk about a father beating his son, and then I won't beat you.' 'All right,' [he would say]. 'It's a father beating his son.' But as soon as the person who was beating him had gone away, he would say it was a son beating his father, and he would once again feel satisfied with himself.

Comrades who have committed mistakes must prepare to listen to some remarks, they must prepare to listen quite a lot. They must be honest and sincere with people, and not lie to people. Another point is that they must stand with the majority. All they have to do is to observe these few points, and I think they can definitely reform. Otherwise, they will not be able to reform. If they aren't prepared to listen to remarks, if they aren't sincere with people, if they tell lies, and if in addition they do not stand with the majority, then it will be very difficult. 'Who save sages and worthies can avoid making mistakes?' In reality, this proverb is not appropriate either, for even the sages made mistakes. 'The faults of the superior man are like the eclipses of the sun and moon. He has his faults, and all men see them; he changes again, and all men look up to him.'[6] We are not Confucius, but we see that even Confucius made mistakes, so we must conclude that all men without exception make some mistakes, more or fewer, bigger or smaller. It doesn't matter if we make mistakes, we must not let mistakes become a burden to us, we mustn't see them as something extraordinary, we should just go ahead and correct them. 'The faults of the superior man are like the eclipses of the sun and moon.' It's like when the celestial dog eats the sun and the moon[7] – he makes a mistake, and everyone sees it. When he corrects his mistake, 'all men look up' to him.

We must learn some things, we must study Marxism–Leninism. I am very much in favour of XXX's proposals regarding our tasks in the domain of study. All of us without exception must study. What shall we do if there isn't enough time? If there isn't enough time, we must squeeze in the time. The problem lies in cultivating the habit of study; once we have done this, we will be able to go on studying. I say these things first of all for the benefit of those comrades who have committed errors, but my words are also directed to all of us comrades, including myself. There are many things I haven't studied. I am a person with many shortcomings, I am by no means perfect. Very often, there are times when I don't like myself. I have not mastered all the various domains of Marxist learning. And, for example, I don't know foreign languages well either. I have only just begun recently to study economic work. But, comrades, I study with determination, and I will go on studying until I die; when I die, that will be the end of it! In sum, as long as I am alive I shall study every day. Let us all create an environment of study. I think I can learn a bit too; otherwise, when the time comes for me to see Marx, I shall be in an embarrassing fix. If he asks me a few questions and I am unable to answer, what will I do? He is certainly very interested in all aspects of the Chinese revolution. I'm not very good either in natural science or engineering.

There are so many things to study now, how shall we go about it? Just keep on in the same way, learning a bit, persevering and penetrating a bit deeper. I say that, if you are resolved to do it, you can certainly learn, whether you are young or old. I will give you an example. I really learned to swim well only in 1954; previously I had not mastered it. In 1954, there was an indoor swimming-pool at Tsinghua University. I went there every evening with my bag, changed my clothes, and for three months without interruption I studied the nature of the water. Water doesn't drown people! Water is afraid of people, people aren't afraid of water; of course, there are exceptions, but it should be possible to swim in all kinds of water. This is a major premise. For example, the Yangtse at Wuhan is water, so it's possible to swim in the Yangtse at Wuhan. So I refuted those comrades who opposed my swimming in the Yangtse. I said, 'You haven't studied formal logic.' If it's water, you can swim in it, except in certain conditions: for example, if the water is only an inch deep you can't swim in it; if it's frozen solid you can't swim in it; you can't swim in places where there are sharks, nor where there are whirlpools, as in the three gorges of the Yangtse. Apart from certain circumstances, it should be possible to swim wherever there is water, this is the major premise, the major premise derived from practice. Thus, for example, the Yangtse at Wuhan is water; hence, the conclusion follows that it is possible to swim in the Yangtse at Wuhan. The Milo and Pearl rivers are water, you can swim in them. You can swim in [the sea off] Peitaiho; it's water, isn't it? Wherever there's water, you should be able to swim. This is the major premise; apart from the fact that you can't swim in one inch of water, and you can't swim in water that's at a temperature of over 100 degrees, or in water that's so cold it's frozen, or where there are sharks or whirlpools – apart from these circumstances, all water can be swum in; this is a fact. Do you believe it? If you are resolute, if you only have the will, I am convinced that all things can be successfully accomplished. I exhort you comrades to study.

Recently, we have seen the great ceremonial hall at the T'ien An Men. It's really quite a thing. Would you all like to go and have a look? (*All those present loudly shout: 'Yes!'*) Get Comrade Wan Li to tell you about it. This chap's name is Wan, isn't it? He should be able to run ten thousand *li* in a day.[8] It has been only ten months; so many people said they didn't believe it [could be done], the Soviet experts we called in said they didn't believe it. By June of this year, the Soviet experts said it might be possible, and when September came, they expressed great admiration, saying that China really had a Great Leap Forward. 12,000 people, brought from all over the country, [representing] the force, the technical capacity, the human capacity, of all the provinces in the country, taking no Sundays off at all, working three shifts a day, and not working on any piecework wage system; many of them began working eight hours a day, and ended up working twelve hours, without a stop. Did they want to be paid for the extra four hours? They didn't. There were also people who would not stop work as long as [a particular] project was not completed, who did not sleep for two days and nights; they remained at their place of work not for eight hours, or twelve hours, but for forty-eight hours. Did they need material incentives? Did they want a few extra *yüan*? Say one *yüan* for each hour? They didn't want it, these people did not want it. The material incentive remained just the material incentive, it was nothing but those 50 *yüan* of [monthly] wages, just that little bit – but they were striving for a common cause. 12,000 staff and workers completed this big piece of work in the space of ten months; this is not merely 'to each according to his work', but it also involved Lenin's great contribution called the 'communist Saturday', it included work which was not compensated for.

Comrades, go and have a look ... There is also the Miyün reservoir ... I think the combination of politics in command and material incentives, of political work and the necessary remuneration according to work, is a good thing. We are all resolute, and firm of will. That which people thought could not be successfully completed has in fact been completed; I'm talking about this big auditorium, which a great many people thought could not be completed. Very many people are hurling insults at our Great Leap Forward and people's communes, but they will nevertheless succeed, and indeed have already succeeded, or are going to continue achieving results. For example, we will progress rapidly in iron and steel, in industry, and also in agriculture. Studying is like this too; if only we are resolute, I think we can study well. We need not fear that there will be too much to do, and that the time will be too short, we can fit it in! Let us develop this habit. We must conquer this world, our objective is this world; as for how we should go about our work on the sun, we won't talk about that for the present. As for the moon, Mercury or Venus, and any of the other eight planets apart from the earth, we may investigate them in the future, and visit them if we can get up there. As for our work, our struggles, I think they're still going to be on earth. If we're going to build up a strong country, we must definitely be resolute like this, as we have had to be to build this big auditorium, so many dams, factories, etc. I think this is definitely the way.

Let the whole Party and the whole people unite! Proletarians of the world, unite! We can certainly attain our goal!

8 Talk at an Enlarged Central Work Conference
30 January 1962

Comrades! I have a few points to raise (*enthusiastic applause*). Altogether there are six points I want to talk about. The main substance of what I want to say is the problem of democratic centralism, but at the same time I want to talk about a number of other problems.

(1) *The way this conference is being run*

This enlarged central work conference is being attended by over 7,000 people. At the start of the conference Comrade Liu Shao-ch'i and several other comrades prepared a draft report. Before this draft had been discussed by the Political Bureau, I suggested to them that instead of first holding a meeting of the Political Bureau to discuss it, we should rather immediately issue it to the comrades who are participating in this conference so that everyone could comment on it and put forward ideas. Comrades, there are among you people from various fields and localities, various provincial, district and county committees, and from the Party committees of various enterprises. There are people from various departments at the Centre. The majority of you have more contact with the lower levels, and should have more understanding of situations and problems than us comrades on the Standing Committee, the Political Bureau and the Secretariat. Furthermore, since you all hold different positions you can raise problems from different angles. That is why we invited you to put forward ideas and issued the draft report to you. The result has been a lively discussion in which many ideas have been put forward, not all of them along the lines of the basic policy of the Central Committee. Later Comrade Shao-ch'i presided over a drafting committee of twenty-one, including responsible members of the various central bureaux. After eight days of discussion they produced a second draft written report. It should be said that in this second draft report the Centre has collected together the results of over 7,000 people's discussion. Without your ideas this second draft could not have been written. In it both the first and second parts have many revisions. This is due to your efforts. I hear that you all consider the second draft to be not bad, and an improvement on the first. If we had not used this method, but held the conference in the usual manner, we would have heard the report first and held a discussion afterwards. Everyone would have approved it with a show of hands and we wouldn't have done as well as this.

This is a question of how to hold meetings. First of all, draft reports are distributed, and those present are invited to submit their ideas and amendments. Then a new report is prepared. When this report is presented it shouldn't be read out word by word, but some supplementary ideas should be expounded and the changes should be explained. In this way we can promote democracy more fully, gather wisdom from all directions, and compare all the different points of view. Also our meetings will be more lively. The purpose of this conference is to sum up the working experience of the past twelve years and especially the working experience of the last four years. There are many problems, so there may be many ideas being put forward, thus creating conditions favourable for this type of conference. Is it possible for all conferences to adopt this method? No, it is not possible. To use this method we must have plenty of time. We can sometimes use this method at meetings of our people's congresses. Comrades from provincial committees, district committees, and county committees, when you convene conferences in future you may also adopt this method under suitable conditions. Of course when you are busy you usually cannot spend a lot of time on conferences. But when conditions are right, why not try it out?

What sort of method is this? It is a democratic centralist method; it is a mass-line method. First democracy, then centralism; coming from the masses, returning to the masses; the unity of the leadership and the masses. This is the first point I wanted to talk about.

(2) *The problem of democratic centralism*

It seems that some of our comrades still do not understand the democratic centralism which Marx and Lenin talked of. Some of these comrades are already veteran revolutionaries, with a 'three–eight style'[1] or some other style – anyway they have been Party members for several decades, yet they still do not understand this question. They are afraid of the masses, afraid of the masses talking about them, afraid of the masses criticizing them. What sense does it make for Marxist–Leninists to be afraid of the masses? When they have made mistakes they don't talk about themselves, and they are afraid of the masses talking about them. The more frightened they are, the more haunted they become. I think one should not be afraid. What is there to be afraid of? Our attitude is to hold fast to the truth and be ready at any time to correct our mistakes. The question of right or wrong, correct or incorrect in our work has to do with the contradictions among the people. To resolve contradictions among the people we can't use curses or fists, still less guns or knives. We can only use the method of discussion, reasoning, criticism and self-criticism. In short, we can only use democratic methods, the method of letting the masses speak out.

Both inside and outside the Party there must be a full democratic life, which means conscientiously putting democratic centralism into effect. We must conscientiously bring questions out into the open, and let the masses speak out. Even at the risk of being cursed we should still let them speak out. The result of their curses at the worst will be that we are thrown out and cannot go on doing this kind of work – demoted or transferred. What is so impossible about that? Why should a person only go up and never go down? Why should one only work in one place and never be transferred to another? I think that demotion and transfer, whether it is justified or not, does good to people. They thereby strengthen their revolutionary will, are able to investigate and study a variety of new conditions and increase their useful knowledge. I myself have had experience in this respect and gained a great deal of benefit. If you do not believe me, why not try it yourselves. Ssu-ma Ch'ien said:

Wen Wang was imprisoned and the result was the development of the *Chou I*; Confucius was in dire straits and so compiled the *Spring and Autumn Annals*; Ch'ü Yüan was exiled and so wrote the *Li Sao*; Tso Ch'iu became blind and then wrote the *Kuo-yü*; Sun-tzu was mutilated and mastered military strategy; Lü Pu-wei was transferred to the kingdom of Shu and so the world could read his work; Han Fei was imprisoned in the kingdom of Ch'in and wrote because he could not keep his anger to himself. Of the hundreds of poems and prose works written the majority were written by sages who were experiencing anger and frustration.[2]

In modern times people have had doubts about the truth of these statements about Wen Wang developing the *Chou I* and Confucius compiling the *Spring and Autumn Annals*, but we don't have to worry about that – let the experts study these problems! Ssu-ma Ch'ien believed that this was true, and it is a fact that Wen Wang was imprisoned and Confucius was in dire straits. The things which Ssu-ma Ch'ien mentioned, apart from the example of Tso Ch'iu's going blind, all referred to the incorrect handling of the people concerned by the top leadership of the time. In the past we have also handled some cadres in an incorrect way. No matter whether we were completely mistaken in our handling of these people, or only partially mistaken, they should all be cleared and rehabilitated according to the actual circumstances. But generally speaking, this incorrect treatment – having them demoted or transferred – tempers their revolutionary will and enables them to absorb much new knowledge from the masses.

I must point out that I am not advocating the indiscriminate wrong treatment of our cadres, our comrades, or anybody else, in the way in which the ancients detained Wen Wang, starved Confucius, exiled Ch'ü Yüan, or cut off Sun-tzu's kneecaps. I am not in favour of this way of doing things – I oppose it. What I am saying is that in every stage of mankind's history there have always been such cases of mishandling. In class societies such cases are numerous. Even in a socialist society such things cannot be entirely avoided either, whether it be in a period of leadership by a correct or an incorrect line. There is however one distinction: namely, that during a period of correct line of leadership, as soon as it has been discovered that things have been mishandled, people can be cleared and rehabilitated, apologies can be made to them, so that their minds can be set at rest and they can lift up their heads again. But during a time when leadership follows an incorrect line, this way of doing things becomes impossible. Then the only thing is for those who represent the correct line, at a suitable opportunity to use the methods of democratic centralism to take the initiative to set mistakes right. As for those who have themselves made mistakes, after their mistakes have been criticized by comrades and their cases have been appraised by the higher levels and they are given correct treatment, then if they are demoted or transferred one hardly need say that this demotion or transfer may be helpful to them in correcting their mistakes and gaining new knowledge.

Now there are some comrades who are afraid of the masses initiating discussion and putting forward ideas which differ from those of the leaders and leading organizations. As soon as problems are discussed they suppress the activism of the masses and do not allow others to speak out. This attitude is extremely evil. Democratic centralism is written into our Party Constitution and State Constitution, but they don't apply it. Comrades, we are revolutionaries. If we have really committed mistakes of the kind which are harmful to the people's cause, then we should seek the opinions of the masses and of comrades and carry out a self-examination. This sort of self-examination should sometimes be repeated several times over. If once is not enough and people are not satisfied, then it should be done a second time. If they are still not satisfied, it should be done a third time until nobody has any more criticisms. Some provincial Party committees have done this. Some provinces are taking more initiative and letting everyone talk.

Those who started self-criticism earlier did so as early as 1959. The late-starters started self-criticism in 1961. Some provincial Party committees were compelled to carry out self-examinations, such as Honan, Kansu and Chinghai. According to some reports there are other provinces which are only now starting on self-criticism. It does not matter whether you take the initiative on the question of self-examination, or whether you are forced into it. It does not matter whether you do it earlier or later, provided you look squarely at your mistakes and are willing to admit them and correct them, and you are willing to let the masses criticize you – provided only that you adopt this kind of attitude you will be welcomed.

Criticism and self-criticism is a kind of method. It is a method of resolving contradictions among the people and it is the only method. There is no other. But if we do not have a full democratic life and do not truly implement democratic centralism, then this method of criticism and self-criticism cannot be applied.

Do we not now have many difficulties? Unless we rely on the masses, and mobilize the enthusiasm of the masses and of the cadres, we cannot overcome these difficulties. But if you do not explain the situation to the masses and to the cadres, if we do not offer our hearts to them and let them voice their own opinions, they will still be afraid of you and not dare to speak out. It would then be impossible to mobilize their enthusiasm. In 1957 I said: 'We must bring about a political climate which has both centralism and democracy, discipline and freedom, unity of purpose and ease of mind for the individual, and which is lively and vigorous.' We should have this political climate both within the Party and outside. Without this political climate the enthusiasm of the masses cannot be mobilized. We cannot overcome difficulties without democracy. Of course, it is even more impossible[3] to do so without centralism, but if there's no democracy there won't be any centralism.

Without democracy there cannot be any correct centralism because people's ideas differ, and if their understanding of things lacks unity then centralism cannot be established. What is centralism? First of all it is a centralization of correct ideas, on the basis of which unity of understanding, policy, planning, command and action are achieved. This is called centralized unification. If people still do not understand problems, if they have ideas but have not expressed them, or are angry but still have not vented their anger, how can centralized unification be established? If there is no democracy we cannot possibly summarize experience correctly. If there is no democracy, if ideas are not coming from the masses, it is impossible to establish a good line, good general and specific policies and methods. Our leading organs merely play the role of a processing plant in the establishment of a good line and good general and specific policies and methods. Everyone knows that if a factory has no raw material it cannot do any processing. If the raw material is not adequate in quantity and quality it cannot produce good finished products. Without democracy, you have no understanding of what is happening down below; the situation will be unclear; you will be unable to collect sufficient opinions from all sides; there can be no communication between top and bottom; top-level organs of leadership will depend on one-sided and incorrect material to decide issues, thus you will find it difficult to avoid being subjectivist; it will be impossible to achieve unity of understanding and unity of action, and impossible to achieve true centralism. Is not the main item for discussion at this session of our conference opposition to dispersionism and the strengthening of centralized unification? If we fail to promote democracy in full measure, then will this centralism and this unification be true or false? Will it be real or empty? Will it be correct or incorrect? Of course it must be false, empty and incorrect.

Our centralism is built on democratic foundations; proletarian centralism is based on broad democratic foundations. The Party committee at various levels is the organ which implements centralized leadership. But the leadership of the Party committees is a collective leadership; matters cannot be decided arbitrarily by the first secretary alone. Within Party committees democratic centralism should be the sole mode of operation. The relationship between the first secretary and the other secretaries and committee members is one of the minority obeying the majority. For example, in the Standing Committee and the Political Bureau situations like this often arise: when I say something, no matter whether it is correct or incorrect, provided that everyone disagrees with me, I will accede to their point of view because they are the majority. I am told that the situation exists within some provincial Party committees, district Party committees and county Party committees, whereby in all matters whatever the first secretary says goes. This is quite wrong. It is nonsense if whatever one person says goes. I am referring to important matters, not to the routine work which comes in the wake of decisions. All important matters must be discussed collectively, different opinions must be listened to seriously, and the complexities of the situation and partial opinions must be analysed. Account must be taken of various possibilities and estimates made of the various aspects of a situation: which are good, which bad, which easy, which difficult, which possible and which impossible. Every effort must be made to be both cautious and thorough. Otherwise you have one-man tyranny. Such first secretaries should be called tyrants and not 'squad leaders' of democratic centralism. Once upon a time there was a certain Hsiang Yü, who was called the Tyrant of Western Ch'u. He hated listening to opinions which differed from his. He had a man called Fan Tseng working for him who offered him advice, but Hsiang Yü did not listen. There was another man called Liu Pang, who became Emperor Kao-tsu of Han, who was better at accepting ideas different from his own. An intellectual called Li I-chi went to see Liu Pang, and announced himself as a scholar of the school of Confucius. Liu Pang said: 'There's a war on, I don't want to see scholars.' Li I-chi flared up. He said to the gatekeeper: 'You bloody well go in and say that I am a drinking man from Kaoyang and not a scholar at all.' The gatekeeper went in and announced him as he was told. Liu Pang said: 'Good, ask him in.' He was invited in. Liu Pang was washing his feet at the time, but he quickly got up to welcome him. But Li I-chi was still furious because Liu Pang had refused to see a scholar and he gave Liu Pang a telling off. 'Do you want to conquer the world or don't you? Why do you look down on your elders? At that time Li I-chi was over sixty and Liu Pang was younger, so Li called himself 'your elder'. At these words Liu Pang apologized and at once accepted his plan of seizing the county of Ch'en-liu. This incident can be read in the biographies of Li I-chi and Chu Chien in the *Shi-chi*.[4]

Liu Pang was a hero whom the historians of the feudal period called a straightforward, open-minded man, who listened to advice and was as relaxed as a flowing river. Liu Pang fought Hsiang Yü for many years. In the end Liu Pang won and Hsiang Yü was defeated. This was no mere chance. We now have some first secretaries who cannot even match Liu Pang of the feudal period, and are somewhat like Hsiang Yü. If these comrades don't reform, they will lose their jobs. You all know the play called *The Tyrant Bids His Lady Farewell*;[5] if these comrades don't reform, the day will surely come when they too will be saying farewell to their ladies (*laughter*). Why do I say this so bluntly? It is because I intend to be mean and make some comrades feel sore so that they think over things properly. It wouldn't be a bad thing if they couldn't sleep for a night or two. If they were able to sleep, then I wouldn't be pleased because it would mean that they have not yet felt sore.

There are some comrades who cannot bear to listen to ideas contrary to their own, and cannot bear to be criticized. This is very wrong. During this conference one province held a meeting which started off in a very lively manner, but as soon as the provincial Party secretary arrived a hush fell on the proceedings and nobody spoke. Comrade provincial Party secretary, what is the purpose of your attendance at meetings? Why don't you stay in your own room and think about problems and let others all take part in the discussion? When this kind of atmosphere is engendered and people don't dare to speak in your presence, then it is up to you to keep away. If you have made mistakes, then you should carry out self-criticism, let others speak, let others criticize you. On 12 June last year, during the last day of the Peking Conference called by the Central Committee, I talked about my own shortcomings and mistakes. I said I wanted the comrades to convey what I said to their various provinces and districts. I found out later that many districts did not get my message, as if my mistakes could be hidden and ought to be hidden. Comrades, they mustn't be hidden. Any mistakes that the Centre has made ought to be my direct responsibilty, and I also have an indirect share in the blame because I am the Chairman of the Central Committee. I don't want other people to shirk their responsibility. There are some other comrades who also bear responsibility, but the person primarily responsible should be me. All you who are our provincial committee secretaries, district Party committee secretaries, county Party committee secretaries, down to ward Party and other secretaries, enterprise committee secretaries and commune Party committee secretaries, since you have taken on the job of first secretary you must bear the responsibility for mistakes and shortcomings in the work.

Those of you who shirk responsibility or who are afraid of taking responsibility, who do not allow people to speak, who think you are tigers, and that nobody will dare to touch your arse, whoever has this attitude, ten out of ten of you will fail. People will talk anyway. You think that nobody will really dare to touch the arse of tigers like you? They damn well will!

Unless we fully promote people's democracy and inner-Party democracy in our country, and unless we fully implement the system of proletarian democracy, it will be impossible to achieve a true proletarian centralism. Without a high degree of democracy, it is impossible to achieve a high degree of centralism, and without a high degree of centralism, it is impossible to establish a socialist economy. If our country does not establish a socialist economy, what kind of situation shall we be in? We shall become a country like Yugoslavia, which has actually become a bourgeois country; the dictatorship of the proletariat will be transformed into a bourgeois dictatorship, into a reactionary fascist type of dictatorship. This is a question which demands the utmost vigilance. I hope comrades will give a great deal of thought to it.

Without the system of democratic centralism, the proletarian dictatorship cannot be consolidated. To practise democracy among the people and to practise dictatorship over the enemies of the people, these two aspects are inseparable. When these two aspects are combined, this is then proletarian dictatorship, or it may be called people's democratic dictatorship. Our slogan is: 'A people's democratic dictatorship, led by the proletariat, and based on the alliance of the workers and peasants.' How does the proletariat exercise leadership? It leads through the Communist Party. The Communist Party is the vanguard of the proletariat. The proletariat unites with all classes and strata who approve of, support and participate in the socialist revolution and socialist construction, and exercises dictatorship over the reactionary classes or the remnants thereof. In our country the system of exploitation of man by man has already been eliminated. The economic foundations of the landlord class and the bourgeoisie have been eliminated. The reactionary classes are now no longer as ferocious as hitherto. For example, they are no longer as ferocious as in 1949 when the People's Republic was founded, nor as ferocious as in 1957 when the right-wing bourgeosie madly attacked us.[6] Therefore we speak of them as the remnants of the reactionary classes. But we may on no account underestimate these remnants. We must continue to struggle against them. The reactionary classes which have been overthrown are still planning a come-back. In a socialist society, new bourgeois elements may still be produced. During the whole socialist stage there still exist classes and class struggle, and this class struggle is a protracted, complex, sometimes even violent affair. Our instruments of dictatorship should not be weakened; on the contrary they should be strengthened. Our security system is in the hands of comrades who follow the correct line. It is possible that the security departments in some places may be in the hands of bad people. There are also some comrades engaged on security work who do not rely on the masses or on the Party. In the work of purging counter-revolutionaries, they do not follow the line of purging them with the help of the masses under the leadership of the Party committee. They rely solely on secret work, on so-called professional work. Professional work is necessary; it is absolutely necessary to use the methods of detection and trial to deal with counter-revolutionary elements, but the most important thing is to carry out the mass line under the leadership of the Party committee. When we are concerned with dictatorship over the whole reactionary class, it is especially important to rely on the masses and the Party. To exercise dictatorship over the reactionary classes does not mean that we should totally eliminate all reactionary elements, but rather that we should eliminate the classes to which they belong. We should use appropriate methods to remould them and transform them into new men. Without a broad people's democracy, proletarian dictatorship cannot be consolidated and political power would be unstable. Without democracy, without the mobilization of the masses, without mass supervision, it will be impossible to exercise effective dictatorship over the reactionary and bad elements, and it will be impossible effectively to remould them. Thus they would continue to make trouble and might still stage a come-back. This problem demands vigilance, and I hope comrades will give a great deal of thought to this too.

(3) Which classes should we unite with?

Which classes should we unite with? Which classes should we repress? This is a question of basic standpoint.

The working class should unite with the peasant class, the urban petit bourgeoisie, and the patriotic national bourgeoisie; first of all it should unite with the peasant class. The intellectuals such as, for example, scientists, engineers and technicians, professors, writers, artists, actors, medical workers and journalists, do not constitute a class; they are either appendages of the bourgeoisie or of the proletariat. As regards the intellectuals, do we unite only with those who are revolutionary? No. As long as they are patriotic we will unite with them and let them get on with their work. Workers, peasants, urban petit-bourgeois elements, patriotic intellectuals, patriotic capitalists and other patriots together comprise more than ninety-five per cent of the whole country's population. Under our people's democratic dictatorship, all of these come within the classification of the people. And among the people we must practise democracy.

Those whom the people's democratic dictatorship should repress are: landlords, rich peasants, counter-revolutionary elements, bad elements and anti-communist rightists. The classes which the counter-revolutionary elements, bad elements and anti-communist rightists represent are the landlord class and the reactionary bourgeoisie. These classes and bad people comprise about four or five per cent of the population. These are the people we must compel to reform. They are the people whom the people's democratic dictatorship is directed against.

On which side do we stand? Do we stand on the side of the popular masses, who comprise over ninety-five per cent of the whole country's population? Or do we stand on the side of the landlords, rich peasants, counter-revolutionary elements, bad elements and rightists who comprise four or five per cent of the whole country's population? We must stand on the side of the popular masses and absolutely mustn't stand on the side of the people's enemies; this is a question of the basic standpoint of a Marxist–Leninist.

This holds true both within our country and in the international sphere. The people of all countries, the great masses of the people who comprise more than ninety-five per cent of the [world's] population certainly want revolution, they certainly support Marxism–Leninism and cannot support revisionism. Some may support revisionism temporarily, but later they will finally reject it. They will all gradually awaken and oppose imperialism and the reactionaries of various nations; they will all oppose revisionism. A true Marxist–Leninist must stand resolutely on the side of the popular masses who comprise over ninety-five per cent of the world's population.

(4) *Acquiring an understanding of the objective world*

In acquiring an understanding of the objective world, in making a flying leap from the realm of necessity to the realm of freedom, man must pass through a process. On the question of how China was to carry out the democratic revolution, from the founding of the Party in 1921 to the Seventh Congress in 1945 it was altogether twenty-four years before our Party's understanding reached complete unity. In the meantime we had the experience of the Rectification Movement on an all-party scale which lasted from the spring of 1942 to the summer of 1945, altogether three and a half years. This was a very searching movement, which adopted the method of democracy, which is to say that no matter who it was who had made mistakes, provided he acknowledged them and corrected them, things would be all right, and everybody helped him to acknowledge and correct his mistakes. This is called 'taking warning from the past in order to be more careful in future; treating the illness in order to save the patient', 'taking the desire for unity as a starting-point, passing through criticism or struggle, distinguishing between right and wrong, and reaching a new unity on a new basis'. The formula 'unity–criticism–unity' was created at that time. The Rectification Movement helped the comrades of the whole Party to reach unity of understanding. The question of how to carry out the democratic revolution, how to devise the Party line and various concrete policies were all completely solved at that time, and especially after the Rectification Movement.

Between the founding of the Party and the War of Resistance to Japan came the Northern Expeditionary War and the ten years' Agrarian Revolutionary War, when we experienced two victories and two defeats. The Northern Expeditionary War was victorious, but in 1927 the revolution suffered a defeat. In the Agrarian Revolutionary War we won great victories, the Red Army grew to a strength of 300,000, but later we again met with setbacks and after the Long March these 300,000 men were reduced to some 20,000-odd. After we reached North Shensi the numbers increased a little, but still did not reach 30,000; that is to say they were still less than a tenth of the original 300,000. In the final analysis which was the stronger – the army of 300,000 or the army of under 30,000? Having suffered such great setbacks and encountered such hardships we had become hardened, we had acquired experience, we had corrected our wrong line and restored the correct line. Therefore the army of under 30,000 was stronger than the previous army of 300,000. Comrade Liu Shao-ch'i said in his report that in the past four years our line was correct, and that our achievements were the main feature; we made some mistakes in our practical work and suffered some hardships, but we gained experience; therefore we are stronger than before, not weaker. This is how things actually are. During the period of the democratic revolution, it was only after experiencing first victory, then defeat, victory again and again defeat, and after comparing the two [victories and defeats], that I came to understand this objective world of China. On the eve of the War of Resistance to Japan and during that war I wrote a number of articles, such as 'Strategic Problems of China's Revolutionary War', 'On Protracted War', 'On New Democracy', 'Forward to the *Communist*', and I drafted a number of documents on policy and strategy for the Central Committee. All these served to summarize revolutionary experience. These articles and documents could only have been produced at that time, and not before, because until I had been through these great storms and had been able to compare our two victories with our two defeats, I did not yet have sufficient experience, and could not yet fully understand the laws of the Chinese revolution.

Speaking generally, it is we Chinese who have achieved understanding of the objective world of China, not the comrades concerned with Chinese questions in the Communist International. These comrades in the Communist International simply did not understand, or we could say they utterly failed to understand[7] Chinese society, the Chinese nation, or the Chinese revolution. For a long time even we did not have a clear understanding of the objective world of China, let alone the foreign comrades!

It was not until the period of the Resistance to Japan that we formulated a general line for the Party and a complete set of concrete policies which were appropriate to the actual situation. By this time we had been making revolution for more than twenty years. For so many years previously we were working very much in the dark. If anyone were to claim that any comrade, for example any member of the Central Committee, or I myself, completely understood the laws of the Chinese revolution right from the beginning, then that comrade would be talking through his hat. He should definitely not be believed. It was not like that at all. In the past, and especially at the beginning, all our energies were directed towards revolution, but as for how to make revolution, what we wanted to change, which should come first and which later, and which should wait until the next stage – for a fairly long time none of these questions were properly understood, or we could say they were not thoroughly understood.

When I explain how our Chinese Communist Party during the period of democratic revolution, after much difficulty successfully came to understand the laws of the Chinese revolution, my aim in bringing up these historical facts is to help our comrades to appreciate one thing: that understanding the laws of socialist construction must pass through a process. It must take practice as its starting-point, passing from having no experience to having some experience; from having little experience to having more experience; from the construction of socialism, which is in the realm of necessity as yet not understood, to the gradual overcoming of our blindness and the understanding of objective laws, thereby attaining freedom, achieving a flying leap in our knowledge and reaching the realm of freedom.

With regard to socialist construction we still lack experience. I have discussed this problem with delegations of fraternal parties from quite a few countries, and I said to them that we have no experience of the construction of a socialist economy.

I have also discussed this problem with several journalists from capitalist countries, among whom there was an American called Snow. For a long time he had wanted to come to China, and in 1960 we let him come. I had a discussion with him. I said: 'As you know, we have a set of experiences, general and specific policies and methods on politics, military affairs and class struggle; but as for socialist construction we have never done any in the past, and we still have no experience. You may say: "Haven't you done it for eleven years?" Yes, we have done it for eleven years, and we still lack knowledge and experience. Even if we are beginning to have a little, it still isn't much.' Snow wanted me to say something about China's long-term construction plan. I said: 'I don't know.' He said: 'You are being too prudent.' I said: 'It's not a question of being prudent. It's just that I really don't know, we just haven't any experience, that's all.' Comrades, it's true that we don't know; we really do lack experience and it is a fact that we have no such long-term plan. 1960 was the year when we ran into a lot of difficulties. In 1961 I had a discussion with Montgomery, at which we talked about these ideas again. He said: 'In another fifty years you will be terrific.' What he meant was that after fifty years we might become powerful and 'invade' other countries, but not within fifty years. He had expounded his opinions to me when he came to China in 1960. I said: 'We are Marxist–Leninists, our state is a socialist state, not a capitalist state, therefore we wouldn't invade others in a hundred years, or even ten thousand years. As for the construction of a strong socialist economy, in China fifty years won't be enough; it may take a hundred years or even longer. In your country the development of capitalism took several hundred years. We won't count the sixteenth century, which was still in the Middle Ages. From the seventeenth century to now is already 360 years. In our country, the construction of a great and mighty socialist economy I reckon will take more than one hundred years.' What period was the sevententh century? It was the end of the Ming and the beginning of the Ch'ing dynasties in China. A century later, in the first half of the eighteenth century, was the Ch'ien-lung period of the Ch'ing dynasty. The author of the *Dream of the Red Chamber,* Ts'ao Hsüeh-ch'in, lived in that period. It was the period which produced the character Chia Pao-yü, who was dissatisfied with the feudal system. In China, in the Ch'ien-lung period, the sprouts of capitalist relationships of production already existed, but it was still a feudal society. This is the social background of the characters who appeared in Prospect Garden.[8] Before this, in the seventeenth century, a number of European countries were already in the process of developing capitalism. It has taken over 300 years for capitalist productive forces to develop to their present pattern. Socialism is superior in many respects to capitalism, and the economic development of our country may be much faster than that of capitalist countries. But China has a large population, our resources are meagre, and our economy backward so that in my opinion, it will be impossible to develop our productive power so rapidly as to catch up with, and overtake, the most advanced capitalist countries in less than one hundred years. If it requires only a few decades, for example only fifty years as some have conjectured, then that will be a splendid thing, for which heaven and earth be praised. But I would advise, comrades, that it is better to think more of the difficulties and so to envisage it as taking a longer period. It took from three to four hundred years to build a great and mighty capitalist economy; what would be wrong with building a great and mighty socialist economy in our country in about fifty or a hundred years? The next fifty or hundred years from now will be an epic period of fundamental change in the social system of the world, an earth-shaking period, with which no past era can be compared. Living in such a period, we must be prepared to carry out great struggles, differing in many respects from the forms of struggle of previous periods. In order to carry out this task, we must do our very best to combine the universal truth of Marxism–Leninism with the concrete reality of Chinese socialist construction and with the concrete reality of future world revolution and, through practice, gradually come to understand the objective laws of the struggle. We must be prepared to suffer many defeats and set-backs as a result of our blindness, thereby gaining experience and winning final victory. When we see things in this light, then there are many advantages in envisaging it as taking a long period; conversely, harm would result from envisaging a short period.

In our work of socialist construction, we are still to a very large extent acting blindly. For us the socialist economy is still in many respects a realm of necessity not yet understood. Take me as an example: there are many problems in the work of economic construction which I still don't understand. I haven't got much understanding of industry and commerce. I understand a bit about agriculture, but this is only relatively speaking – I still don't understand much. In order to have a deeper understanding of agriculture one should understand pedology, botany, crop cultivation, agricultural chemistry, agricultural mechanization, etc. There are also different forms of agricultural production such as food grains, cotton, oil, hemp, silk, tea, sugar, vegetables, tobacco, fruit, medical herbs, and miscellaneous grain crops, etc. There are also animal husbandry and forestry. I myself am a believer in Vilensky's pedology. In his works on pedology Vilensky advocated the combination of farming, forestry and animal husbandry. I think we must have this three-way combination or agriculture will suffer. I advise, comrades, when you have some moments to spare after work, please will you seriously study all these problems of agricultural production. I myself also would like to study more. Up to now however my knowledge of these matters has been very scanty. I have paid rather more attention to problems relating to the system, to the productive relationships. As for the productive forces, I know very little. As regards our Party as a whole, our knowledge of socialist construction is extremely inadequate. We should from now on spend a period of time in summarizing our experiences and in hard study, and in the course of practice gradually deepen our understanding of it through clarifying its laws. We must put in a lot of hard work and make thorough investigations. We must go down to the countryside to squat on a selected spot. We must go and squat in the production brigades and production teams, and go to the factories and shops. As to making investigations and studies, we used to do them rather well but since we came into the cities we have no longer taken them seriously. In 1961 we did advocate it once again, and now there have already been some changes. But amongst the leading cadres, especially the higher-level leading cadres, some districts, departments and enterprises still haven't adopted this style. There are some provincial Party secretaries who have still not gone down to squat on selected spots. If the provincial Party secretaries don't go, how can they ask district Party secretaries and county Party secretaries to go down to squat? This is no good – it must be changed.

Since the founding of the Chinese People's Republic, twelve years have already gone by. These twelve years can be divided into a first period of eight years and a second period of four years: 1950 to the end of 1957 constitute the first eight years; 1958 to now is the second four years. In this conference of ours, we have already initially summarized the experiences of our past work, mainly the experiences of the second period of four years. This summary is reflected in the report by Comrade Liu Shao-ch'i. We have already formulated, or are formulating, or shall formulate, concrete policies in various fields. What we have already formulated are things such as sixty regulations on work in the countryside, seventy regulations on industrial enterprises, sixty regulations on higher education, and forty regulations on scientific research. All these draft regulations have already been implemented or are being experimented with; they will be revised in future – some may have to be greatly revised. Among those regulations which are in the process of formulation are the regulations on commerce. Among the regulations which are going to be formulated in future are the regulations on middle-school and primary-school education.[9] We should also formulate some regulations on the work of our Party, government and mass organizations. The army has already formulated some regulations. In short, in industry, agriculture, commerce, education, army, government and Party, in these seven aspects of the work we must properly summarize experience and formulate a complete set of general and specific policies and methods suited to our conditions, so that they may progress along correct lines.

It is not enough to have the General Line; it is also necessary that, under the leadership of the General Line, in the domains of industry, agriculture, commerce, education, army, government and Party, there should be a complete set of concrete general and specific policies and methods which are suited to our conditions. Only then is it possible to persuade the masses and the cadres. We should use these as teaching materials to educate them, so that they may be united in understanding and action. Only then will it be possible to attain victory in the task of revolution and construction; otherwise it is impossible. On this point, even as far back as the War of Resistance to Japan, we already had a profound understanding. At that time we acted in this way, and therefore the cadres and masses had a unified understanding of the complete set of concrete general and specific policies and methods of the democratic revolutionary period, and thus there was unified action and we therefore attained victory in the democratic revolutionary task of that period. This everybody knows. During the period of socialist revolution and construction, our revolutionary tasks in the first few years were: in the countryside to complete the reform of the feudal land system and then to implement agricultural cooperation; in the cities to implement the socialist transformation of capitalist industrial and commercial enterprises. In the field of economic construction our task then was to rehabilitate the economy and implement the first five-year plan. Both in the revolution and in construction at that time we had a General Line which was appropriate to the objective conditions and which had abundant persuasive power. We also had a complete set of general and specific policies and methods under the leadership of the General Line. Therefore we could educate the cadres and masses, unify their understanding, and the work was carried out relatively well. This everybody also knows. But in those days the situation was such that, since we had no experience in economic construction, we had no alternative but to copy the Soviet Union. In the field of heavy industry especially, we copied almost everything from the Soviet Union, and we had very little creativity of our own. At that time it was absolutely necessary to act thus, but at the same time it was also a weakness – a lack of creativity and lack of ability to stand on our own feet. Naturally this could not be our long-term strategy. From 1958 we decided to make self-reliance our major policy and striving for foreign aid a secondary aim. At the Second Session of the Party's Eighth Congress in 1958, we adopted the General Line of 'going all out and aiming high to achieve greater, faster, better and more economical results in building socialism'. In the same year the people's communes were also established, and the slogan of a 'Great Leap Forward' was issued. For a certain period after the General Line of socialist construction was proclaimed, we still hadn't had the time nor the possibility to formulate a complete set of concrete general and specific policies and methods which were appropriate to the conditions, since our experience was still not sufficient. Under these circumstances the cadres and the masses still did not have a complete set of teaching materials, nor had they received any systematic education on policy and so it wasn't possible to have genuinely unified understanding and action. It only became possible after the passage of time, the experience of setbacks and difficulties, and the gaining of both positive and negative experience. Now it's all right, we already have these things or are now formulating them. Thus we can now more judiciously carry out the socialist revolution and socialist construction. In order to formulate a complete set of concrete general and specific policies and methods under the guidance of the General Line, it is necessary to allow ideas to come from the masses and to adopt the method of systematic and thorough investigation and study, and examine historically the successful and unsuccessful experiences in our work. Only then may we discover the laws inherent in objective things and not created by people's subjective imaginations; and only then may we be able to formulate various regulations which are appropriate to the circumstances. This is a very important matter. Will you comrades please pay attention to this point.

In industry, agriculture, commerce, education, military affairs, government and Party, in all these seven domains the Party leads in all things. The Party has to lead industry, agriculture, commerce, culture, education, the army and government. Generally speaking, our Party is very good. Our Party is mainly composed of workers and poor peasants. The great majority of our cadres are good, they all work industriously, but we must also see that in our Party there still exist some problems; we mustn't imagine that everything is good with the state of our Party. At present we have over seventeen million Party members, and among these members almost eighty per cent became members after the founding of the state: they joined the Party in the fifties. Only twenty per cent joined before the founding of our state, and among these twenty per cent of our members, those who joined the Party before 1930 – that is to say those who joined the Party during the twenties – according to the estimate of eight years ago were some 800-odd people. Some of these have died in the past two years so now I am afraid there may only be 700-odd people left. Among both old and new Party members – especially among the new members – there are always some people whose characters and working styles are impure. Those people are individualists, bureaucrats, subjectivists: some have even become degenerate elements. There are some people who adopt the guise of Communist Party members, but they in no way represent the working class; instead they represent the bourgeoisie. All is not pure within the Party. We must see this point, otherwise we shall suffer.

The above is my fourth point. Our understanding of the objective world must pass through a process. First of all we do not understand, or do not completely understand it, but after repeated practice and after we have obtained results through practice, when we have won victories and also had tumbles and setbacks, we are able to compare our victories and defeats. Only then is there a possibility of developing to the point of achieving complete understanding or relatively complete understanding. By that time we shall be exercising more initiative, we shall be more free and we shall become more intelligent. Freedom means the recognition of necessity and it means transforming the objective world. Only on the basis of recognizing necessity can man enjoy freedom of activity; this is the dialectical law of freedom and necessity. What we call necessity is an objectively existing law. Before we recognize it our behaviour cannot be conscious; it has elements of blindness. At this time we are stupid; during the last few years haven't we made many stupid blunders?

(5) The international communist movement

On this question I am only going to say a few simple sentences. No matter whether in China or in other countries of the world, over ninety per cent of the people will support Marxism–Leninism in the long run. In this world at present there are still many people being deceived by social-democratic parties, by the revisionists, the imperialists, or by the reactionary elements of various countries, who have not yet awakened.

But eventually little by little they will awaken, they will support Marxism–Leninism. Marxism–Leninism is truth; it cannot be resisted. The masses want revolution; the world revolution will finally be victorious. Those who forbid revolution such as the characters in Lu Hsün's book, Squire Chao, Squire Ch'ien and the Fake Foreign Devil who did not allow Ah Q to make revolution, will finally be defeated.

The Soviet Union was the first socialist country, and the Soviet Communist Party was the party created by Lenin. Although the Party and the state leadership of the Soviet Union have now been usurped by the revisionists, I advise our comrades to believe firmly that the broad masses, the numerous Party members and cadres of the Soviet Union are good; that they want revolution, and that the rule of the revisionists won't last long. No matter when: now, in the future, in our generation or our descendants', we should all learn from the Soviet Union, study the experiences of the Soviet Union. If we don't learn from the Soviet Union, we will make mistakes. People may ask: since the Soviet Union is under the rule of the revisionists, should we still learn from them? What we should learn is about the good people and good things of the Soviet Union, the good experiences of the Soviet Communist Party. As for the bad people and bad things of the Soviet Union and the Soviet revisionists, we should treat them as teachers by negative example and learn lessons from them.

We should always uphold the principle of the unity of proletarian internationalism. We always advocate that the socialist countries and the world communist movement must unite firmly on the basis of Marxism–Leninism. The international revisionists are ceaselessly cursing us. Our attitude is, let them go on cursing us. When it becomes necessary we can give them some appropriate answers. Our Party has become accustomed to being cursed. Leaving aside those who attacked us in the past, what about the present? Abroad, the imperialists curse us, the reactionary nationalists curse us, the revisionists curse us; in our country Chiang Kai-shek curses us, the landlords, rich peasants, reactionaries, bad elements and rightists curse us. They had always done so in the past ... Are we isolated? I myself don't feel isolated. In this room alone there are already over 7,000 people; how can we be isolated with over 7,000 people? The popular masses of all countries of the world are already standing, or are going to stand, together with us. Can we be isolated?

(6) *We must unite the whole Party and the whole people*

We must unite the progressive elements and active elements within and without the Party, and unite the middle elements in order to bring forward those who lag behind. Only in this way can we unite the whole Party and the whole country; only by relying on such unity can we carry out our work, overcome difficulties and properly build up China. To unite the whole Party and the whole people is not at all to suggest that we do not have our own definite orientation. Some people say that the Communist Party is 'a party of the whole people', but we do not see things in this way. Our Party is a proletarian party; it is the vanguard of the proletariat; it is a fighting force armed with Marxism–Leninism. We stand on the side of the popular masses who comprise over ninety-five per cent of the total population. We definitely don't stand on the side of the landlords, rich peasants, reactionaries, bad elements and rightists who constitute four to five per cent of the total population. It is the same in the international sphere, we speak of unity with all Marxist–Leninists, all revolutionary comrades, the whole people. We definitely do not speak of unity with the anti-communist, anti-popular imperialists and reactionaries of various countries. Whenever possible we also want to establish diplomatic relations with these people, and strive to have peaceful coexistence with them on the basis of the five principles. But these matters are in a different category from the matter of uniting with the people of all countries. In order to unite the whole Party and the whole people it is necessary to promote democracy and let the people speak out. It should be so within the Party; it should also be so outside the Party. Comrades from provincial Party committees, comrades from district Party committees, and comrades from county Party committees, when you return, you must definitely let people speak out. Those of you who are present here must act and those who are not here must also act thus. All leading members within the Party must promote democracy and let people speak out. What are the limits? One is that we must observe Party discipline, the minority must obey the majority, and the whole Party should obey the Centre.

Another limit is the prohibition on organizing secret factions. We are not afraid of open opposition groups, we are only afraid of secret opposition groups. Such people do not speak the truth to your face; what they say to your face is all falsehood and deceit. They do not express their real aims. But as long as they do not break discipline, as long as they are not carrying on any secret factional activities, we should always allow them to speak and even if they should say the wrong things we should not punish them. If people say the wrong things they can be criticized, but we should use reason to convince them. What should we do if we persuade them and they are not convinced? We can let them reserve their opinions. As long as they obey resolutions and obey decisions taken by the majority, the minority can be allowed to reserve their various opinions. Both within and outside the Party there is advantage in allowing the minority to reserve their opinions. If they have incorrect opinions they can reserve them temporarily and they will change their minds in future. Very often the ideas of the minority will prove to be correct. History abounds with such instances. In the beginning truth is not in the hands of the majority of people, but in the hands of a minority. Marx and Engels held the truth in their hands, but in the beginning they were in the minority. Lenin for a very long period was also in the minority. We had this kind of experience within our own Party. Both under the rule of Ch'en Tu-hsiu and during the period of rule of the 'Left-wing' Line truth was not in the hands of the majority in the leading organs, but rather in the hands of the minority. In history doctrines of natural scientists such as Copernicus, Galileo and Darwin were for a very long period not recognized by the majority of people, but instead were thought to be incorrect. In their time they were in the minority. When our Party was founded in 1921 we only had a few dozen members; we were also in the minority, but these few people represented the truth and represented China's destiny.

There is also the question of arrests and executions on which I want to say something. At present, only a dozen or so years after the victory of the Revolution, while elements of the overthrown reactionary classes have not yet been reformed, and while there are people still attempting a restoration, a few people have to be arrested and executed; otherwise the people's anger cannot be appeased and the people's dictatorship cannot be consolidated. But we must not arrest people lightly, and we must especially not execute people lightly. There are some bad people, bad elements and degenerate people who have infiltrated into our ranks, and degenerate elements who sit on the heads of the people and piss and shit on them, behaving in a vicious and unrestrained way, seriously disobeying laws and discipline. These people are petty Chiang Kai-sheks. We must find a way to deal with this type of people, and arrest some and execute a few of the worst who have committed the biggest crimes and the greatest evils, because if we do not arrest or execute any of this type of people, we won't be able to appease the anger of the people. This is what we mean when we say: 'We cannot refrain from arresting them, we cannot refrain from executing them.' But we must not on any account arrest too many and must not execute too many. All those who might be arrested but need not be arrested, and all those who might be executed but need not be executed, we must resolve not to arrest or to execute. There was a man called P'an Han-nien who had once been vice-mayor of Shanghai. In the past he had secretly surrendered to the Kuomintang. He was a man of the C.C. Clique.[10] Now he is detained in custody; we have not executed him. If we kill one person like P'an Han-nien and thereby break the ban on executions, then we would have to kill all people like him. There was another man called Wang Shih-wei who was a secret agent working for the Kuomintang. When he was in Yenan, he wrote a book called *The Wild Lily*, in which he attacked the revolution and slandered the Communist

Party.[11] Afterwards he was arrested and executed. That incident happened at the time when the army was on the march, and the security organs themselves made the decision to execute him; the decision did not come from the Centre. We have often made criticisms on this very matter; we thought that he shouldn't have been executed. If he was a secret agent and wrote articles to attack us and refused to reform till death, why not leave him there or let him go and do labour? It isn't good to kill people. We should arrest and execute as few people as possible. If we arrest people and execute people at the drop of a hat, the end result would be that everybody would fear for themselves and nobody would dare to speak. In such an atmosphere there wouldn't be much democracy.

Also we mustn't put hats on people indiscriminately. Some of our comrades are in the habit of persecuting people with hats. As soon as they open their mouths hats come flying out; they frighten people so that they don't dare speak. Of course one cannot avoid hats altogether. Are there not many hats in the report made by Comrade Liu Shao-ch'i? Isn't 'dispersionism' a hat? But we mustn't put hats on people without due consideration, so that every Tom, Dick and Harry is labelled with 'dispersionism', and everybody becomes labelled with 'dispersionism'. It is better that hats should be put on by people themselves and they should fit the wearers, rather than that they should be put on them by others. If people put a few hats on themselves and other people don't agree that they should wear those hats, then they should be removed. This will make for a very good democratic atmosphere. We advocate not to grasp at others' faults, not to put hats on people, not to flourish the big stick. The aim is to make people unafraid in their hearts and let them dare to express their opinions.

We should adopt a well-intentioned helpful attitude towards those who have made mistakes, and towards those who do not allow people to speak out. We must not create the kind of atmosphere in which people feel that they cannot afford to make mistakes and that there would be terrible consequences if they made any mistakes, and if once they made mistakes they would never raise their heads again. When a person has made mistakes, as long as he sincerely wants to make amends, as long as he has really made a self-criticism, then we must show that we accept him. When people make their self-criticism the first or second time, we must not ask too much of them. It does not matter if their self-examinations are not yet thorough, we should allow them to think again and give them well-intentioned help. People need help from others; we should help those comrades who have made mistakes to understand their mistakes. If people sincerely carry out self-criticism and are willing to correct mistakes, then we should forgive them and adopt a lenient policy towards them. As long as their achievements are still of primary importance, as long as they are competent, they can be allowed to continue in their posts.

Here in my speech I have criticized certain phenomena and criticized certain comrades, but I have not named them. I have not pointed out who Tom, Dick and Harry are. You yourselves must have some ideas in your minds (*laughter*). For shortcomings and mistakes made in the last few years, the primary responsibility should be borne by the Centre; at the Centre the primary responsibility is mine; next the responsibility belongs to the provincial committees, municipal committees, and autonomous region Party committees; and third, to the regional committee level; fourth, to county committee level; and fifth, to the enterprise Party committees and commune Party committees. In short everyone has his share of the responsibility.

Comrades, when you have gone back you must build up democratic centralism. The comrades of the county committees should lead the commune Party committees to build up and strengthen democratic centralism. First of all we must establish and strengthen collective leadership, and not practise the type of leadership which has long been diagnosed as 'dispersionism'. Under this method the Party committee secretaries and members do their bits separately; they cannot have real collective discussions, nor can they have real collective leadership.

If we are to promote democracy we must encourage others to criticize us and listen to their criticisms. To be able to withstand criticism we must first take measures to carry out self-criticism.

We must examine whatever needs examining for one hour or at most two hours. If everything is to be brought out in the open, it will take as long as that. If others consider we have not done enough, then let them say so. If what they say is right, we will accept their opinion. When we allow others to speak, should we be active or passive in our attitude? Of course it is better to be active. What can we do if we are forced on to the defensive? In the past we were undemocratic and so we find ourselves on the defensive. No matter. Let everybody criticize us. As for me, I will not go out during the day; I will not go to the theatre at night. Please come and criticize me day and night (*laughter*). Then I will sit down and think about it carefully, not sleep for two or three nights, think about it until I understand it, and then write a sincere self-examination. Isn't that the way to deal with it? In short, let other people speak out. The heavens will not fall and you will not be thrown out. If you do not let others speak, then the day will surely come when you are thrown out.

Today I will confine myself to the above matters. The central point that I have spoken about is the question of how to realize democratic centralism and how to promote democracy within and without the Party. I recommend comrades to consider this question carefully. Some comrades still do not think in terms of democratic centralism. Now is the time to adopt this way of thinking and begin to acquire some understanding of this question. If we do our utmost to promote democracy, then we can mobilize the enthusiasm of the broad masses of people within and without the Party. We can unite the broad popular masses who comprise more than ninety-five per cent of our total population. When we have achieved this, our work will get better and better and we will more quickly overcome the difficulties we encounter. Our cause will develop much more favourably (*enthusiastic applause*).

9 Speech at the Tenth Plenum of the Eighth Central Committee
The morning of 24 September 1962 in the Huai-jen Hall

It is now ten o'clock. The meeting is in session.

This plenary session of the Central Committee has solved a number of important problems. One is the problem of agriculture, another is that of commerce. Both of these are important problems. There are also the problems of industry and of planning which are secondary problems. The third is the problem of inner-Party unity. Several comrades have made speeches. The agricultural problem was explained by Comrade Ch'en Po-ta, the problem of commerce by Comrade Li Hsien-nien, and the problems of industry and planning by Comrades Li Fu-ch'un and XXX. In addition to these problems we also had the questions of increasing the membership of the Control Commission and of the vertical and horizontal interchange of cadres.

This conference did not open today: it has already been in session for over two months. It met for a month in Peitaiho and has continued for almost a month since transferring to Peking. The practical problems were discussed and clarified in August and September by various small groups (all of you present participated) which were in fact large groups. So now the plenary session will not take too long – three to five days will probably suffice. If we cannot finish by the twenty-seventh, we will stay over until the twenty-eighth, by which date the meeting must adjourn.

At Peitaiho I presented three problems: those of class, the situation and contradictions. I raised the problem of class because this problem had not been solved. Leaving aside the internal situation, internationally there are imperialism, nationalism, and revisionism. I am talking about capitalist countries which have not solved the class problem. So we have an anti-imperialist task. We have the task of supporting national liberation movements, that is to say we must support the broad masses of people in Asia, Africa, and Latin America, including workers, peasants, the revolutionary national bourgeoisie, and the revolutionary intellectuals. We want to unite with so many people. But they do not include the reactionary national bourgeoisie like Nehru, nor the reactionary bourgeois intellectuals like the Japanese renegade communist Shojiro Kasuga[1] who, with seven or eight others, supports the theory of structural reforms.

Now then, do classes exist in socialist countries? Does class struggle exist? We can now affirm that classes do exist in socialist countries and that class struggle undoubtedly exists. Lenin said: After the victory of the revolution, because of the existence of the bourgeoisie internationally, because of the existence of bourgeois remnants internally, because the petit bourgeoisie exists and continually generates a bourgeoisie, therefore the classes which have been overthrown within the country will continue to exist for a long time to come and may even attempt restoration. The bourgeois revolutions in Europe in such countries as England and France had many ups and downs. After the overthrow of feudalism there were several restorations and reversals of fortune. This kind of reversal is also possible in socialist countries. An example of this is Yugoslavia which has changed its nature and become revisionist, changing from a workers' and peasants' country to a country ruled by reactionary nationalist elements. In our country we must come to grasp, understand and study this problem really thoroughly. We must acknowledge that classes will continue to exist for a long time. We must also acknowledge the existence of a struggle of class against class, and admit the possibility of the restoration of reactionary classes. We must raise our vigilance and properly educate our youth as well as the cadres, the masses and the middle- and basic-level cadres. Old cadres must also study these problems and be educated. Otherwise a country like ours can still move towards its opposite. Even to move towards its opposite would not matter too much because there would still be the negation of the negation, and afterwards we might move towards our opposite yet again. If our children's generation go in for revisionism and move towards their opposite, so that although they still nominally have socialism it is in fact capitalism, then our grandsons will certainly rise up in revolt and overthrow their fathers, because the masses will not be satisfied. Therefore, from now on we must talk about this every year, every month, every day. We will talk about it at congresses, at Party delegate conferences, at plenums, at every meeting we hold, so that we have a more enlightened Marxist–Leninist line on the problem.

The situation in our country has not been very good for the past few years, but now it is starting to take a turn for the better. In 1959 and 1960 a number of things were done wrongly, mainly because most people had no experience to enable them to understand the problems. The most serious fault was that our requisitioning was excessive. When we did not have very much grain, we insisted on saying that we had. Blind commands were issued in both industry and agriculture. There were also some other large-scale mistakes. In the second half of 1960 we started to put these right – in point of fact it was quite early on, starting at the First Chengchow Conference in October 1958. Next came the Wuhan Conference in November and December 1958, while in February and March 1959 we held the Second Chengchow Conference. At the Shanghai Conference in April of that year we also paid attention to correcting our mistakes. Meanwhile there was a period in 1960 when we did not pay enough attention to it because revisionism came and put pressure on us. Our attention was diverted to opposing Khrushchev. From the second half of 1958 he wanted to blockade the Chinese coastline. He wanted to set up a joint fleet so as to have control over our coastline and blockade us. It was because of this question that Khrushchev came to our country. After this, in September 1959 during the Sino–Indian border dispute, Khrushchev supported Nehru in attacking us and Tass issued a communiqué. Then Khrushchev came to China and at our Tenth Anniversary Celebration banquet in October, he attacked us on our own rostrum. At the Bucharest Conference in 1960 they tried to encircle and annihilate us.[2] Then came the conference of the Two Communist Parties, the Twenty-six-Country Drafting Committee, the Eighty-one-Country Moscow Conference, and there was also a Warsaw Conference, all of which were concerned with the dispute between Marxism–Leninism and revisionism. We spent the whole of 1960 fighting Khrushchev. So you see that among socialist countries and within Marxism–Leninism a question like this could emerge. But in fact its roots lie deep in the past, in things which happened very long ago. They did not permit China to make revolution: that was in 1945. Stalin wanted to prevent China from making revolution, saying that we should not have a civil war and should cooperate with Chiang Kai-shek, otherwise the Chinese nation would perish. But we did not do what he said. The revolution was victorious. After the victory of the revolution he next suspected China of being a Yugoslavia, and that I would become a second Tito. Later when I went to Moscow to sign the Sino–Soviet Treaty of Alliance and Mutual Assistance, we had to go through another struggle. He was not willing to sign a treaty. After two months of negotiations he at last signed. When did Stalin begin to have confidence in us? It was at the time of the Resist America, Aid Korea campaign, from the winter of 1950. He then came to believe that we were not Tito, not Yugoslavia. But now we have become 'left adventurists', 'nationalists', 'dogmatists', 'sectarians', while the Yugoslavs have become 'Marxist–Leninists'. Nowadays Yugoslavia is quite all right, she's doing fine. I hear that she has become 'socialist' again. So the socialist camp is internally highly complicated too. It is, in fact, also very simple. There is only one principle involved: that is the problem of the class struggle – the problem of the struggle between the proletariat and the bourgeoisie, the problem of the struggle between Marxism–Leninism and anti-Marxism–Leninism, the problem of the struggle between Marxism–Leninism and revisionism.

As for the situation, it is good both internationally and domestically. In the initial period after the founding of our state, some people, including myself as well as Comrade X X, took the view that the parties and trade unions of Asia and the parties of Africa might suffer serious damage. It was later proved that this point of view was incorrect: it did not turn out as we expected. Since the Second World War, thriving national liberation struggles have developed in Asia, Africa and Latin America year by year. There was the Cuban revolution, the independence of Algeria, the Asian Games in Indonesia; tens of thousands of people demonstrated and smashed the Indian consulate and India became isolated; West Irian was handed over by the Netherlands; armed struggle developed in South Vietnam – a very good armed struggle. There was also the victory of armed struggle in Algeria, the victorious struggle in Laos, the Suez Canal affair, the independence of Egypt. The United Arab Republic is inclined towards the right, but then Iraq emerged. Both are to the right of centre, but both oppose imperialism. Although the population of Algeria is less than ten million, and France had an army of 800,000 fighting for seven or eight years, yet Algeria won in the end. Thus the international situation is excellent. Comrade Ch'en I has given a very good report on this.

The contradiction I want to talk about is that between us and imperialism. The contradiction between the people of the whole world and imperialism is the primary one. There is the opposition of the people of all countries to the reactionary bourgeoisie and to reactionary nationalism. There are also the contradictions between the people of all countries and revisionism, the contradictions among imperialist countries, the contradiction between nationalist countries and imperialism, internal contradictions within imperialist countries, and the contradiction between socialism and imperialism. I think that right-wing opportunism in China should be renamed: it should be called Chinese revisionism. The two months' conference at Peitaiho and Peking has been concerned with problems of two different kinds. One kind was the problem of political work; the other was the problem of class struggle – that is to say, the struggle between Marxism–Leninism and revisionism. The problem of work is also the problem of struggle against bourgeois ideas, which is identical with struggle between Marxism–Leninism and revisionism. There are several documents on problems of work: in industry, agriculture, commerce, etc. Various comrades have spoken on these questions.

As for how the Party should tackle the problem of revisionism within the country and within the Party and the problem of the bourgeoisie, I think we should adhere to former policies without changing them. No matter what sort of errors a comrade has committed, we should follow the line of the Rectification Campaign of 1942–5.[3] So long as comrades admit their mistakes and reform, we will welcome them. We must unite with them and cure the disease in order to save the patient; take warning from the past in order to safeguard the future. Unity–criticism–unity. But we must be quite specific about what is right and what is wrong. We must not mince words, or only spit out one word at a time. Why does the monk knock the wooden fish drum when he chants his sutra? The *Journey to the West* explains it by telling how the sutras collected in India were devoured by the black fish demon, who would spit out just one word each time it was knocked. This is the explanation of the wooden fish. We must not take this attitude and behave like the black fish demon. We must think things over carefully. We will unite with you, comrades, who have made mistakes, provided that you recognize your errors and return to a Marxist standpoint. Some of you comrades here present, I welcome you too. Do not be shy because you have made mistakes. We permit people to make mistakes and, having made them, we also permit you to correct them. Do not be intolerant of mistakes and do not prevent people from correcting them. Many comrades have corrected them well, which is excellent. The speech of Comrade Li Wei-han[4] is a case in point. Comrade Li Wei-han has corrected his mistakes and we trust him. We must be resolute first in observing people, and then in helping them. There are many other comrades. I have also committed mistakes. I talked about that last year. You must also let me make mistakes, and let me correct them. When I correct them, you should welcome it. Last year I said that we must be analytical towards people. No man can be without error. Consider the sages: to say that they were without shortcomings would be a metaphysical point of view, not a Marxist dialectical-materialist point of view. Anything can be analysed. I urge comrades, no matter whether you have had connections with foreign countries, or whether you belong to secret anti-Party groups – as long as you spill the beans and tell the whole truth we welcome you and will give you work to do. We must on no account take the attitude of ignoring such people, still less resort to the method of execution. We cannot break our ban on executions so there have been many counter-revolutionaries whom we have not killed. Wasn't the Hsüan T'ung emperor[5] a counter-revolutionary? There were also war criminals like Wang Yao-wu, K'ang Tse, Tu Yü-ming, Yang Kuang, and a whole lot of others whom we did not kill. Many people corrected their mistakes and we reprieved them. We didn't kill them. Those rightists who have corrected their mistakes have had their hats removed.[6] The recent trend towards the reversal of verdicts is incorrect. Only those verdicts which were truly incorrect can be reversed. Those verdicts which were correct cannot be reversed. As for the reversal of those verdicts which were truly wrong, when they were wholly wrong they should be wholly reversed, when they were partly wrong they should be partly reversed. When they were not wrong they should not be reversed. We cannot reverse all of them indiscriminately.

On the question of work, comrades will please take care that the class struggle does not interfere with our work. The first Lushan Conference of 1959 was originally concerned with work. Then up jumped P'eng Te-huai and said: 'You fucked my mother for forty days, can't I fuck your mother for twenty days?' All this fucking messed up the conference and the work was affected. Twenty days was not long enough and we abandoned the question of work. We really mustn't do that this time, we must really pay attention. In transmitting their reports of the conference, all localities and departments should take care to put work first. Work and the class struggle should proceed simultaneously. The class struggle must not be placed in a very prominent position. We have now formed two Special Case Review Commissions to clarify problems, to elucidate the problems and then convince people. We have to engage in the class struggle, but there are special people to take care of this kind of work. The security departments are specially charged with carrying on the class struggle. P'an Han-nien[7] is a counter-revolutionary! Hu Feng and Jao Shu-shih are also counter-revolutionaries! We haven't killed any of them! We must not let the class struggle interfere with our work. We can wait until the next Plenum or the one after that and then make another attempt to clarify these matters. The main task [of the security organs] is to deal with enemy sabotage.[8] If people engage in sabotage, then we will break our ban on executions. But this is only directed at people who destroy factories or bridges, throw bombs in the vicinity of Canton, who kill people or commit arson. The task of security is to defend our cause, to defend factories, enterprises, communes, production brigades, schools, the government, the army, the Party, mass organizations, and also cultural organs such as newspapers, publishing houses and news agencies; i.e. to protect the superstructure.

Writing novels is popular these days, isn't it? The use of novels for anti-Party activity is a great invention. Anyone wanting to overthrow a political régime must create public opinion and do some preparatory ideological work. This applies to counter-revolutionary as well as to revolutionary classes. Our ideology is revolutionary Marxism–Leninism; it is the combination of the universal truth of Marxism with the concrete practice of the Chinese revolution. If these are well combined, then the problems will be more easily solved. If they are not well combined, then we will meet with failure and setbacks. As regards socialist construction, this is also a combination of universal truth with the practice of construction. Have we combined them well or not? We are in the process of solving this problem. The same thing is true in military construction. For example, the military line of a few years ago is not the same as the military line today. Comrade Yeh Chien-ying[9] wrote a book which is very sharp; it is never confused on crucial points. I have always criticized you for not being sharp enough, but this time you were sharp. Here are a couple of sentences for you: 'Chu-ko Liang was cautious all his life, while Lü Tuan was clear-headed in big matters.'[10]

Will Comrade XX please announce the names of those who

are not attending this plenum? The Standing Committee of the Politburo decided that five people should not attend.

(Comrade XX intervened to say: The Standing Committee of the Politburo decided that five people should not attend the Plenum. P'eng, Hsi, Chang, Huang and Chou[11] are important individuals presently under investigation. While they are under investigation, they are not qualified to attend meetings.)

Because their crimes are really too great, they are not qualified to attend meetings, and should not attend important meetings, nor be allowed to appear on the T'ien An Men, until the situation has been clarified through investigation. We must distinguish through analysis between important and unimportant individuals, there is a difference between them. Unimportant individuals have attended our meeting today. When unimportant individuals have thoroughly corrected their errors, they should be given work to do. If important individuals have thoroughly corrected their errors, they should also be given work to do. We are particularly hopeful that unimportant individuals will become conscious [of their errors]; naturally we hope that important elements will also become conscious.

10 Remarks at the Spring Festival

Summary Record. 13 February 1964

CHAIRMAN MAO: Today is the Spring Festival, and we are holding a forum to discuss both foreign and domestic problems[1] ... Do you think our state is likely to collapse or not? Imperialism and revisionism, in concert, have struck right up to our borders, do [you] democratic personages[2] fear the atom bomb? If the atom bomb should explode, we would simply find ourselves back in Yenan. The whole Shen–Kan–Ning Border Area had a population of 1·5 millions, and in the city of Yenan there were 30,000. People cannot reply publicly unless they are first attacked. There was a time when the Kuomintang was cleverer than usual, and did not denounce us publicly. They put out a document using the method of restraining 'alien' parties, of restraining the Communist Party.[3] Do you know about that?

CHANG SHIH-CHAO:[4] I don't know about it.

CHAIRMAN MAO: You people aren't very well informed. In January 1941, the Kuomintang launched the South Anhwei Incident, in which we lost more than 17,000 men. After this, they staged several more anti-communist high tides, and thus taught [our] Party a lesson. Chiang Kai-shek is no good, every time he had a chance he tried to regiment us. After the end of the anti-Japanese war, Chiang talked about peace, and invited me to go to Chungking for negotiations, but he also gave underhand orders. During the negotiations, he carried out a campaign against our Party and annihilated the three divisions of Kao Shu-hsün.[5]

xxx: Kao has already joined the Party. People can change.

K'ANG SHENG: The Hsüan T'ung emperor has come to present his New Year's greetings (at the Political Consultative Conference).

CHAIRMAN MAO: We must unite very well with the Hsüan T'ung emperor. Both Kuang Hsü and Hsüan T'ung used to be our bosses.[6] Hsüan T'ung's monthly salary of a little over a hundren *yüan* is too small – this man is an emperor.

CHANG SHIH-CHAO: Hsüan T'ung's uncle, Tsai-t'ao,[7] is in wretched straits.

CHAIRMAN MAO: This fellow Tsai-t'ao is a high military official. He was a student in France. I know him, though not intimately. Would it be all right to aid him through you, so that he can eat a bit better? After all, he is our guest. We should improve his standard of living.

It's no fun being a running dog. Nehru is in bad shape, imperialism and revisionism have robbed him blind. Revisionism is being rebuffed everywhere. It was rebuffed in Romania, it is not listened to in Poland. In Cuba they listen to half and reject half; they listen to half because they can't do otherwise, since they don't produce oil or weapons. Imperialism is having a hard time, too. Japan is opposing the United States, and it's not only the Japanese Communist Party and the Japanese people that are opposing the United States – the big capitalists are doing so too. Not long ago, the Kita— iron works rejected an American inspection. De Gaulle's opposition to the United States is also in response to the demands of the capitalists. They are also behind his establishment of diplomatic relations with China. China opposes the United States; formerly in Peking there was Shen Ch'ung[8], the whole country opposed US imperialism. The Khrushchevite revisionists abuse us as dogmatists, pseudo-revolutionaries – they really curse us. Not long ago, a letter from the Central Committee of the Communist Party of the Soviet Union to the Central Committee of the Chinese Communist Party put forward four points: (1) An end to open polemics; (2) The return of the [Soviet] experts [to China]; (3) Talks on the Sino–Soviet border; (4) The expansion of commerce. We can have talks about the border; they will begin on 25 February. We can do a little business, but we can't do too much, for Soviet products are heavy, crude, high-priced, and they always keep something back.[9]

K'ANG SHENG: The quality is inferior.

CHAIRMAN MAO: They are first crude, second expensive, third inferior, and fourth they keep something back, so it's not so good to deal with them as with the French bourgeoisie, who still have some notion of business ethics.

In the past there have been mistakes in our work. The first was issuing blind commands, the second was excessive requisitioning; these have now been corrected. Now we have gone to the opposite extreme; we have gone from issuing blind commands to no commands, and as a result we are not doing our utmost. So we must emulate the Liberation Army, we must emulate the Petroleum Ministry's Tach'ing.[10] In the Tach'ing oilfields they have invested more than — and in the space of three years they have built up an oilfield producing — tons, and a processing plant for — tons of oil. The investment has been small, the time has been short, the successes have been great, and the many writings on this subject are worth having a look at. All ministries should learn from the Petroleum Ministry, learn from the Liberation Army, and get some good experience, so as to be a combat brigade in relation to the enemy, and a work brigade in relation to ourselves. University students should also learn from the Liberation Army. They should make full use of their successes, set up models for emulation, praise them extensively, and at the same time criticize mistakes. Praise should be the main thing, and criticism should be supplementary. Among those working for our cause, there are many good people, and many good models, which should be praised.

Last year in Hopei there were great natural disasters. In the south there was a drought; originally the harvest was good, but there were heavy rains causing the loss of 20,000 million *chin* [approximately 12 million metric tons] of grain; nevertheless, last year the total production rose by more than 10,000 million *chin,* and this year we want to do even better. At present we are learning from the Liberation Army, we are learning from the Petroleum Ministry, we are learning from models in the cities, the villages, the factories and the schools, we are overcoming mistakes in our work, and endeavouring to do our work somewhat better this year.

At this forum today, we have discussed international problems, but our basic concern is with internal problems. If we don't deal effectively with our internal problems, there's no good talking about international affairs. At present, there are some countries that want to establish relations with our country, such as the Congo. The Congo of Lumumba launched a guerrilla war, but they have no modern weapons at all – only things like Kuan Kung's Black Dragon Crescent Sword, and Chang Fei's eighteen-foot spear.[11]

XXX: There are also Huang Chung's arrows.

CHAIRMAN MAO: It is nothing but the weapons of Kuan, Chang, Chao, Ma and Huang – they have no modern weapons. In the past, we didn't have any either. After the Nanchang Uprising, we lost two divisions; then Chu Te, Ch'en I, and Lin Piao led the remnant up the Chingkangshan. I didn't know how to fight myself. In 1918 I worked in the library of Peking University; I was paid eight dollars a month, and got along without worrying about clothing, food, or lodging. Chang Shih-chao didn't want to be an official for Yüan Shih-k'ai, so he let him be President of Peking University, he went to Peking University to run a journal. Old Huang, are you a constitutionalist?

HUANG YEN-P'EI: I am a revolutionary, not a constitutionalist, I participated in the T'ung Meng Hui.

CHANG SHIH-CHAO: He's a revolutionary.

CHAIRMAN MAO: Old Ch'en,[12] you belonged to the Research Clique; Chang Shih-chao participated in the Second Revolution, and in 1925 he was a minister.[13] Now all of you are marching together with us, participating in socialist construction in the new China. When I say we hope to do our work somewhat better this year, this is not merely the Central Committee's hope, it is also your hope. Hsü Te-heng, are you in charge of an industrial ministry?[14]

XXX: There is great hope for his ministry.

CHAIRMAN MAO: Old Huang, your family seems to include every possible party and faction – the Democratic League, the

Association for Promoting Democracy,[15] the Communist Youth League. The poem by your son Huang Wan-li, entitled 'Greetings to the Bridegroom', is very well written. I admire it. There is a member of the September Third Society who also writes good poems. I admire him too. You don't know your ten-odd children very well, you are like Kuo Tzu-i.[16]

All Ministries should learn from the Liberation Army, set up a political department, and strengthen their political work. They must encourage achievement, set up model workers for emulation, praise them extensively, and at the same time criticize mistakes. Praise should be the main thing, and criticism should be supplementary. Among those working for our cause, there are many good people and good things, there are many good models which we must praise.

Today I want to talk to you about the problem of education. Progress has been made in industry, and I think that there should be some changes in education too. The present state of affairs won't do. In my opinion the line and orientation [fang-chen] in education are correct, but the methods are wrong, and must be changed. Present here today are comrades from the Central Committee, comrades from within the Party, comrades from outside the Party, comrades from the Academy of Sciences. Comrade XXX[17] will now give a talk.

xxx: At present, an urgent problem in the domain of education is that of the educational system, i.e., the fact that the prescribed length of studies is excessive. At present, children begin school at the age of seven, and spend six years in primary school, six years in middle school, and in some cases six years at university, generally five, thus making in all seventeen or eighteen years. They graduate from university only at the age of twenty-four or twenty-five, and afterwards they engage in manual labour for a year, and then undergo a further period of one year's on-the-job training, so that they finally emerge [from the whole process] when they are already twenty-six or twenty-seven. This is two or three years longer than it takes in the Soviet Union. In the Soviet Union, primary and middle school last for ten years, and the university for four or five, so that at twenty-three or twenty-four they take up a post and begin work.

In the study of the humanities, there is no great problem about students growing too old. In the case of the natural sciences they manifestly [remain at their studies] too long. This is particularly the case with the science of atomic energy, with the most advanced sciences, the students are too old when they graduate. On the basis of the experience of all countries of the world, it is possible to make a contribution to the natural sciences by the time one reaches the age of twenty-four or twenty-five. For example, in the United States and in the Soviet Union, those who have some achievements to their credit in the natural sciences, in the field of atomic energy, are commonly all twenty-four or twenty-five. At that age, the brain functions most effectively, but at that age our students are still at university, and have not taken up a post and begun work. They start working only at twenty-six or twenty-seven; this is not advantageous to the development of the sciences. The prescribed course length is exceedingly great, we must give some thought to the system of education.

CHAIRMAN MAO: The period of schooling should be shortened somewhat.

XXX: Recently Comrade XX had an idea: there should be five years of primary school and four years of middle school, so that students would graduate from middle school at sixteen. If there were six years of primary school, they would graduate from middle school at seventeen. The problem is that the facilities for higher education are inadequate; each year, the universities take only 120,000 or 130,000 students, or 150,000 at the outside. The others could begin work at sixteen. They could receive two years of vocational training after graduating from middle school, and then at eighteen they could go to work in the factories or the villages; in this way, they would be more in touch [with reality]. Or they could attend two years of preparatory courses, thus establishing links with the university, and begin work at twenty-four or twenty-five. In a word, studies must be shortened somewhat. At present, the Central Committee has set up a small group [hsiao-tsu] under the leadership of Comrade XX, especially to study the question of the educational system.

If we adopt this suggestion for improving our national education, then students could graduate in general at fifteen or sixteen. There is, however, one problem – that of military service. They would be too young for this, but they could undergo preliminary training.

CHAIRMAN MAO: That's not important; those who are not old enough for military service can also experience military life. Not only male students, but also female students can undergo military service. We can form a red women's detachment. Girls of sixteen or seventeen can also experience six months to a year of military life, and at seventeen they can also serve as soldiers.

XXX: Thus, the problem of schools teaching literary subjects is not so great. The problems with faculties of science and engineering are somewhat greater. The universities have preparatory courses of one or two years; after graduating from middle school, students can either go on to the university preparatory courses, or enter a vocational school, and after two years' training they can go on to work in a factory or in the countryside at eighteen, thus they will be relatively in touch [with reality]. If they study engineering, they will also be relatively in touch, when they graduate at twenty-three or twenty-four they can take up a post and begin work.

CHAIRMAN MAO: At present, there is too much studying going on, and this is exceedingly harmful. There are too many subjects at present, and the burden is too heavy, it puts middle-school and university students in a constant state of tension. Cases of short sight are constantly multiplying among primary and middle-school students. This can't be allowed to go on unchanged.

XXX: The subjects covered by the syllabus are too many and too complicated. Many old teachers have remained at their posts. The students are not able to bear it; they are tense in the extreme, and they have no extra-curricular activities, and no time for extra-curricular reading.

CHAIRMAN MAO: The syllabus should be chopped in half. The students should have time for recreation, swimming, playing ball, and reading freely outside their course work. Confucius only professed the six arts – rites, music, archery, chariot-driving, poetry and history – but he produced four sages: Yen Hui, Tseng-tzu, Tzu Lu and Mencius. It won't do for students just to read books all day, and not to go in for cultural pursuits, physical education, and swimming, not to be able to run around, or to read things outside their courses, etc.

xxx: The students are extremely tense. When I'm at home the children say, what's the point in getting top marks in everything?

CHAIRMAN MAO: Throughout history, very few of those who came first in the imperial examination have achieved great fame. The celebrated T'ang dynasty poets Li Po and Tu Fu were neither *chin-shih* nor *han-lin*.[18] Han Yü and Liu Tsung-yüan[19] were only *chin-shih* of the second rank. Wang Shih-fu, Kuan Han-ch'ing,[20] Lo Kuan-chung,[21] P'u Sung-ling, Ts'ao Hsüeh-ch'in were none of them *chin-shih* or *han-lin*. P'u Sung-ling was a *hsiu-ts'ai* who had received promotion, he wanted to rise to the next higher rank, but he was not a *chü-jen*.[22] None of those who became *chin-shih* or *han-lin* were successful. Only two of the emperors of the Ming dynasty did well, T'ai-tsu and Ch'eng-tsu. One was illiterate, and the other only knew a few characters. Afterwards, in contrast, in the Chia-ch'ing reign, when the intellectuals had power, things were in a bad state, the country was in disorder.[23] Han Wu Ti and Li Hou-chu[24] were highly cultivated, and ruined the country. It is evident that to read too many books is harmful. Liu Hsiu[25] was an academician, whereas Liu Pang was a country bumpkin.

xxx: There is too much on the syllabus, and there are too many exercises to hand in, the students cannot reflect independently. The present method of examination –

CHAIRMAN MAO: Our present method of conducting examinations is a method for dealing with the enemy, not a method for dealing with the people. It is a method of surprise attack, asking oblique or strange questions. This is still the same method as the old eight-legged essay. I do not approve of this. It should be changed completely. I am in favour of publishing the questions in advance and letting the students study them and answer them with the aid of books. For instance, if one sets twenty questions on the *Dream of the Red Chamber*, and some students answer half of them and answer them well, and some of the answers are very good and contain creative ideas, then one can give them 100 per cent. If some other students answer all twenty questions and answer them correctly, but answer them simply by reciting from their textbooks and lectures, without any creative ideas, they should be given 50 or 60 per cent. At examinations whispering into each other's ears and taking other people's places ought to be allowed. If your answer is good and I copy it, then mine should be counted as good. Whispering in other people's ears and taking examinations in other people's names used to be done secretly. Let it now be done openly. If I can't do something and you write down the answer, which I then copy, this is all right. Let's give it a try. We must do things in a lively fashion, not in a lifeless fashion. There are teachers who ramble on and on when they lecture; they should let their students doze off. If your lecture is no good, why insist on others listening to you? Rather than keeping your eyes open and listening to boring lectures, it is better to get some refreshing sleep. You don't have to listen to nonsense, you can rest your brain instead.

xxx: If we shorten the period of schooling, there will be time for engaging in labour, or for military service. We can also consider having the outstanding students skip a grade, we don't have to keep them eternally in the same place. In the same grade as my child there is a classmate who was originally an outstanding student; afterwards, he skipped a grade, and he is still an outstanding student. Thus we see that it is possible to skip grades. Ask Comrade XX to organize a small group to conduct a thorough study of this problem of the school system.

CHAIRMAN MAO: Let both XX and XXX participate in this small group. At present we are doing things in too lifeless a manner. There is too much on the syllabus, and examinations are conducted in too rigid a manner. I cannot approve this. The present method of education ruins talent and ruins youth. I do not approve of reading so many books. The method of examination is a method for dealing with the enemy, it is most harmful, and should be stopped.

xxx: At present, the head of the Department of Education[26] has just called a meeting, at which two questions are being considered: one is that the students' burden is too heavy, and there is homework in every subject: the second is that there are three pedagogical systems, those of Confucius, the Soviets, and Dewey.

CHAIRMAN MAO: Confucius wasn't really like that. We have cast aside the mainstream of Confucianism. He had only the six subjects: rites, music, archery, chariot-driving, '*shu*', and mathematics. (*Chairman Mao asked XXX whether* 'shu' *meant calligraphy or history.*)[27]

xxx: It means calligraphy.

CHAIRMAN MAO: It means history. As in the *Shu Ching* or the *Han Shu*.[28]

xxx: At present, middle-school students take continuing their studies as their sole aim. After graduating, they are not willing to engage in labour; this is a very big question, and we must solve it. We must put into practice the union of education and productive labour; in addition, we must also walk on two legs.[29] Last year there was flooding in Hopei, and the Department of Education was under great strain. Many buildings collapsed, and they had to set up simple schools as best they could. As a result, the number of primary- and middle-school pupils actually increased.

CHAIRMAN MAO: The flood engulfed dogmatism. We must get rid of dogmas, both foreign and indigenous.

xxx: Other places have carried out a regularization, and introduced teaching all in one class, rather than separately according to subject. The number of students has declined, and the number of poor and lower-middle peasants has declined, very many poor and lower-middle peasants do not continue their schooling. In Hopei Province they have some good experience. In Hsin-hui *hsien* in Kwangtung Province, they have investigated ten-odd agricultural middle schools, and ordinary middle schools. In an ordinary middle school, the state spends 120 *yüan* per year on each student, whereas in an agricultural middle school they spend only 6·80 *yüan* a year on each student. There is no problem at all about the graduates of an agricultural middle school filling a job, whereas if a graduate of an ordinary middle school does not succeed in the university entrance examinations, there is a great deal of difficulty about placing him in employment. Thus, primary and middle schools should all walk on two legs. At the same time, we must pay attention to improving quality. Previously, everything was done according to Soviet methods, but in 1958 we struck a blow at this, and more provision was made for labour, but then study was neglected in turn, but now that things have been further altered it is all right. It is the same with literature and art, the level is relatively high now, but if there had not been 1958, we would not have attained our present level.[30]

CHAIRMAN MAO: We must drive actors, poets, dramatists and writers out of the cities, and pack them all off to the countryside. They should all periodically go down in batches to the villages and to the factories. We must not let writers stay in the government offices; they will never get anything written if they do not go down. Whoever does not go down will get no dinner; only when they go down will they be fed.

XXX: At present, there are a little over two per cent bad elements among the primary- and middle-school teachers, and there are also notoriously bad elements among the primary- and middle-school students.

CHAIRMAN MAO: That doesn't matter, they can change jobs.

XXX: At present, the worst students go to normal school; the good students go into engineering. Henceforth, we might think about not taking graduates of higher middle school directly into normal school or faculties of letters, but accepting only higher middle-school graduates who have engaged in labour for a year or two. The students of the natural sciences should also go down. They have some experience at the XX School in Harbin; they send the teachers down for a year or two. Those who were not so good originally are all pretty good when they come back from labour, they become part of the core.

CHAIRMAN MAO: They must go down. At present, there are some people who do not attach much importance to going to work in the countryside. In the Ming dynasty, Li Shih-chen[31] went hither and thither, and climbed the mountains to gather herbs. Tsu Ch'ung-chih[32] never went to middle school or university. Confucius was from a poor peasant family; he herded sheep, and never attended middle school or university either. He was a musician, he did all sorts of things. When someone had a death in the family, he would be invited to play at the funeral. He may also have been an accountant. He could play the *ch'in*[33] and drive a chariot, ride a horse and shoot with bow and arrow. '*Yü*' means to drive a chariot; it is like being the chauffeur of an automobile. He produced seventy-two sages, such as Yen Hui and Tseng-tzu, and he had 3,000 disciples. In his youth, he came from the masses, and understood something of the suffering of the masses. Later he became an official in the state of Lu, though not a terribly high official. The population of Lu was over a million, and for a long time people looked down on him. When he travelled around to different countries, people cursed him. This person liked to talk frankly, and said he had not experienced misery, and could not bear insults. Later, Tzu Lu acted as Confucius' bodyguard, and did not allow people to speak ill of Confucius, but would beat anyone who opened his mouth. From this time forward, no more unpleasant sounds entered his ears, and the masses did not dare approach him. We must not cast aside the tradition of Confucius. Our general policy is correct, but our methods are wrong. There are quite a few problems regarding the present school system, curriculum, methods of teaching, and examination methods, and all this must be changed. They are all exceedingly destructive of people.

xxx: We can get by with five years of primary school.

CHAIRMAN MAO: Primary-school teaching should not go on too long, either. Gorki had only two years of primary school; his learning was all self-taught. Franklin of America was originally a newspaper seller, yet he discovered electricity. Watt was a worker, yet he invented the steam-engine. Both in ancient and modern times, in China and abroad, many scientists trained themselves in the course of practice.

xx: When the school system has been reformed in the future, students will be able to take up a post when they reach the age of twenty-three or twenty-four. Seven is a rather late age for beginning school, we can bring it forward to six. There is a problem with buildings, but if primary school is changed to five years we can dispense with some. Then four years of middle school, and one or two years of a preparatory course at university. In view of the different nature of the various courses at university, we can diversify, and take in 140,000 or 150,000 students each year for a one or two-year preparatory course.

xxx: Before entering university, they can take off a period and go to work in a factory or in a village.

CHAIRMAN MAO: They can also go to the army for training.

xx: This is all right as regards literary subjects, but in physics there is the problem of the use of mathematics, and if they work for two years they might forget it.

xx: In the Soviet Union they work for two years after graduating from middle school, and then enter the faculties of physics and chemistry, they don't take them directly.

xx: Except for some special schools, the universities are divided into three course-lengths: six years, especially for medicine, five years for engineering, and four years for literary subjects. In most cases of university courses, four years is sufficient. In the future, the system should be diversified, there should be different course-lengths. In the cities, there should be two kinds of middle schools, one leading to university, and the other where students graduate in two years, after which they enter specialized training.

CHAIRMAN MAO: That's right, we must diversify.

xx: The main problem with the curriculum is a lack of centralization, and there are also those problems we studied in the past, many subjects are studied several times, every semester there are eight or nine subjects to study, there are many examinations, and this creates great tension.

CHAIRMAN MAO: Nowadays, first, there are too many classes; second, there are too many books. The pressure is too great. There are some subjects which it is not necessary to examine. For example, it is not necessary to examine the little logic and grammar which is learned in middle school. Real understanding must be acquired gradually through experience at work. It is enough to know what logic and grammar are.

xx: At present it's all cramming, mechanical memorizing and reciting.

xxx: There are two schools of thought nowadays. One school advocates teaching subjects thoroughly, while the other advocates teaching them in outline, teaching how to go about mastering subjects, though teaching somewhat less. At present many schools follow the first pattern, but isn't it true that this won't work. By advocating doing things in this way, they petrify thought.

CHAIRMAN MAO: This is scholasticism. The annotations to the Four Books and the Five Classics are exceedingly scholastic, and nowadays they have all become completely indigestible. Scholasticism must inevitably die out. For example, in the study of the classics very many commentaries were written, but now they have disappeared. I think that students trained by this method, no matter whether it be in China, in America or in the Soviet Union, will all disappear, will all move towards their opposites. The same applies to the Buddhist classics, of which there are so many. The version of the *Diamond Sutra* edited by Hsüan-tsang[34] of the T'ang dynasty was comparatively simplified, only a thousand-odd words, and it still exists. Another version, edited by Kumarajiva,[35] was too long, and has died out. Won't the Five Classics and the Thirteen Classics also come to the end of the road? They have been very copiously annotated, and as a result nobody reads them. In the fourteenth and fifteenth centuries they indulged in scholastic philosophy; only in the seventeenth, eighteenth and nineteenth centuries did [the world] enter the age of enlightenment and the Renaissance take place. We shouldn't read too many books. We should read Marxist books, but not too many of them either. It will be enough to read a dozen or so. If we read too many, we can move towards our opposites, become bookworms, dogmatists, revisionists. In the writings of Confucius, there is nothing about agriculture. Because of this, the limbs of his students were not accustomed to toil, and they could not distinguish between the five grains. We must do something about this.

xxx: There is another question, which is a political question, that of the students' nourishment, which must be improved. Each student eats food costing 12·5 *yüan* every month. We should spend another 40 million *yüan*.

CHAIRMAN MAO: It is all right to spend another 40 million *yüan*.

XXX: We should increase it by 2 to 4 *yüan*.[36]

CHAIRMAN MAO: If you read too many books, they petrify your mind in the end. Emperor Wu of the Liang dynasty did pretty well in his early years, but afterwards he read many books, and didn't make out so well any more. He died of hunger in T'ai Ch'eng.[37]

11 Talk on Questions of Philosophy
18 August 1964

It is only when there is class struggle that there can be philosophy. It is a waste of time to discuss epistemology apart from practice. The comrades who study philosophy should go down to the countryside. They should go down this winter or next spring to participate in the class struggle. Those whose health is not good should go too. Going down won't kill people. All they'll do is catch a cold, and if they just put on a few extra suits of clothes it'll be all right.

The way they go about it in the universities at present is no good, going from book to book, from concept to concept. How can philosophy come from books? The three basic constituents of Marxism are scientific socialism, philosophy, and political economy.[1] The foundation is social science, class struggle. There is a struggle between the proletariat and the bourgeoisie. Marx and the others saw this. Utopian socialists are always trying to persuade the bourgeoisie to be charitable. This won't work, it is necessary to rely on the class struggle of the proletariat. At that time, there had already been many strikes. The English parliamentary inquiry recognized that the twelve-hour day was less favourable than the eight-hour day to the interests of the capitalists.[2] It is only starting from this viewpoint that Marxism appeared. The foundation is class struggle. The study of philosophy can only come afterwards. Whose philosophy? Bourgeois philosophy, or proletarian philosophy? Proletarian philosophy is Marxist philosophy. There is also proletarian economics, which has transformed classical economics. Those who engage in philosophy believe that philosophy comes first.

The oppressors oppress the oppressed, while the oppressed need to fight back and seek a way out before they start looking for philosophy. It is only when people took this as their starting-point that there was Marxism–Leninism, and that they discovered philosophy. We have all been through this. Others wanted to kill me; Chiang Kai-shek wanted to kill me. Thus we came to engage in class struggle, to engage in philosophizing.

University students should start going down this winter – I am referring to the humanities. Students of natural science should not be moved now, though we can move them for a spell or two. All those studying the humanities – history, political economy, literature, law – must every one of them go. Professors, assistant professors, administrative workers, and students should all of them go down, for a limited period of five months. If they go to the countryside for five months, or to the factories for five months, they will acquire some perceptual knowledge. Horses, cows, sheep, chickens, dogs, pigs, rice, sorghum, beans, wheat, varieties of millet – they can have a look at all these things. If they go in the winter, they will not see the harvest, but at least they can still see the land and the people. To get some experience of class struggle – that's what I call a university. They argue about which university is better, Peking University or People's University.[3] For my part I am a graduate of the university of the greenwoods, I learned a bit there. In the past I studied Confucius, and spent six years on the Four Books and the Five Classics.[4] I learned to recite them from memory, but I did not understand them. At that time, I believed deeply in Confucius, and even wrote essays [expounding his ideas]. Later I went to a bourgeois school for seven years. Seven plus six makes thirteen years. I studied all the usual bourgeois stuff – natural science and social science. They also taught some pedagogy. This includes five years of normal school, two years of middle school, and also the time I spent in the library.[5] At that time I believed in Kant's dualism, especially in his idealism. Originally I was a feudalist and an advocate of bourgeois democracy. Society impelled me to participate in the revolution. I spent a few years as a primary-school teacher and principal of a four-year school. I also taught history and

Chinese language in a six-year school. I also taught for a short period in a middle school, but I did not understand a thing. When I joined the Communist Party I knew that we must make revolution, but against what? And how would we go about it? Of course we had to make revolution against imperialism and the old society. I did not quite understand what sort of a thing imperialism was, still less did I understand how we could make revolution against it. None of the stuff I had learned in thirteen years was any good for making revolution. I used only the instrument – language. Writing essays is an instrument. As for the content of my studies, I didn't use it at all. Confucius said: 'Benevolence is the characteristic element of humanity.' 'The benevolent man loves others.'[6] Whom did he love? All men? Nothing of the kind. Did he love the exploiters? It wasn't exactly that, either. He loved only a part of the exploiters. Otherwise, why wasn't Confucius able to be a high official? People didn't want him. He loved them, and wanted them to unite. But when it came to starving, and to [the precept] 'The superior man can endure poverty,' he almost lost his life, the people of K'uang wanted to kill him.[7] There were those who criticized him for not visiting Ch'in in his journey to the West. In reality, the poem 'In the Seventh Month the Fire Star Passes the Meridian' in the *Book of Odes* refers to events in Shensi. There is also 'The Yellow Bird', which talks about the affair in which three high officials of Duke Mu of Ch'in were killed and buried with him on his death.[8] Ssu-ma Ch'ien had a very high opinion of the *Book of Odes*. He said the 300 poems it contains were all written by sages and worthies of ancient times when they were aroused. A large part of the poems in the *Book of Odes* are in the manner of the various states, they are the folk songs of the common people, the sages and worthies are none other than the common people. 'Written when they were aroused' means that when a man's heart was filled with anger, he wrote a poem!

> You sow not nor reap;
> How do you get the paddy for your three hundred round binns?
> You do not follow the chase;
> How do we see the quails hanging in your courtyards?

O that superior man!
He would not eat the bread of idleness![9]

The expression 'to neglect the duties of an office while taking the pay' comes from here. This is a poem which accuses heaven and opposes the rulers. Confucius, too, was rather democratic, he included [in the *Book of Odes*] poems about the love between man and woman. In his commentaries, Chu Hsi characterized them as poems about clandestine love affairs.[10] In reality, some of them are and some of them aren't; the latter borrow the imagery of man and woman to write about the relations between prince and subject. In Shu [present-day Szechwan] at the time of the Five Dynasties and Ten Countries, there was a poem entitled 'The Wife of Ch'in Laments the Winter', by Wei Chuang.[11] He wrote it in his youth, and it is about his longing for his prince.

To return to this matter of going down, people should go beginning this winter and spring, in groups and in rotation, to participate in the class struggle. Only in this way can they learn something, learn about revolution. You intellectuals sit every day in your government offices, eating well, dressing well, and not even doing any walking. That's why you fall ill. Clothing, food, housing and exercise are the four great factors causing disease. If, from enjoying good living conditions, you change to somewhat worse conditions, if you go down to participate in the class struggle, if you go into the midst of the 'four clean-ups' and the 'five antis',[12] and undergo a spell of toughening, then you intellectuals will have a new look about you.

If you don't engage in class struggle, then what is this philosophy you're engaged in?

Why not go down and try it? If your illness gets too severe you should come back – you have to draw the line at dying. When you are so ill that you are on the verge of dying, then you should come back. As soon as you go down, you will have some spirit. (*K'ang Sheng interjects: 'The research institutes in the Departments of Philosophy and Social Science of the Academy of Science should all go down too. At present, they are on the verge of turning into institutes for the study of antiquities, of turning into a fairyland nourishing itself by inhaling offerings of incense. None of the people in the Institute of Philosophy read the* Kuang-ming jih-pao.') I read only the *Kuang-ming jih-pao* and the *Wen-hui pao*,[13] I don't read *People's Daily*, because the *People's Daily* doesn't publish theoretical articles; after we adopt a resolution, then they publish it. The *Liberation Army Daily* is lively, it's readable. (*Comrade K'ang Sheng: 'The Institute of Literature pays no attention to Chou Ku-ch'eng,*[14] *and the Economics Institute pays no attention to Sun Yeh-fang*[15] *and to his going in for Libermanism, going in for capitalism.'*)

Let them go in for capitalism. Society is very complex. If one only goes in for socialism and not for capitalism, isn't that too simple? Wouldn't we then lack the unity of opposites, and be merely one-sided? Let them do it. Let them attack us madly, demonstrate in the streets, take up arms to rebel – I approve all of these things. Society is very complex, there is not a single commune, a single *hsien*, a single department of the Central Committee, in which one cannot divide into two. Just look, hasn't the Department of Rural Work been disbanded?[16] It devoted itself exclusively to accounting on the basis of the individual household, and to propagating the 'four great freedoms' – freedom to lend money, to engage in commerce, to hire labour, and to buy and sell land. In the past, they put out a proclamation [to this effect]. Teng Tzu-hui had a dispute with me. At a meeting of the Central Committee, he put forward the idea of implementing the four great freedoms.[17]

To consolidate New Democracy, and to go on consolidating it for ever, is to engage in capitalism. New Democracy is a bourgeois-democratic revolution under the leadership of the proletariat. It touches only the landlords and the comprador bourgeoisie, it does not touch the national bourgeoisie at all. To divide up the land and give it to the peasants is to transform the property of the feudal landlords into the individual property of the peasants, and this still remains within the limits of the bourgeois revolution. To divide up the land is nothing remarkable – MacArthur did it in Japan. Napoleon divided up the land too. Land reform cannot abolish capitalism, nor can it lead to socialism.

In our state at present approximately one third of the power is in the hands of the enemy or of the enemy's sympathizers. We have been going for fifteen years and we now control two thirds of the realm. At present, you can buy a [Party] branch secretary for a few packs of cigarettes, not to mention marrying a daughter to him. There are some localities where land reform was carried out peacefully, and the land reform teams were very weak; now you can see that there are a lot of problems there.

I have received the materials on philosophy.* I have had a look at the outline,† I have not been able to read the rest. I have also looked at the materials on analysis and synthesis.

It is a good thing to collect materials like this on the law of the unity of opposites, what the bourgeoisie says about it, what Marx, Engels, Lenin and Stalin say about it, what the revisionists say about it. As for the bourgeoisie, Yang Hsien-chen talks about it, and Hegel of old talked about it. Such people existed in the olden days. Now they are even worse. There were also Bogdanov and Lunacharsky, who used to talk about deism. I have read Bogdanov's economics.[19] Lenin read it, and it seems he approved of the part on primitive accumulation. (*K'ang Sheng: 'Bogdanov's economic doctrines were perhaps somewhat more enlightened than those of modern revisionism. Kautsky's economic doctrines were somewhat more enlightened than those of Khrushchev, and Yugoslavia is also somewhat more enlightened than the Soviet Union. After all, Djilas said a few good things about Stalin, he said that on Chinese problems Stalin made a self-criticism.'*)

Stalin felt that he had made mistakes in dealing with Chinese problems, and they were no small mistakes. We are a great country of several hundred millions, and he opposed our revolution, and our seizure of power. We prepared for many years in order to seize power in the whole country, the whole of the Anti-Japanese War constituted a preparation. This is quite clear

*This refers to the materials on the problem of contradictions – note by stenographer.

† This refers to the outline of an article criticizing 'two combine into one'[18] – note by stenographer.

if you look at the documents of the Central Committee for that period, including *On New Democracy*. That is to say that you cannot set up a bourgeois dictatorship, you can only establish New Democracy under the leadership of the proletariat, you can only set up a people's democratic dictatorship led by the proletariat. In our country, for eighty years, all the democratic revolutions led by the bourgeoisie failed. The democratic revolution led by us will certainly be victorious. There is only this way out, there is no other way out. This is the first step. The second step will be to build socialism. Thus, *On New Democracy* was a complete programme. It discussed politics, economics, and culture as well; it failed to discuss only military affairs. (*K'ang Sheng*: 'On New Democracy *is of great significance for the world communist movement. I asked Spanish comrades, and they said the problem for them was to establish bourgeois democracy, not to establish New Democracy. In their country, they did not concern themselves with the three points: army, countryside, political power. They wholly subordinated themselves to the exigencies of Soviet foreign policy, and achieved nothing at all.*') These are the policies of Ch'en Tu-hsiu! (*Comrade K'ang Sheng*: 'They say the Communist Party organized an army, and then turned it over to others.*') This is useless.

(*Comrade K'ang Sheng*: 'They also did not want political power, nor did they mobilize the peasantry. At that time, the Soviet Union said to them that if they imposed proletarian leadership, England and France might oppose it, and this would not be in the interests of the Soviet Union.*')

How about Cuba? In Cuba they concerned themselves precisely to set up political power and an army, and also mobilized the peasants, as [we did] in the past; therefore they succeeded.

(*Comrade K'ang Sheng*: 'Also, when they [the Spanish] fought, they waged regular war, in the manner of the bourgeoisie, they defended Madrid to the last.[20] In all things, they subordinated themselves to Soviet foreign policy.*')

Even before the dissolution of the Third International, we did not obey the orders of the Third International. At the Tsunyi Conference we didn't obey, and afterwards, for a period

of ten years, including the Rectification Campaign and down to
the Seventh Congress, when we finally adopted a resolution
('Resolution on Certain Questions in the History of our
Party'),[21] and corrected [the errors of] 'leftism', we didn't
obey them at all. Those dogmatists utterly failed to study
China's peculiarities; ten-odd years after they had betaken
themselves to the countryside, they utterly failed to study the
land, property, and class relationships in the countryside. You
can't understand the countryside just by going there, you must
study the relations between all the classes and strata in the
countryside. I devoted more than ten years to these problems
before I finally clarified them for myself. You must make contact with all kinds of people, in tea houses and gambling dens,
and investigate them. In 1925 I was active at the Peasant Movement Training Institute,[22] and carried out rural surveys. In my
native village, I sought out poor peasants to investigate them.
Their life was pitiable, they had nothing to eat. There was one
peasant whom I sought out to play dominoes (the kind with
heaven, earth, man, harmony, Mei Ch'ien, Ch'ang Sang, and the
bench), afterwards inviting him to have a meal. Before, after,
and during the meal, I talked to him, and came to understand
why the class struggle in the countryside was so acute. The
reasons he was willing to talk to me were: first, that I looked on
him as a human being; second, that I invited him to have a
meal; and third, that he could make a bit of money. I kept
losing; I lost one or two silver dollars, and as a result he was
very well satisfied. There is a friend who still came to see me
twice, after Liberation. Once, in those days, he was really in a
bad way, and he came looking for me to borrow a dollar. I gave
him three, as non-refundable assistance. In those days, such non-
refundable assistance was hard to come by. My father took the
view that if a man did not look after himself, heaven and earth
would punish him. My mother opposed him. When my father
died, very few people followed the funeral procession. When
my mother died, a great many followed the procession. One
time the Ko Lao Hui robbed our family. I said they were right
to do so, for people had nothing. Even my mother could not
accept this at all.[23]

Once there broke out in Changsha rice riots in which the provincial governor was beaten up. There were some hawkers from Hsiang Hsiang who had sold their broad beans and were straggling back home. I stopped them and asked them about the situation. The Red and Green Gangs in the countryside also held meetings, and ate up big families. This was reported in the Shanghai newspapers, and the troubles were only stamped out when troops were sent from Changsha. They did not maintain good discipline, they took the rice of the middle peasants, and so isolated themselves. One of their leaders fled hither and thither, finally taking refuge in the mountains, but he was caught there and executed. Afterwards, the village gentry held a meeting, and killed a few more poor peasants.[24] At that time, there was as yet no Communist Party; these were spontaneous class struggles.

Society pushed us on to the political stage. Who ever thought of indulging in Marxism previously? I hadn't even heard of it. What I had heard of, and also read of, was Confucius, Napoleon, Washington, Peter the Great, the Meiji Restoration, the three distinguished Italian [patriots] – in other words, all those [heroes] of capitalism. I had also read a biography of Franklin. He came from a poor family; afterwards, he became a writer, and also conducted experiments on electricity. (*Ch'en Po-ta: 'Franklin was the first to put forward the proposition that man is a tool-making animal.'*)

He talked about man being a tool-making animal. Formerly, they used to say that man was a thinking animal, 'the organ of the heart can think'[25]; they said that man was the soul of all creation. Who called a meeting and elected him [to that position]? He conferred this dignity on himself. This proposition existed in the feudal era. Afterwards, Marx put forward the view that man is a tool-maker, and that man is a social animal. In reality it is only after undergoing a million years [of evolution] that man developed a large brain and a pair of hands. In the future, animals will continue to develop. I don't believe that men alone are capable of having two hands. Can't horses, cows, sheep evolve? Can only monkeys evolve? And can it be, moreover, that of all the monkeys only one species can evolve, and all the others are incapable of evolving? In a million years, ten million years, will horses, cows and sheep still be the same as those today? I think they will continue to change. Horses, cows, sheep, and insects will all change. Animals have evolved from plants, they have evolved from seaweed. Chang T'ai-yen knew all this. In the book in which he argued about revolution with K'ang Yu-wei, he expounded these principles.[26] The earth was originally dead, there were no plants, no water, no air. Only after I don't know how many tens of millions of years was water formed; hydrogen and oxygen aren't just transformed immediately in any old way into water. Water has its history too. Earlier still, even hydrogen and oxygen did not exist. Only after hydrogen and oxygen were produced was there the possibility that these two elements could combine to give water.

We must study the history of the natural sciences, it won't do to neglect this subject. We must read a few books. There is a great difference between reading because of the necessities of our present struggles, and reading aimlessly. Fu Ying[27] says that hydrogen and oxygen form water only after coming together hundreds and thousands of times; it is not at all a simple case of two combining into one. He was right about this, too; I want to look him up and have a talk. (*Speaking to Lu P'ing:*[28]) You people should not oppose absolutely everything by Fu Ying.

Hitherto, analysis and synthesis have not been clearly defined. Analysis is clearer, but there hasn't been much said about synthesis. I had a talk with Ai Ssu-ch'i.[29] He said that nowadays they only talk about conceptual synthesis and analysis, and do not talk about objective practical synthesis and analysis. How do we analyse and synthesize the Communist Party and the Kuomintang, the proletariat and the bourgeoisie, the landlords and the peasants, the Chinese and the imperialists? How do we do this, for example, in the case of the Communist Party and the Kuomintang? The analysis is simply a question of how strong we are, how much territory we have, how many members we have, how many troops, how many bases such as Yenan, what are our weaknesses? We do not hold any big cities, our army numbers only 1,200,000, we have no foreign aid, whereas the Kuomintang has a great amount of foreign aid. If you compare Yenan to Shanghai, Yenan has a population of only 7,000; adding to this the persons from the [Party and government] organs and from the troops [stationed in Yenan], the total comes to 20,000. There is only handicrafts and agriculture. How can this be compared with a big city? Our strong points are that we have the support of the people whereas the Kuomintang is divorced from the people. You have more territory, more troops, and more arms, but your soldiers have been obtained by impressment, and there is opposition between officers and soldiers. Naturally there is also a fairly large portion of their armies which has considerable fighting capacity, it is not at all the case that they will all just collapse at one blow. Their weak point lies here, the key is their divorce from the people. We unite with the popular masses; they are divorced from the popular masses.

They say in their propaganda that the Communist Party establishes community of property and community of wives, and they propagate these ideas right down to the primary schools. They composed a song: 'When Chu Te and Mao Tse-tung appear, killing and burning and doing all kinds of things, what will you do?' They taught the primary-school pupils to sing it, and as soon as they had sung it, the pupils went and asked their fathers and mothers, brothers and sisters, thus producing the opposite effect of propaganda for us. There was a little child who heard [the song] and asked his daddy. His daddy replied: 'You mustn't ask; after you have grown up, you will see for yourself and then you'll understand.' He was a middle-of-the-roader. Then the child also asked his uncle. The uncle scolded him, and replied: 'What is this about killing and burning? If you ask me again, I'll beat you!' Formerly, his uncle was a member of the Communist Youth League. All the newspapers and radio stations attacked us. There were a lot of newspapers, several dozen in each city, every faction ran one, and all of them without exception were anti-communist. Did the common people all listen to them? Nothing of the kind! We have some experience of Chinese affairs, China is a 'sparrow'.[30] In foreign countries, too, it's nothing else but the rich and the poor, counter-

revolution and revolution, Marxism–Leninism and revisionism.
You mustn't believe at all that everybody will take in anti-
communist propaganda, and join in opposing communism.
Didn't we read newspapers at the time? Yet we were not
influenced by them.

I have read the *Dream of the Red Chamber* five times, and
have not been influenced by it. I read it as history. First I read it
as a story, and then as history. When people read the *Dream of
the Red Chamber*, they don't read the fourth chapter carefully,
but in fact this chapter contains the gist of the book. There is
also Leng Tzu-hsing who describes the Jung-kuo mansion,
and composes songs and notes. The fourth chapter, 'The Bottle-
Gourd Monk decides the affair of the bottle gourd', talks about
the 'Talisman for Officials', it introduces the four big families:

> Shout hip hurrah
> For the Nanking Chia!
> They weigh their gold out
> By the jar.
> The Ah-pang Palace
> Scrapes the sky,
> But it could not house
> The Nanking Shih.
> The King of the Ocean
> Goes along,
> When he's short of gold beds,
> To the Nanking Wang.
> The Nanking Hsüeh
> So rich are they,
> To count their money
> Would take all day . . .[31]

The *Dream of the Red Chamber* describes each of the four
big families. It concerns a fierce class struggle, involving the
fate of many dozens of people, though only twenty or thirty of
these people are in the ruling class. (It has been calculated that
there are thirty-three [in this category].) The others are all
slaves, over three hundred of them, such as Yüeh Yang, Ssu-
ch'i, Second Sister Yu, Third Sister Yu, etc. In studying history,
unless you take a class-struggle view as the starting-point, you

will get confused. Things can only be analysed clearly by the use of class analysis. More than 200 years have elapsed since the *Dream of the Red Chamber* was written, and research on the book has not clarified the issues, even down to the present day; from this we can see the difficulty of the problem. There are Yü P'ing-po and Wang K'un-lun, who are both of them specialists.[32] Ho Ch'i-fang[33] also wrote a preface. A fellow called Wu Shih-ch'ang[34] has also appeared on the scene. All this refers to recent research on the *Dream of the Red Chamber,* I won't even enumerate the older studies. Ts'ai Yüan-p'ei's view of the *Dream of the Red Chamber* was incorrect; Hu Shih's was somewhat more correct.[35]

What is synthesis? You have all witnessed how the two opposites, the Kuomintang and the Communist Party, were synthesized on the mainland. The synthesis took place like this: their armies came, and we devoured them, we ate them bite by bite. It was not a case of two combining into one as expounded by Yang Hsien-chen, it was not the synthesis of two peacefully coexisting opposites. They didn't want to coexist peacefully, they wanted to devour you. Otherwise, why would they have attacked Yenan? Their army penetrated everywhere in North Shensi, except in three *hsien* on the three borders. You have your freedom, and we have our freedom. There are 250,000 of you, and 25,000 of us.[36] A few brigades, something over 20,000 men. Having analysed, how do we synthesize? If you want to go somewhere, you go right ahead; we still swallow your army mouthful by mouthful. If we could fight victoriously, we fought; if we could not win, we retreated. From March 1947 to March 1948, one whole army [of the enemy] disappeared into the landscape, for we annihilated several tens of thousands of their troops. When we surrounded I-ch'uan, and Liu K'an came to relieve the city, the commander-in-chief Liu K'an was killed, two of his three divisional commanders were killed and the other taken prisoner, and the whole army ceased to exist. This was synthesis. All of their guns and artillery were synthesized over to our side, and the soldiers were synthesized too. Those who wanted to stay with us could stay, and to those who didn't want to stay we gave money for their travelling expenses. After we had annihilated Liu K'an, the brigade stationed in I-ch'uan surrendered without fighting. In the three great campaigns – Liao–Shen, Huai–Hai, and Peking–Tientsin – what was our method of synthesis? Fu Tso-i was synthesized over to our side, with his army of 400,000 men, without fighting, and they handed over all their rifles.[37] One thing eating another, big fish eating little fish, this is synthesis. It has never been put like this in books. I have never put it this way in my books either. For his part, Yang Hsien-chen believes that two combine into one, and that synthesis is the indissoluble tie between two opposites. What indissoluble ties are there in this world? Things may be tied, but in the end they must be severed. There is nothing which cannot be severed. In the twenty-odd years of our struggle, many of us have also been devoured by the enemy. When the 300,000-strong Red Army reached the Shen–Kan–Ning area, there were only 25,000 left. Of the others, some had been devoured, some scattered, some killed or wounded.

We must take life as our starting-point in discussing the unity of opposites. (*Comrade K'ang Sheng: 'It won't do merely to talk about concepts.'*)

While analysis is going on, there is also synthesis, and while synthesis is going on, there is also analysis.

When people eat animals and plants, they also begin with analysis. Why don't we eat sand? When there's sand in rice, it's not good to eat. Why don't we eat grass, as do horses, cows and sheep, but only things like cabbage? We must analyse everything. Shen Nung tasted the hundred herbs,[38] and originated their use for medicine. After many tens of thousands of years, analysis finally revealed clearly what could be eaten, and what could not. Grasshoppers, snakes, and turtles can be eaten. Crabs, dogs, and aquatic creatures can be eaten. There are some foreigners who don't eat them. In North Shensi they don't eat aquatic creatures, they don't eat fish. They don't eat cat there either. One year there was a big flood of the Yellow River, which cast up on shore several tens of thousands of pounds of fish, and they used it all for fertilizer.

I am a native philosopher, you are foreign philosophers.

(Comrade K'ang Sheng: 'Could the Chairman say something about the problem of the three categories?')

Engels talked about the three categories, but as for me I don't believe in two of those categories. (The unity of opposites is the most basic law, the transformation of quality and quantity into one another is the unity of the opposites quality and quantity, and the negation of the negation does not exist at all.) The juxtaposition, on the same level, of the transformation of quality and quantity into one another, the negation of the negation, and the law of the unity of opposites is 'triplism', not monism. The most basic thing is the unity of opposites. The transformation of quality and quantity into one another is the unity of the opposites quality and quantity. There is no such thing as the negation of the negation. Affirmation, negation, affirmation, negation . . . in the development of things, every link in the chain of events is both affirmation and negation. Slave-holding society negated primitive society, but with reference to feudal society it constituted, in turn, the affirmation. Feudal society constituted the negation in relation to slave-holding society but it was in turn the affirmation with reference to capitalist society. Capitalist society was the negation in relation to feudal society, but it is, in turn, the affirmation in relation to socialist society.

What is the method of synthesis? Is it possible that primitive society can exist side-by-side with slave-holding society? They do exist side-by-side, but this is only a small part of the whole. The overall picture is that primitive society is going to be eliminated. The development of society, moreover, takes place by stages; primitive society, too, is divided into a great many stages. At that time, there was not yet the practice of burying women with their dead husbands, but they were obliged to subject themselves to men. First men were subject to women, and then things moved towards their opposite, and women were subject to men. This stage in history has not yet been clarified, although it has been going on for a million years and more. Class society has not yet lasted 5,000 years, Cultures such as that of Lung Shan and Yang Shao[39] at the end of the primitive era had coloured pottery. In a word, one devours another, one overthrows another, one class is eliminated, another class rises, one society is eliminated, another society rises. Naturally, in the process of development, everything is not all that pure. When it gets to feudal society, there still remains something of the slave-holding system, though the greater part of the social edifice is characterized by the feudal system. There are still some serfs, and also some bond-workers, such as handicraftsmen. Capitalist society isn't all that pure either, and even in more advanced capitalist societies there is also a backward part. For example, there was the slave system in the Southern United States. Lincoln abolished the slave system, but there are still black slaves today, their struggle is very fierce. More than 20 million people are participating in it, and that's quite a few.

One thing destroys another, things emerge, develop, and are destroyed, everywhere is like this. If things are not destroyed by others, then they destroy themselves. Why should people die? Does the aristocracy die too? This is a natural law. Forests live longer than human beings, yet even they last only a few thousand years. If there were no such thing as death, that would be unbearable. If we could still see Confucius alive today, the earth wouldn't be able to hold so many people. I approve of Chuang-tzu's approach.[40] When his wife died, he banged on a basin and sang. When people die there should be parties to celebrate the victory of dialectics, to celebrate the destruction of the old. Socialism, too, will be eliminated, it wouldn't do if it were not eliminated, for then there would be no communism. Communism will last for thousands and thousands of years. I don't believe that there will be no qualitative changes under communism, that it will not be divided into stages by qualitative changes! I don't believe it! Quantity changes into quality, and quality changes into quantity. I don't believe that it can remain qualitatively exactly the same, unchanging for millions of years! This is unthinkable in the light of dialectics. Then there is the principle, 'From each according to his ability, to each according to his needs'. Do you believe they can carry on for a million years with the same economics? Have you thought about it? If that were so, we wouldn't need economists, or in any case we could get along with just one textbook, and dialectics would be dead.

The life of dialectics is the continuous movement toward opposites. Mankind will also finally meet its doom. When the theologians talk about doomsday, they are pessimistic and terrify people. We say the end of mankind is something which will produce something more advanced than mankind. Mankind is still in its infancy. Engels spoke of moving from the realm of necessity to the realm of freedom, and said that freedom is the understanding of necessity. This sentence is not complete, it only says one half and leaves the rest unsaid. Does merely understanding it make you free? Freedom is the understanding of necessity *and* the transformation of necessity – one has some work to do too. If you merely eat without having any work to do, if you merely understand, is that sufficient? When you discover a law, you must be able to apply it, you must create the world anew, you must break the ground and edify buildings, you must dig mines, industrialize. In the future there will be more people, and there won't be enough grain, so men will have to get food from minerals. Thus it is that only by transformation can freedom be obtained. Will it be possible in the future to be all that free? Lenin said that in the future, aeroplanes would be as numerous in the skies as flies, rushing hither and thither. Everywhere they will collide, and what will we do about it? How will we manoeuvre them? And if we do, will things be all that free? In Peking at present there are 10,000 buses; in Tokyo there are 100,000 [vehicles] (or is it 800,000?), so there are more automobile accidents. We have fewer cars, and we also educate the drivers and the people, so there are few accidents. What will they do in Peking 10,000 years hence? Will there still be 10,000 buses? They may invent something new, so that they can dispense with these means of transport, so that men can fly, using some simple mechanical device, and fly right to any place, and land wherever they like. It won't do just to understand necessity, we must also transform things.

I don't believe that communism will not be divided into stages, and that there will be no qualitative changes. Lenin said that all things can be divided. He gave the atom as an example, and said that not only can the atom be divided, but the electron, too, can be divided. Formerly, however, it was held that it could not be divided; the branch of science devoted to splitting the atomic nucleus is still very young, only twenty or thirty years old. In recent decades, the scientists have resolved the atomic nucleus into its constituents, such as protons, anti-protons, neutrons, anti-neutrons, mesons and anti-mesons. These are the heavy ones; there are also the light ones. For the most part, these discoveries only got under way during and after the Second World War. As for the fact that one could separate the electrons from the atomic nucleus, that was discovered some time ago. An electric wire makes use of dissociated electrons from the outside of copper or aluminium. In the 300 *li* of the earth's atmosphere, it has also been discovered that there are layers of dissociated electrons. There, too, the electrons and the atomic nucleus are separated. As yet, the electron has not been split, but some day they will certainly be able to split it. Chuang-tzu said, 'A length of one foot, which is divided in half each day, will never be reduced to zero.' (*Chuang-tzu*, Chapter [33 G] 'On the various schools', quoting Kung-sun Lung.) This is the truth. If you don't believe it, just consider. If it could be reduced to zero, then there would be no such thing as science. The myriad things develop continuously and limitlessly, and they are infinite. Time and space are infinite. As regards space, looking at it both macroscopically and microscopically, it is infinite, it can be divided endlessly. So even after a million years scientists will still have work to do. I very much appreciate the article on basic particles in the *Bulletin of Natural Science* by Sakata.[41] I have never seen this kind of article before. This is dialectical materialism. He quotes Lenin.

The weakness of philosophy is that it hasn't produced practical philosophy, but only bookish philosophy.

We should always be bringing forward new things. Otherwise what are we here for? What do we want descendants for? New things are to be found in reality, we must grasp reality. In the last analysis, is Jen Chi-yü[42] Marxist or not? I greatly appreciate those articles of his on Buddhism. There is some research [behind them], he is a student of T'ang Yung-t'ung. [43] He discusses only the Buddhism of the T'ang dynasty, and does not touch directly on the Buddhism of later times. Sung and Ming metaphysics developed from the Ch'an School of the T'ang dynasty, and it was a movement from subjective idealism to objective idealism.[44] There is both Buddhism and Taoism, and it is wrong not to distinguish between them. How can it be proper not to pay attention to them? Han Yü didn't talk sense. His slogan was, 'Learn from their ideas, but not from their mode of expression.' His ideas were entirely copied from others, he changed the form, the mode of composition of the essays. He didn't talk sense, and the little bit he did talk was basically taken from the ancients. There is a little something new in writings like the *Discourse on Teachers*. Liu Tzu-hou was different, he knew the ins and outs of Buddhist and Taoist materialism.[45] And yet, his *Heaven Answers* is too short, just that little bit. His *Heaven Answers* is a product of Ch'ü Yüan's *Heaven Asks*.[46] For several thousand years, only this one man has written a piece such as *Heaven Answers*. What are *Heaven Asks* and *Heaven Answers* all about? If there are no annotations, to explain it clearly, you can't understand it if you read it, you'll only get the general idea. *Heaven Asks* is really fantastic, thousands of years ago it raised all kinds of questions, relating to the universe, to nature, and to history.

(*Regarding the discussion on the problem of two combining into one:*) Let *Hung Ch'i* reprint a few good items, and write a report.

12 China's Great Leap Forward[1]
December 1964

We cannot follow the old paths of technical development of every other country in the world, and crawl step by step behind the others. We must smash conventions, do our utmost to adopt advanced techniques, and within not too long a period of history, build our country up into a powerful modern socialist state. When we talk of a Great Leap Forward we mean just this. Is this really impossible? Are we boasting or shooting off our mouths? Certainly not. It can be done. We need only take a look at our history to realize this. Haven't we basically overthrown seemingly powerful imperialism, feudalism and capitalism within our own country? From a poor and blank start haven't we through fifteen years of endeavour reached an appreciable level of development in all aspects of socialist revolution and socialist construction? Haven't we also exploded an atomic bomb? Haven't we flung off the title of 'sick man of East Asia' applied to us in the past by the Westerners? Why is it that what the Western bourgeoisie could achieve, the Eastern proletariat cannot achieve also? The great Chinese revolutionary, our precursor Mr Sun Yat-sen, said at the beginning of the century that in China there would come a Great Leap Forward. This prediction of his will certainly be realized within a few decades. This is an inevitable trend which cannot be stopped by any reactionary force.

13 Directive on Public Health
26 June 1965

Tell the Ministry of Public Health that it only works for fifteen per cent of the total population of the country and that this fifteen per cent is mainly composed of gentlemen,[1] while the broad masses of the peasants do not get any medical treatment. First they don't have any doctors; second they don't have any medicine. The Ministry of Public Health is not a Ministry of Public Health for the people, so why not change its name to the Ministry of Urban Health, the Ministry of Gentlemen's Health, or even to Ministry of Urban Gentlemen's Health?

Medical education should be reformed. There's no need to read so many books. How many years did Hua T'o[2] spend at college? How many years' education did Li Shih-chen of the Ming dynasty receive? In medical education there is no need to accept only higher middle school graduates or lower middle school graduates. It will be enough to give three years to graduates from higher primary schools. They would then study and raise their standards mainly through practice. If this kind of doctor is sent down to the countryside, even if they haven't much talent, they would be better than quacks and witch doctors and the villages would be better able to afford to keep them. The more books one reads the more stupid one gets. The methods of medical examination and treatment used by hospitals nowadays are not at all appropriate for the countryside, and the way doctors are trained is only for the benefit of the cities. And yet in China over 500 million of our population are peasants.

They work divorced from the masses, using a great deal of manpower and materials in the study of rare, profound and difficult diseases at the so-called pinnacle of science, yet they either ignore or make little effort to study how to prevent and improve the treatment of commonly seen, frequently occurring and widespread diseases. I am not saying that we should ignore the advanced problems, but only a small quantity of manpower and material should be expended on them, while a great deal of manpower and material should be spent on the problems to which the masses most need solutions.

There is another peculiar thing. Whenever a doctor makes an examination, he always has to wear a mask no matter what the illness is. Is this because they are afraid they might catch a disease and thus transmit it to others? I am afraid that it is primarily because they are afraid of catching an illness themselves. Different diseases should be dealt with separately. If they wear masks no matter what the illness, this creates a distance between doctor and patient from the start.

We should leave behind in the city a few of the less able doctors who graduated one or two years ago, and the others should all go into the countryside. The 'four clean-ups' movement was wound up in the year xx and has been basically completed[3] but even though the 'four clean-ups' has been completed, medical and health work in the villages has not yet been completed!

In medical and health work put the emphasis on the countryside!

14 Speech at Hangchow
21 December 1965

I have read three articles in this issue of *Che-hsüeh yen-chiu** [*Philosophical Research*]. Those of you who are engaged in philosophy should go in for practical philosophy, otherwise nobody will read it. Bookish philosophy is very difficult to understand. For whom is it written? Some intellectuals like Wu Han[1] and Chien Po-tsan[2] are going from bad to worse. Someone called Sun Ta-jen[3] has written an article refuting Chien Po-tsan's idea of the feudal landlord class adopting a policy of concessions towards the peasants. After peasant wars the landlord class would only counter-attack and seek revenge; there was never any question of concessions. The landlord class made no concessions to the Taiping Heavenly Kingdom. The Boxers first said: 'Oppose the Ch'ing and eliminate the foreigners,' and later, 'Support the Ch'ing and eliminate the foreigners,' thus gaining the support of the Empress Dowager Tz'u-hsi. After the Ch'ing dynasty had suffered defeat at the hands of imperialism the Dowager Empress and the Emperor ran away, and Tz'u-hsi started to 'support the foreigners and eliminate the Boxers'. Some people say that the *Inside Story of the Ching Court* is patriotic, but I think it is treasonable – out-and-out treason.[4] Why is it that some say it is patriotic? Merely because they think that the Kuang Hsü emperor was a pitable man who, together with K'ang Yu-wei, opened schools, formed the New Armies and put into effect a few enlightened measures.

At the end of the Ch'ing dynasty some people advocated

* i.e., the special issue of philosophical articles written by workers, peasants and soldiers, 1965, No. 6.

'Chinese learning for the substance, Western learning for practical application'. The substance was like our General Line, which cannot be changed. We cannot adopt Western learning as the substance, nor can we use the substance of the democratic republic. We cannot use 'the natural rights of man' nor the 'theory of evolution'. We can only use Western technology. 'The natural rights of man' represents, of course, an erroneous line of thought. Is there such a thing as rights bestowed by nature? Isn't it man who bestows rights on man? Were the rights we enjoy bestowed by nature? Our rights were bestowed by the common people, and primarily by the working class and the poor and lower-middle peasants.

If you study a little modern history you will see that there was no such thing as a 'policy of concession'. The only concessions were made by the revolutionary forces to the reactionaries. The reactionaries always counter-attacked and sought revenge. Whenever a new dynasty emerged in history they adopted a policy of 'decreased labour service and taxation'. This was because people were very poor and there was nothing to take from them. This policy was of advantage to the landlord class.

I hope that those who are engaged in philosophical work will go to the factories and the countryside for a few years. The system of philosophy should be reformed. You should not write in the old manner and you should not write so much.

A student of Nanking University who came from a peasant family, a student of history, took part in the 'four clean-ups' movement. Afterwards he wrote some articles on the subject of the necessity for those engaged in history to go down to the countryside. In these articles, which were published in the *Nanking University Journal*, he made a confession saying: 'I have studied now for several years and have lost all notion of manual labour.' In the same issue of the *Nanking University Journal* is an article which says: 'The essence is the major contradiction and, in particular, the major aspect of the major contradiction.' Even I have not made such a statement before. The outward appearance is visible; it stimulates the senses. The essence is invisible and intangible; it is hidden behind the outward appearance. The essence can only be discovered through investigation and study. If we could touch and see the essence there would be no need for science.

You should gradually get into contact with reality, live for a while in the countryside, learn a bit of agricultural science, botany, soil technology, fertilizer technology, bacteriology, forestry, water conservancy, etc. There's no need to read big tomes. It's sufficient to read little books and get a bit of general knowledge.

Now about this university education. From entering primary school to leaving college is altogether sixteen or seventeen years. I fear that for over twenty years people will not see rice, mustard, wheat or millet growing; nor will they see how workers work, nor how peasants till the fields, nor how people do business. Moreover their health will be ruined. It is really terribly harmful. I said to my own child: 'You go down to the countryside and tell the poor and lower-middle peasants, "My dad says that after studying a few years we became more and more stupid. Please, uncles and aunts, brothers and sisters, be my teachers. I want to learn from you." ' In point of fact pre-school children have a lot of contact with society up to the age of seven. At two they learn to speak and at three they have noisy quarrels. When they grow a little bigger, they dig with toy hoes to imitate grown-ups working. This is the real world. By then the children have already learned concepts. 'Dog' is a major concept. 'Black dog' and 'yellow dog' are minor concepts. His family's yellow dog is concrete. Man is a concept which has shed a great deal of meaning. Man or woman, great or small, Chinese or foreigner, revolutionary or counter-revolutionary – all these distinctions are absent. What is left are only the characteristics which differentiate man from the other animals. Who has ever seen 'man'? You can only see Mr Chang and Mr Li. You cannot see the concept 'house' either, only actual houses, such as the foreign-style buildings of Tientsin or the courtyard houses of Peking.

We should reform university education. So much time should not be spent attending classes. Not to reform arts faculties would be terrible. If they are not reformed, can they produce philosophers? Can they produce writers? Can they produce historians? Today's philosophers can't turn out philosophy, writers can't write novels, and historians can't produce history. All they want to write about is emperors, kings, generals and ministers. Ch'i Pen-yü's article[5] is excellent, I read it three times. Its defect is that it does not name names. Yao Wen-yüan's article[6] is also very good: it has had a great impact on theatrical, historical and philosophical circles. Its defect is that it did not hit the crux of the matter. The crux of *Hai Jui Dismissed from Office* was the question of dismissal from office. The Chia Ch'ing emperor dismissed Hai Jui from office. In 1959 we dismissed P'eng Te-huai from office. And P'eng Te-huai is Hai Jui too.

We must reform the arts faculties in the universities. The students must go down and engage in industry, agriculture and commerce. The engineering and science departments are different. They have factories for practical work and also laboratories. They can work in their factories and do experiments in their laboratories. After they have finished high school they should first do some practical work. Only to go to the countryside is not enough. They should also go to factories, shops, army companies. They can do this kind of work for a few years and then study for two years. This will be enough. If the university has a five-year system, they should go down for three years. Teachers should also go down and work and teach at the same time. Can't they teach philosophy, literature and history there too? Must they have big foreign-style buildings to teach them in?

Many great inventors, such as Watt and Edison, came from workers' families. Franklin, who discovered electricity, sold newspapers: he started as a newspaper boy. Many of the great scholars and scientists did not go through college. Not many of the comrades in our Party's Central Committee are university graduates.

You cannot go on writing books the way you write them now. Take the example of analysis and synthesis. In the past books did not explain them clearly. They said, 'Within analysis there is synthesis; analysis and synthesis are indivisible.' This sort of statement may be correct, but it has its inadequacy. One should say, 'Analysis and synthesis are both divisible and indivisible.' Everything can be divided. It is all a case of 'one divides into two'. Analysis has to be applied in differing circumstances. Take, for example, an analysis of the Kuomintang and the communists. How did we analyse the Kuomintang in the past? We said that it occupied extensive territory with a large population, it controlled the large and medium-sized cities, enjoyed the support of imperialism and had large well-equipped armies. But the fundamental point was that it was divorced from the masses – the peasants and soldiers. Also it had internal contradictions. Our armies were small, our weapons inferior (only millet and rifles), our territory was small, we had no big cities and no foreign aid, but we had close links with the masses; we had democracy in the three main fields, we had the three–eight working style, and we represented the demands of the masses. This was the fundamental thing.

Those Kuomintang officers who had graduated from military academies could not fight battles, while those who had studied in the Whampoa Military Academy for only a few months could fight. Among our own marshals and generals there are very few who have been to college. I had never studied military books. I had read the *Tso Commentary*,[7] the *Mirror of Good Government*[8] and the *Romance of the Three Kingdoms*. These books all described battles, but when I actually went into battle I forgot all about them. When we fought we did not take a single book with us. We only analysed the situation of ourselves and the enemy, analysed the concrete situation.

To synthesize the enemy is to eat him up. How did we synthesize the Kuomintang? Did we not do it by taking enemy material and remoulding it? We did not kill prisoners, but released some of them and retained most of them to replenish our own armies. We took all the weapons, food and fodder and equipment of all kinds. Those we did not use we have '*aufgehoben*', to use a philosophical term, as in the case of people like Tu Yü-ming.[9] The process of eating is also one of analysis and synthesis. For example when eating crabs you eat the meat but not the shell. The stomach will absorb the nutritious part and get rid of the useless part. You are all foreign-style philosophers. I am a native-style philosopher. Synthesizing the Kuomintang means eating it up, absorbing most of it and eliminating a small part. I've learnt this from Marx. Marx removed the shell of Hegel's philosophy and absorbed the useful inner part, transforming it into dialectical materialism. He absorbed Feuerbach's materialism and criticized his metaphysics. The heritage had always to be passed on. In his treatment of French utopian socialism and English political economy, Marx absorbed the good things and abandoned the bad.

Marx's *Capital* started with the analysis of the dual nature of commodities. Our commodities also have a dual nature. In a hundred years' time commodities will still have a dual nature. Things which are not commodities have a dual nature too. Our comrades likewise have a dual nature, correct and incorrect. Don't you have a dual nature? I know I have. Young people easily make the mistake of being metaphysical: they cannot bear to talk about their shortcomings. People improve with experience. In recent years, however, it is the young who have made progress; the hopeless cases are some of the old professors. Wu Han is mayor of a city. It would be better if he were demoted to being head of a county. It would be better if Yang Hsien-chen and Chang Wen-t'ien were demoted too. This is the only way we can really help them.

Recently an article was written about the law of adequate justification. What law of adequate justification? I don't think such a thing exists. Different classes have different ways of justifying their actions. Which class does not have adequate justification? Doesn't Russell? He recently sent me a pamphlet which should be translated and read. Russell is now a bit better politically. He is anti-revisionist and anti-American and he supports Vietnam. This idealist has acquired a little materialism. I am talking about his actions.[10]

A man should work in many fields, have contact with all sorts of people. Leftists should not only meet leftists but also rightists. They should not be afraid of this and that. I myself have met all sorts of people; I have met big officials and small ones.

In writing philosophy can you change your methods? You

must write in a popular style, using the language of the labouring masses. We all talk like students. (*Comrade Ch'en Po-ta interrupts: 'The Chairman excepted.'*) I have been involved in the peasant movement, the workers' movement, the student movement, the Kuomintang movement, and I have done military work for over twenty years, so I am somewhat better.

In tackling the study of Chinese philosophy, we must study Chinese history and the historical process of Chinese philosophy. One should first study the history of the past 100 years. Isn't the historical process the unity of opposites? Modern history is a continual process of one dividing into two and continual struggle. In these struggles some people compromised, but the people were dissatisfied with them and went on struggling. Before the 1911 Revolution we had the struggle between Sun Yat-sen and K'ang Yu-wei. After the 1911 Revolution had overthrown the emperor there was the struggle between Sun and Yüan Shih-k'ai. Afterwards the Kuomintang had continual internal schisms and struggles.

The Marxist–Leninist classics not only need to have prefaces written, but also annotations. Political prefaces are easier to write than philosophical ones, which are none too easy. It used to be said that there were three great laws of dialectics, then Stalin said that there were four. In my view there is only one basic law and that is the law of contradiction. Quality and quantity, positive and negative, external appearance and essence, content and form, necessity and freedom, possibility and reality, etc., are all cases of the unity of opposites.

It has been said that the relationship of formal logic to dialectics is like the relationship between elementary mathematics and higher mathematics. This is a formulation which should be studied further. Formal logic is concerned with the form of thought, and is concerned to ensure that there is no contradiction between successive stages in an argument. It is a specialized science. Any kind of writing must make use of formal logic.

Formal logic does not concern itself with major premises: it is incapable of so doing. The Kuomintang call us 'bandits'. 'Communists are bandits', 'Chang San is a communist', therefore 'Chang San is a bandit'. We say 'The Kuomintang are bandits',

'Chiang Kai-shek is Kuomintang', therefore we say 'Chiang Kai-shek is a bandit'. Both of these syllogisms are in accordance with formal logic.

One cannot acquire much fresh knowledge through formal logic. Naturally one can draw inferences, but the conclusion is still enshrined in the major premise. At present some people confuse formal logic and dialectics. This is incorrect.

15 Talks with Mao Yüan-hsin* (1964–6)

First Talk
5 July 1964[1]

THE CHAIRMAN: Have you made any progress in the course of the past half year? Have you raised [your level]?
YÜAN-HSIN: I'm a bit mixed up about it myself, I wouldn't venture to say that I have made any progress; if I have, it is merely superficial.
THE CHAIRMAN: I think you have after all made some progress, your way of looking at problems is no longer so simple. Have you read the 'Ninth Reply' or not?[2] Have you seen the five criteria for successors?
YÜAN-HSIN: I have seen them. (*Following on from this, he talked for a while, setting forth the main content of the 'Ninth Reply' as regards successors.*)
THE CHAIRMAN: You have talked about it, all right, but do you understand it? These five criteria are indissolubly linked to one another. The first is theory, or also orientation. The second is the aim – i.e. when you come right down to it, whom do you serve? This is the most important. When you have mastered this point, you can do anything. The third, fourth and fifth criteria relate to questions of methodology. You must unite with the majority, you must implement democratic centralism, you must not allow everything to be settled by the word of one man, you must carry out self-criticism, you must be modest and prudent. Isn't all this methodology?
(*When talking about the first criterion for successors, the*

*Comrade Mao Yüan-hsin is Chairman Mao's nephew who studied at the Harbin Military Engineering Institute.

Chairman said:) Are you going to study Marxism–Leninism, or revisionism?

YÜAN-HSIN: Naturally, I'm studying Marxism–Leninism.

THE CHAIRMAN: Don't be too sure, who knows what you're studying? Do you know what Marxism–Leninism is?

YÜAN-HSIN: Marxism–Leninism means that you must carry on the class struggle, that you must carry out revolution.

THE CHAIRMAN: The basic idea of Marxism–Leninism is that you must carry out revolution. But what is revolution? Revolution is the proletariat overthrowing the capitalists, the peasants overthrowing the landlords, and then afterwards setting up a workers' and peasants' political power, and moreover continuing to consolidate it. At present, the task of the revolution has not yet been completed; it has not yet been finally determined who, in the end, will overthrow whom. In the Soviet Union, is not Khrushchev in power, is not the bourgeoisie in power? We, too, have cases in which political power is in the grip of the bourgeoisie; there are production brigades, factories, and *hsien* committees, as well as district and provincial committees, in which they have their people, there are deputy heads of public security departments who are their men. Who is leading the Ministry of Culture? The cinema and the theatre are entirely in their service, and not in the service of the majority of the people.[3] Who do you say is exercising leadership? To study Marxism–Leninism is to study the class struggle. The class struggle is everywhere; it is in your Institute, a counter-revolutionary has appeared in your Institute, are you aware of this or not? He wrote a reactionary diary filling a dozen or so notebooks, every day he cursed us, shouldn't he be considered a counter-revolutionary element? Are you people not completely insensitive to class struggle? Isn't it right there beside you? If there were no counter-revolution, then why would we still need revolution?

(*Yüan-hsin reports on some circumstances regarding the 'five antis' in the factory where he had gone for practical training, from which he had learned a great deal.*)

THE CHAIRMAN: Everywhere there is counter-revolution, how

could it be absent from the factories? Middle-and low-ranking Kuomintang officers, secretaries of *hsien* [Kuomintang] party offices, etc., have all crept in. No matter what guise they have been transformed into, we must now clean them all out. Everywhere there is class struggle, everywhere there are counter-revolutionary elements. Is not Ch'en Tung-p'ing[4] sleeping right next to you? I have read all the various materials [of his] denounced by your Institute. You were sleeping together with a counterrevolutionary, and yet you did not know it!

(*The Chairman next asked about political and ideological work in the Institute. Mao Yüan-hsin gave his views of this.*)

YÜAN-HSIN: They call meetings and talk a lot; outwardly it's very stirring, but they don't solve many real problems.

THE CHAIRMAN: The whole country is engaged in learning from the People's Liberation Army on a vast scale. You are members of the PLA; why aren't you learning from it? Does the Institute have a political department? What is it doing? Do you have political training or not?

(*Yüan-hsin explains the way political training is carried out at the Institute.*) All this is nothing but attending classes and discussing things, what is the use of it? You should go and study reality. You have not even applied the principle that ideology comes first, you have no real knowledge at all, so when people talk about those things how can you understand them?

(*The Chairman especially advocates swimming in great winds and waves, and moreover urges Mao Yüan-hsin to practise it resolutely every day.*) You have already come to know water, and have mastered it, that is excellent. Do you know how to ride horseback?

YÜAN-HSIN: I don't know how [to ride].

THE CHAIRMAN: To be a soldier, and not to know how to ride – this should not be. (*The Chairman calls on Mao Yüan-hsin to go and learn to ride; the Chairman himself constantly practises riding, and has also made his secretary and staff go and learn.*) Have you done any rifle shooting or not?

YÜAN-HSIN: I haven't touched a gun for four years.

THE CHAIRMAN: At present the militia all shoot very well, but you members of the PLA haven't done any shooting; you discuss this criticism of mine with XXX, what kind of soldier is it that doesn't know how to shoot?

(Once when he was swimming, and the weather was relatively cold, so that it was warmer in the water than above it, Mao Yüan-hsin, after he had come out and felt a bit cold, said: 'It is after all a bit more comfortable in the water.')

THE CHAIRMAN *(staring angrily at Mao Yüan-hsin)*: In fact, you like comfort, and fear difficulties. *(The Chairman, in discussing the second criterion for successors, said:)* You know how to think about yourself, you spend all your time pondering your own problems. Your father *(Comrade Mao Tse-min)* was dauntless and resolute in the face of the enemy, he never wavered in the slightest, because he served the majority of the people.[5] If it had been you, wouldn't you have got down on both knees and begged for your life? Very many members of our family have given their lives, killed by the Kuomintang and the American imperialists. You grew up eating honey, and thus far you have never known suffering. In future, if you do not become a rightist, but rather a centrist, I shall be satisfied. You have never suffered, how can you be a leftist?

YÜAN-HSIN: Is there still some hope for me?

THE CHAIRMAN: Well, yes, there is hope, but if you surpass the criteria I have set, that will be even better.

(The Chairman also talked about the third criterion, saying:) When you people hold a meeting, how do you hold it? You are a squad leader; how does one go about being a squad leader? When everyone criticizes you, can you accept it? Can you accept their criticisms even if they are wrong? Can you accept a false and unjust charge? If you cannot accept it, then how can you unite people? You must especially learn to work with people who disagree with you. If you like to have people praise you, if you like to have honey on your lips, and songs to your glory in your ears, that is the most dangerous thing, and that is exactly what you do like.

(In talking about the fourth criterion, the Chairman said:) Do you unite with the masses or not? Is it not the case that you spend your time with the sons and daughters of cadres, and look

down on other people? You must let people talk, and not be satisfied with letting one person settle everything.

(*In talking about the fifth criterion, the Chairman said:*) In this respect you have already made some progress, you have engaged in a bit of self-criticism, but it's barely a beginning, you mustn't think everything is all right.

(*Afterwards, the Chairman once again talked about the work at the Institute:* The most fundamental defect of your Institute is that you have not applied the 'four firsts'.[6] Didn't you say you wanted to study Marxism–Leninism? What method of study do you employ? How much can you learn merely by relying on listening to lectures? The most important thing is to go and learn from practice.

YÜAN-HSIN: A faculty of science and engineering and faculty of letters are different; [the former] doesn't provide for so much time to go and enter into contact with society.

THE CHAIRMAN: That is wrong; the class struggle is your most important subject, and it is a compulsory subject. I have already discussed this question with XXX. Your Institute should go down to the countryside to carry out the 'four clean-ups', from the cadres to the students all of you should go, and not one should remain. You should go this winter, or in the spring of next year; it is better to go earlier than later, you must definitely go. As for you, you must not only spend five months participating in the 'four clean-ups', you must also go to a factory and spend half a year carrying out the 'five antis'. Isn't it true that you don't understand a thing about society? If you don't carry out the four clean-ups, you won't understand the peasants, and if you don't carry out the five antis, you won't understand the workers. Only when you have completed such a course of political training can I consider you a university graduate. Otherwise, if the Military Engineering Institute lets you graduate, I won't recognize your diploma. If you don't even know about the class struggle, how can you be regarded as a university graduate? If you are to graduate, I will set you this additional subject. Your Institute has not carried out ideological work; so many counter-revolutionaries, and you were not aware of it; Ch'en Tung-p'ing was right next to you and you didn't know it.

(*Mao Yüan-hsin says that while Ch'en Tung-p'ing was at home during the holidays, he listened to the enemy's radio and was thus corrupted.*) How can you believe the enemy's radio if you listen to it? Have you listened to it or not? The enemy doesn't even have food to eat, can you believe what he says? Wei Li-huang[7] was in business in Hong Kong; having lost his money, he returned. Everybody looks down on people like Wei Li-huang; it's hard to imagine that the enemy doesn't despise him (*Ch'en Tung-p'ing*) too.

What are the four firsts? (*Mao Yüan-hsin talks about this.*) You know about this; why, then, do you not grasp living ideology? I hear there are a lot of political cadres in your Institute, but they do not grasp the essential, so naturally they do not grasp ideology. Naturally, your Institute has scored some successes; there's nothing so remarkable if it has a few problems. We've been engaged in military engineering for only a decade. Our army has no experience in running technical schools. It's like when we learned to fight in 1927: at first we didn't know how, and we kept being defeated, but afterwards we learned how.

(*The Chairman also asked:*) How is it with the reform of teaching in your Institute?

YÜAN-HSIN: The last time we had examinations, our unit tried out a new method. Everyone thought it was good, and gave a correct evaluation of the level [of each student]. It also had an influence on the method of study as a whole, making it possible to study in a lively fashion.

THE CHAIRMAN: This should have been done long ago.

YÜAN-HSIN: In the past, the notion of marks prevailed, so that we did not study with initiative.

THE CHAIRMAN: It's good that you are able to recognize this. I can't blame you for this either, for the whole educational system brazenly calls on you to strive for a mark of five. If you don't strive for such a perfect mark, they may block [your advancement] completely. Your elder sister, too, suffered from this kind of thing. There was a student at Peking University who never took notes at ordinary times, and scored between three-and-a-half and four marks in examinations, yet at graduation time the dissertation he presented was of the highest level in the class. There are people who have seen through all this, and have taken the initiative in study. There are some people like that who have seen through marks, and who study boldly, and with initiative. Your teachers teach by inculcation. Every day you attend lectures. Do they really have that much to say? The teachers should distribute their lecture notes to you. What are they afraid of? They should let the students study them by themselves. To keep the lecture notes secret from the students, allowing them only to take notes in class, hampers the students terribly. In the past, when I was teaching at K'ang Ta, I used to distribute lecture notes to my students in advance. I only talked for thirty minutes, and let the students themselves do their own study; afterwards the students would ask questions and the teacher would answer. With university students, especially the senior students, the main thing is to let them study and work out problems. What is the point of talking so much?

In the past they openly called on everyone to strive for perfect marks. People were perfect in school, but they weren't necessarily perfect in their work. In Chinese history, none of the highest graduates of the Hanlin Academy had true talent or learning. These were found rather among those who failed even to pass as second-degree graduates. The two greatest poets of the T'ang dynasty[8] did not even obtain the degree of *chü-jen.* Don't put too much emphasis on marks; you should concentrate your energies on fostering and training your ability to analyse and solve problems. Do not run along behind the teachers and be fettered by them. The problem of educational reform is primarily a problem of teachers. The teachers have so many books, and they can do nothing without their lecture notes. Why don't they distribute their lecture notes to you and study problems together with you? When the students in the senior classes ask questions, the teachers will only answer half of them, and will know nothing about the rest, so they will study and discuss the problems together with the students. This is not bad either. They must not put on arrogant airs to frighten people off. Even the bourgeoisie has opposed the cramming method of teaching. Why shouldn't we oppose it? It will be all right so long as the students are not treated as targets of attack. Teachers are the key to educational reform.

(*Once Mao Yüan-hsin had urged the Chairman to visit an exhibition of new scientific achievements; the Chairman had said: 'I'm busy now, I can't go and look at it. I haven't time to look at it carefully, and to look at flowers while riding by on horseback isn't worth while either.'*)

How is it that you are interested in this, but not in Marxism–Leninism? In any case, I rarely hear you ask questions about this aspect of things most of the time. What newspaper do you usually read?

YÜAN-HSIN: I read the *People's Daily*.

THE CHAIRMAN: There's nothing worth looking at in the *People's Daily*. You should read *Liberation Army Daily*, or *Chinese Youth Daily*.[9] The things the workers and soldiers write are real and lively, and they know how to explain problems. Have you read the discussion on 'two combines into one'?

YÜAN-HSIN: I've read only very little, and I didn't understand much of what I did read.

THE CHAIRMAN: Is that so? Have a look at this newspaper (*the Chairman hands him a copy of* Chinese Youth Daily), see how the workers analyse things, see how the cadres of the Youth League analyse things, they analyse things very well, it's easier to understand than *People's Daily*.

(*The Chairman also said:*) Your political study is nothing but talk. If you want to learn a lot of things, the most important point is to go and study in the midst of reality. Why are you interested in your professional speciality, but not in Marxism–Leninism?

When you study history, if you don't combine it with present reality it's no good. If you study modern history and don't carry out work compiling village histories and family histories, it's a complete waste of time.[10] When you study ancient history, this too must be combined with present reality, and cannot be divorced from excavations and archaeology. Did Yao, Shun, and Yü[11] exist or not? I don't believe it, you don't have any real evidence. There are oracle-bones to provide evidence regarding the Shang dynasty, we can believe in that. If you go and burrow into a pile of books, the more you study, the less knowledge you'll have.

Second Talk

18 February 1966

[*Chairman Mao and his nephew*] *discussed the question of whether the Military Engineering Institute should go in for two or three years of study first and then do another year of part-time work and part-time study; and also the question of coordination and assignment of work.*

CHAIRMAN MAO: The science and engineering faculties should still have their own language. With their six-year syllabus we could start by trying to do it in three years first and see how it works out, and not necessarily be in a hurry to shorten it to two years. With advanced science, if there is a clear-cut objective, then three years of study would perhaps be all right, and if three years are not enough they could later add on a bit.

Only when there is a clear-cut objective can you do less but do it well, and only then can you combine the general and the particular. The six-year system can then be altered into a three-year system, and after we have done that our steps can be sure and steady and our direction will be right.

When you try new things, the only way to do it is to carry on for a few years, constantly summarizing your experience.

The science and engineering faculties have their specific nature and have their own special terminology, so you have to read a few books. But they also have something in common with other subjects, it's no good just to read books. One had only to study at Whampoa Academy for half a year and after graduation one served as a soldier for one year. In that way many talented officers were produced, but after it was changed to the Army University (I have not made a note of how long they studied) the result was that when people graduated, they kept on being defeated in battle and becoming our captives.

I don't know anything about the science and engineering faculties, but I do claim a little knowledge about the medical faculty. When you listen to an eye doctor talk it all sounds very mysterious, but the human body should be viewed as a whole.

The development of science proceeds from a low level to a high level, from the simple to the complex, but when one teaches one cannot follow the sequence of development. When we study history, we should concentrate on modern history. Now we only have three thousand-odd years of recorded history; what will happen when we have ten thousand years of history, how will we teach it then?

Advanced science, including those fundamental theories which practice has proved useful, must get rid of those parts which practice has proved useless and irrational.

When one lectures on nuclear physics it will suffice to talk about the Sakata model; one needn't start from the theories of Bohr of the Danish school; otherwise you won't graduate even after ten years of study. Even Sakata uses dialectics – why don't you use it?

Man's understanding of things always starts from the concrete and proceeds to the abstract. In medicine they start by teaching abstract things such as psychology, the nervous system, etc. I think this is wrong: they should start by teaching anatomy. Mathematics was originally derived from physical models. Nowadays one cannot associate mathematics with physical models: instead one has gone a step further and made it abstract.

Third Talk

1966

[CHAIRMAN MAO:] Formerly, I was principal of a primary school, and a teacher in a middle school. I am also a member of the Central Committee, and was once a department chief for the Kuomintang.[12] But when I went to the rural areas and spent some time with the peasants, I was deeply struck by how many things they knew. I realized their knowledge was wide, and I was no match for them, but should learn from them. To say the least, you are not a member of the Central Committee, are you? How can you know more than the peasants? When you return, tell your political commissar that I said from now on you should go to the countryside once each year. There are great advantages in this!

You don't understand dialectics; you don't understand that one divides into two. Formerly, you thought you were something extraordinary, and now you do not think you are worth a tinker's damn. Both views are wrong.

Those who are guilty of errors should be encouraged. When someone who has made errors sees his mistakes, you should point out his good points. Actually, he will still have many good points. Those who have made errors should be washed clean in warm water. If it is too hot they can't stand it; warm water is most suitable. Young people who make mistakes should not be dismissed. Dismissal harms them, and there cannot be any confrontations. People like Pu-yi and K'ang Tse[13] were transformed. Among the young people who have not been transformed are some Party members and some [Youth] League members. To dismiss them would be to simplify matters to excess.

At the Institute are you a leftist? I saw an article praising you.[14] To have people flatter you is no good at all. Young people like you should be told off. If they tell you off too little it won't do. Everything is subject to this kind of compulsion. When I wrote XXX, I was compelled to do it. If I had to write it now, I could not do it.

What do we mean by advanced? To be advanced is to do the work of the backward, to analyse those who are around us, to be intent on making inquiries and making friends wherever we go. Our young people must study dialectics, and master the use of dialectics in analysing problems. Take me, for example. I am not at all more intelligent than others, but I understand dialectics and I know how to use it in analysing problems. If we use dialectics to analyse an unclear problem, the problem becomes clear in a trice. You must diligently study dialectics, its efficacy is very great.

16 Talk to Leaders of the Centre
21 July 1966

Chairman Mao said that the 'May Twenty-fifth' big-character poster of Nieh Yüan-tzu is a manifesto of the Chinese Paris Commune of the sixties of the twentieth century, the significance of which surpasses the Paris Commune. This kind of big-character poster we are incapable of writing.

(Several Young Pioneers wrote big-character posters about their fathers saying that their fathers had forgotten their past, did not talk to them about Mao Tse-tung thought, but did ask them about the marks they got at school and rewarded them when they got good marks.)

Chairman Mao asked Comrade Ch'en Po-ta to pass on a message to these little friends: 'Your big-character posters are very well-written.' [He continued:]

I say to you all: youth is the great army of the Great Cultural Revolution! It must be mobilized to the full.

After my return to Peking I felt very unhappy and desolate. Some colleges even had their gates shut. There were even some which suppressed the student movement. Who is it who suppressed the student movement? Only the Pei-yang Warlords.[1] It is anti-Marxist for communists to fear the student movement. Some people talk daily about the mass line and serving the people, but instead they follow the bourgeois line and serve the bourgeoisie. The Central Committee of the Youth League should stand on the side of the student movement. But instead it stands on the side of suppression of the student movement. Who opposes the great Cultural Revolution? The American imperialists, the Soviet revisionists, the Japanese revisionists and the reactionaries.

To use the excuse of distinguishing between 'inner' and 'outer'[2] is to fear revolution. To cover over big-character posters which have been put up, such things cannot be allowed. This is a basic error of orientation. They must immediately change direction, and smash all the old conventions.

We believe in the masses. To become teachers of the masses we must first be the students of the masses. The present great Cultural Revolution is a heaven-and-earth-shaking event. Can we, dare we, cross the pass into socialism? This pass leads to the final destruction of classes, and the reduction of the three great differences.

To oppose, especially to oppose 'authoritative' bourgeois ideology, is to destroy. Without this destruction, socialism cannot be established nor can we carry out first struggle, second criticism, third transformation. Sitting in offices listening to reports is no good. The only way is to rely on the masses, trust the masses, struggle to the end. We must be prepared for the revolution to be turned against us. The Party and government leadership and responsible Party comrades should be prepared for this. If you now want to carry the revolution through to the end, you must discipline yourself, reform yourself in order to keep up with it. Otherwise you can only keep out of it.

There are some comrades who struggle fiercely against others, but cannot struggle with themselves. In this way, they will never be able to cross the pass.

It is up to you to lead the fire towards your own bodies, to fan the flames to make them burn. Do you dare to do this? Because it will burn your own heads.

The comrades replied thus: 'We are prepared. If we're not up to it, we will resign our jobs. We live as Communist Party members and shall die as Communist Party members. It doesn't do to live a life of sofas and electric fans.' [Chairman Mao said:]

It will not do to set rigid standards for the masses. When Peking University saw that the students were rising up, they tried to set standards. They euphemistically called it 'returning to the right track'. In fact it was 'diverting to the wrong track'.

There were some schools which labelled the students as counter-revolutionaries. (*Liaison officer Chang Yen went out and labelled twenty-nine people as counter-revolutionary.*) [*Chairman Mao said:*]

In this way you put the masses on the side of the opposition. You should not fear bad people. How many of them are there after all? The great majority of the student masses are good.

Someone raised the question of disturbances. What do we do in such cases about taking legal action? [*Chairman Mao said:*]

What are you afraid of? When bad people are involved you prove that they are bad. What do you fear about good people? You should replace the word 'fear' by the word 'dare'. You must demonstrate once and for all whether or not the pass into socialism has been crossed. You must put politics in command, go among the masses and be at one with them, and carry on the Great Proletarian Cultural Revolution even better.

17 Speech at a Meeting with Regional Secretaries and Members of the Cultural Revolutionary Group of the Central Committee

22 July 1966

Now all the regional secretaries and members of the Cultural Revolution Group are present. The task of this meeting is to attend to our documents, and primarily to change the method of sending out work teams so that revolutionary teachers and students in schools, as well as some middle-of-the-road people, can organize school Cultural Revolution Groups to lead the Great Cultural Revolution. Only they understand the affairs of the schools. The work teams do not understand. There are some work teams who made a mess of things. The purpose of the Great Cultural Revolution in the schools is to carry out struggle, criticism, transformation. The work teams had the effect of obstructing the movement. Can we carry out struggle and transformation? For example, Chien Po-tsan wrote a great many books, yet you still haven't read them. How can you struggle against him and transform him? Where schools are concerned it is a case of 'When the temple is small the gods seem big, and when the pool is shallow the turtles seem plentiful.' Therefore we must rely on internal forces in the schools. The work teams won't do. I won't do, you won't do. The provincial Party committees won't do either. If it's struggle and transformation you want, you must rely on the schools themselves and the units themselves. It is no good relying on the work teams. I wonder whether the work teams can be changed into liaison staff. If they are changed into advisers they will have too much power. Perhaps they can be called observers. The work teams obstruct the revolution, but there are some among them who don't. If they obstruct the revolution they will unavoidably become counter-revolutionary. The Communications University in Sian does not allow people to telephone, and does not allow people to be sent to the Centre. Why should they fear people going to the Centre? Let them come and besiege the State Council. We must draw up documents to the effect that they may telephone or send delegates. Will it do to get so frightened? When the newspapers in Sian and Nanking were besieged for three days, the people concerned were so afraid that their souls left their bodies. Are you afraid like this? You people! If you don't make revolution, the revolution will be directed against you. Some districts do not allow people to besiege newspaper offices, go to the provincial Party committee or go to see the State Council. Why are you so afraid? When they get to the State Council all they see are little unimportant generals, and so nothing can be cleared up. Why are things like this? Even if you won't show your faces I will show mine. This word 'fear' is always coming to the fore – fear of counter-revolution, fear of people using knives and guns. Can there really be so many counter-revolutionaries? These past few days K'ang Sheng,[1] Ch'en Po-ta and Chiang Ch'ing have been going down to the schools to read the big-character posters. How can you get by without perceptual knowledge? None of you go down because you are busy with routine matters; but you should go down even if it means neglecting routine matters, in order to get perceptual knowledge. In Nanking they did things a bit better. They didn't stop students from coming to the Centre.

K'ang Sheng interrupted: 'Nanking had three great debates. The first debate was about whether the New China Daily *was revolutionary or not; the second was about whether the Kiangsu Provincial Party Committee was revolutionary or not. The debate concluded that the Kiangsu Provincial Party Committee was after all revolutionary. The third debate was about whether K'uang Ya-ming should be paraded in the street wearing a dunce's hat.'* [Chairman Mao resumed:]

In the schools the majority is revolutionary, the minority is not revolutionary. As to whether K'uang Ya-ming will parade the streets wearing a dunce's hat, the conclusion of the debate will naturally clarify this point.

During this meeting the comrades who are attending it should go to Peking University and the Broadcasting Institute to read the big-character posters. You should go to the places where there is the most trouble and take a look there. Today you aren't going because we have to attend to the documents. When you read the big-character posters you can say that you are there to learn, to support their revolution; you go there to light the fire of revolution and support the revolutionary teachers and students, not to listen to counter-revolutionaries and right-wing talk. After two months you still haven't got the slightest perceptual knowledge and you are still bureaucratic. If you go there you will be surrounded by the students and should be surrounded by them, and when you start talking to a few of them they will surround you. At the Broadcasting Institute over a hundred people were beaten up. There is one good thing about our era: the left-wingers get beaten up by the right-wingers, and this toughens up the left-wingers. To send the work teams for six months or even a year won't work, only people from on the spot will do. The first thing is struggle, the second is criticism, the third is transformation. Struggle means destruction, and trans-formation means establishing something new. It won't do to change the teaching materials in half a year's time. The thing to do is to delete, to abandon, to condense and to simplify. Materials which are incorrect or repetitious can be cut by one third to one half.

Wang Jen-chung[2] *interrupted: 'We should cut out two thirds and study* Quotations from Chairman Mao.' [*Chairman Mao continued:*]

Political teaching materials, central directives and newspaper editorials are guidelines for the masses; they mustn't be re-garded as dogmas. The problem of beatings-up hasn't been men-tioned in our circulars. This won't do. This is a matter of our basic direction and of laying down guidelines. Our general policy should be quickly established. In carrying out transform-ation we must rely on the revolutionary teachers and students and leftists in the schools. It doesn't matter if rightists join the cultural revolutionary committees of the schools; they can be useful as teachers by negative example, but the rightists shouldn't be concentrated together. The Peking Municipal Party Committee doesn't need so many people. When there are too many people around there will be telephoning and the issuing of orders. There should be a wholesale cut in secretaries. When I was working on the Front Committee[3] I had a secretary called Hsiang Pei. Later during our retreat we did not have secretaries any more. It's enough just to have someone to receive and dispatch documents.

K'ang Sheng interrupted: 'The Chairman has talked about four things. One is the reorganization of the Peking Municipal Party Committee. This has been done. The second is the reorganization of the Propaganda Department of the Central Committee, which has also been carried out. The third is the elimination of the five-man Cultural Revolution Group, which has also been done.[4] The fourth is the transformation of certain ministries into departments, which hasn't been done. [Chairman Mao replied:]

That's right, regarding ministers, those who can manage their work don't have to be changed. They can be called ministers, heads of departments, heads of bureaux, heads of offices, but those who don't do their jobs should be changed into the Department of Metallurgy, the Department of Coal.

Someone interrupted: 'Peking University carried out four big debates. Was the incident of 18 June a counter-revolutionary affair?[5] Some say yes, because there were riff-raff involved in it, but some say no, and that the work team made mistakes. Over forty people in the Peking University Middle School propose sacking the head of the work team, Chang Ch'eng-hsien.' [Chairman Mao replied:]

There are many work teams which obstruct the movement and they include Chang Ch'eng-hsien. But we mustn't arrest people indiscriminately. What constitutes counter-revolutionary activity? It's simply murder, arson, and spreading poison. Such people you can arrest. You can let those who write reactionary slogans go free for the time being so that you can have a confrontation. You can consider the matter again when you have struggled against them.

18 A Letter to the Red Guards of Tsinghua University Middle School

1 August 1966

Red Guard comrades of Tsinghua University Middle School:

I have received both the big-character posters which you sent on 28 July as well as the letter which you sent to me, asking for an answer. The two big-character posters which you wrote on 24 June and 4 July[1] express your anger at, and denunciation of, all landlords, bourgeois, imperialists, revisionists, and their running dogs who exploit and oppress the workers, peasants, revolutionary intellectuals and revolutionary parties and groupings. You say it is right to rebel against reactionaries; I enthusiastically support you. I also give enthusiastic support to the big-character poster of the Red Flag Combat Group of Peking University Middle School which said that it is right to rebel against the reactionaries; and to the very good revolutionary speech given by comrade P'eng Hsiao-meng representing their Red Flag Combat Group at the big meeting attended by all the teachers, students, administration and workers of Peking University on 25 July. Here I want to say that I myself as well as my revolutionary comrades-in-arms all take the same attitude. No matter where they are, in Peking or anywhere in China, I will give enthusiastic support to all who take an attitude similar to yours in the Cultural Revolution movement. Another thing, while supporting you, at the same time we ask you to pay attention to uniting with all who can be united with. As for those who have committed serious mistakes, after their mistakes have been pointed out you should offer them a way out of their difficulties by giving them work to do, and enabling them to correct their mistakes and become new men. Marx said: the proletariat must emancipate not only itself but all mankind. If it cannot emancipate all mankind, then the proletariat itself will not be able to achieve final emancipation. Will comrades please pay attention to this truth too.

19 Speech at the Closing Ceremony of the Eleventh Plenum of the Eighth Central Committee

12 August 1966

With regard to the Ninth Congress, I think it's time we made some preparations. We should prepare to make a decision as to when the Ninth Congress will be held. It has been a good many years; in two years' time it will be ten years since the Second Session of the Eighth Congress. Now the Ninth Congress must be held, probably at a suitable time next year. We must now prepare for it. May I propose that we entrust the necessary preparations to the Politburo and its Standing Committee?

Whether the decisions taken by this conference are correct or incorrect will be shown by future events. But it seems that our decisions are welcomed by the masses. For example one of the important decisions of the Central Committee concerns the Great Cultural Revolution. The broad masses of students and revolutionary teachers support us and resist the policies of the past. Our decision was based on their resistance to past policies. But whether this decision can be implemented will ultimately depend on the action of leaders at all levels, including those present today and those who are not. Take for example the question of reliance on the masses. One way is to implement the mass line. Another way is not to implement the mass line. It must by no means be taken for granted that everything which is written down in our resolutions will be implemented by all our Party committees and all our comrades. There will always be some who are unwilling to do so. Things are perhaps better than in the past, since in the past we had no such publicly taken decisions. Furthermore, there are organizational guarantees for the implementation of these decisions. This time our organization has undergone some changes. The adjustments in the full and alternate membership of the Politburo, in the Secretariat and in the membership of the Standing Committee have guaranteed the implementation of the Decision and Communiqué of the Central Committee.

Comrades who have made mistakes should always be offered a way out. They should be allowed to correct their mistakes. You should not first take the view that they have made mistakes and then deny them the chance to correct them. Our policy is 'punish first offences to avoid their recurrence and cure the disease to save the patient', 'first watch and then help', and 'unity–criticism–unity'. Do we have a party outside our Party? I think that we do, and that we have factions inside the Party. We used to criticize the Kuomintang, who said: 'No party outside the Party and no factions inside the Party.' Some people put it, 'No party outside the Party is autocracy; no factions inside the Party is nonsense.' The same applies to us. You may say that there are no factions in our Party, but there are. For instance, there are two factions as regards attitude toward the mass movements. It is just a question of which faction is the majority and which is the minority. If we had delayed holding this meeting a few months longer, things would have been in much more of a mess. So it is a good thing that this meeting was held. It has produced results.

20 Talk at the Report Meeting
24 October 1966

The Chairman said: 'What is there to be frightened of? Have you read the brief report by Li Hsüeh-feng[1]? His two children ran off and when they came back they gave Li Hsüeh-feng a lecture. "Why are you old leaders so frightened of the Red Guards? They haven't beat you up and yet you just won't examine yourselves." Wu Hsiu-ch'üan has four children and they all belong to different factions and lots of their school-mates go to his home, sometimes ten or more at a time. When you have had more contact with them then you realize there is nothing to be afraid of; instead you think they are quite lov-able. If one wants to educate others the educationist should first be educated. You are not clear-headed and dare not face the Red Guards, nor speak the truth to the students; you act like officials and big shots. First of all you don't dare to see people and then you don't dare to speak. You have been making revo-lution for many decades, but the longer you do it the stupider you get. In the letter Shao-ch'i wrote to Chiang Wei-ch'ing, he criticized Chiang Wei-ch'ing* and said that he was stupid, but is he himself any cleverer?'

The Chairman asked Liu Lan-t'ao[2]: 'When you have gone back, what do you have in mind to do?'

Liu replied: 'I first want to go back and have a look.'

The Chairman said: 'When you speak you always mince your words.'

Chairman Mao asked Premier Chou about the progress of the meeting. The Premier said: 'It's almost finished. We will

* First Secretary of the Kiangsu Provincial Committee.

meet for another half-day tomorrow. As for the concrete problems, we can solve them according to basic principles when we get back.'

Chairman Mao asked Li Ching-ch'üan:[3] 'How's Liao Chih-kao* getting on?'

Li replied: 'In the beginning he wasn't very clear, but in the latter part of the meeting he was somewhat better.'

The Chairman said: 'What's all this about being consistently correct? You yourself did a bunk. You were frightened out of your wits and rushed off to stay in the military district. When you get back you must pull yourself together and work properly. It's bad to paste up big-character posters about Liu and Teng in the streets. Mustn't we allow people to make mistakes, allow people to make revolution, allow them to change? Let the Red Guards read *The True Story of Ah Q*.'

The Chairman said: 'The meeting this time is somewhat better. At the last meeting it was all indoctrination and no progress. Moreover we had no experience. Now we have had two months' more experience. Altogether we have had less than five months' experience. The democratic revolution was carried on for twenty-eight years; we made many mistakes and many people died. The socialist revolution has been carried on for seventeen years, but the cultural revolution has only been carried on for five months. It will take at least five years to get some experience. One big-character poster, the Red Guards, the great exchange of revolutionary experience, and nobody – not even I – expected that all the provinces and cities would be thrown into confusion. The students also made some mistakes, but the mistakes were mainly made by us big shots.'

The Chairman asked Li Hsien-nien: 'How did your meeting go today?'

Li replied: 'The Institute of Finance and Economics held an accusation meeting, and I wanted to make a self-examination, but they wouldn't let me speak.'

The Chairman said: 'You should go there again tomorrow and make your examination, otherwise people will say you have done a bunk.'

* First Secretary of the Szechuan Provincial Committee.

Li said: 'Tomorrow I have to go abroad.'

The Chairman said: 'You should also tell them that in the past it used to be San-niang who taught her son.[4] Nowadays it's the son who teaches San-niang. I think you are a bit lacking in spirit.

'If they don't want to listen to your self-examination, you must still go ahead and make one. If they accuse you, you should admit your mistakes. The trouble was stirred up by the Centre, the responsibility rests with the Centre, but the regions also have some responsibility. What I'm responsible for is the division into first and second lines. Why did we make this division into first and second lines? The first reason is that my health is not very good; the second was the lesson of the Soviet Union. Malenkov was not mature enough, and before Stalin died he had not wielded power. Every time he proposed a toast, he fawned and flattered. I wanted to establish their prestige before I died; I never imagined that things might move in the opposite direction.'

Comrade T'ao Chu[5] said: 'Supreme power (*ta ch'üan*) has slipped from your hands.'

The Chairman said: 'This is because I deliberately relinquished it. Now, however, they have set up independent kingdoms; there are many things I have not been consulted about, such as the land problem, the Tientsin speeches, the cooperatives in Shansi, the rejection of investigation and study, the big fuss made of Wang Kuang-mei. All these things should really have been discussed at the Centre before decisions were taken. Teng Hsiao-p'ing never came to consult me: from 1959[6] to the present he has never consulted me over anything at all. In 1962 suddenly the four vice-premiers, Li Fu-ch'un, T'an Chen-lin, Li Hsien-nien and Po I-po[7] came to look me up in Nanking, and afterwards went to Tientsin. I immediately gave my approval, and the four went back again, but Teng Hsiao-p'ing never came. I was not satisfied with the Wuchang Conference; I could do nothing about the high targets. So I went to Peking to hold a conference, but although you had met for six days, you wouldn't let me hold mine even for a single day. It's not so bad that I am not allowed to complete my work, but I don't like being treated as a dead ancestor.

'After the Tsunyi conference the Centre was more concentrated, but after the Sixth Plenum in 1938, Hsiang Ying and P'eng Te-huai* tried to set up an independent kingdom. They didn't keep me informed about any of these things. After the Seventh Congress there was nobody at the Centre. When Hu Tsung-nan marched on Yenan[10] the Centre was divided into two armies; I was in North Shensi with En-lai and Jen Pi-shih;[11] Liu Shao-ch'i and Chu Te were in the north-east. Things were still relatively centralized. But once we entered the cities, we were dispersed, each devoting himself to his own sphere. Especially when the division was made into first and second lines, there was even more dispersal. In 1953, after the financial and economic conference, I told everybody to communicate with one another, to communicate with the Centre and communicate with the regions. Liu and Teng acted openly, not in secret, they were not like P'eng Chen. In the past Ch'en Tu-hsiu, Chang Kuo-t'ao, Wang Ming, Lo Lung-chang, Li Li-san all acted openly; that's not so serious. But Kao Kang, Jao Shu-shih, P'eng Te-huai were two-faced. P'eng Te-huai colluded with them, but I did not know it. P'eng Chen, Lo Jui-ch'ing,[12] Lu Ting-i[13] and Yang Shang-k'un[14] were acting secretly, and those who are secretive will come to no good end. Those who follow the wrong line should reform, but Ch'en, Wang and Li did not reform.'

Chou En-lai remarked: 'Li Li-san did not change his thinking.'

[Chairman Mao resumed:] 'Cliques and factions of whatever description should be strictly excluded. The essential thing is that they should reform, that their ideas should conform, and that they should unite with us. Then things will be all right. We should allow Liu and Teng to make revolution and to reform themselves. You say that I am the kind of person that mixes with thin mud. I am the kind of person that mixes with thin mud. During the Seventh Congress Ch'en Ch'i-han[15] said, one

* The New Fourth Army Incident in Southern Anhwei[8], P'eng's Hundred Regiments Offensive[9].

shouldn't elect people who have followed Wang Ming's line to the Central Committee. Wang Ming and several others were all elected members of the Central Committee. At present only Wang Ming has left, the others are all still here! Lo Fu is no good. I have a favourable impression of Wang Chia-hsiang,[16] for he approved of the battle at Tungku.[17] During the Ningtu conference,[18] Lo Fu wanted to expel me, but Chou and Chu did not agree. During the Tsunyi Conference he played a useful role, and at that time one couldn't have got by without them.[19] Lo Fu was obstinate. Comrade Shao-ch'i opposed them, and Nieh Jung-chen[20] also opposed them. We shouldn't condemn Liu Shao-ch'i out of hand. If they have made mistakes they can change, can't they? When they have changed it will be all right. Let them pull themselves together, and throw themselves courageously into their work. This meeting was held at my suggestion, but the time has been so short that I don't know whether things are clear or not. Still, it may be better than the last meeting. I had no idea that one big-character poster, the Red Guards and big exchange of revolutionary experience would have stirred up such a big affair. Some of the students did not have a terribly good family background, but were our own family backgrounds all that good? Don't enlist deserters and turncoats. I myself have many right-wing friends such as Chou Ku-ch'eng and Chang Chih-chung.[21] Will it do not to have a few right-wing contacts? How can one be so pure? To enter into contact with them is to investigate and study them, and understand their behaviour. The other day on the T'ien An Men I deliberately drew Li Tsung-jen[22] over towards me. It's better not to give this fellow a post; it's better for him not to have any position or power. Do we want to have democratic parties? Can't we have just one party? The Party organizations in the schools shouldn't be restored too early. After 1957, the Party added many new members; Chien Po-tsan, Wu Han, Li Ta were all Party members. Were they all so good? Are the democratic parties all so very bad? I think the democratic parties are better than P'eng, Lo, Lu and Yang. We still want the democratic parties, the Political Consultative Conference; we should explain this clearly to the Red Guards. The

Chinese democratic revolution was started by Sun Yat-sen. At that time there was no Communist Party. Under the leadership of Sun Yat-sen, they fought against K'ang, Liang,[23] and the imperial system. This year makes the hundredth anniversary of Sun Yat-sen's birth. How shall we celebrate it? We should discuss this with the Red Guards, and we should hold commemorative meetings. The division which I introduced into first and second lines has led to the opposite result.'

Comrade K'ang Sheng interrupted: 'The political report at the Eighth Congress contains the theory of the disappearance of classes.'

[Chairman Mao replied:] 'I read the report, and it was passed by the congress; we cannot make those two – Liu and Teng – solely responsible.

'Factories and villages should be dealt with by stages and in batches. Go back and clarify the thinking of your fellow-students in the provinces and municipalities, and hold good meetings. Find a quiet place in Shanghai in which to meet. If the students stir things up, let them. We have met for seventeen days, and it has been worth while. As Lin Piao says, we should do careful political and ideological work among them. In 1936 Stalin talked about the elimination of class struggle, but in 1939 he carried out another purge of counter-revolutionaries. Wasn't that class struggle too?

'When you go back you should pull yourselves together and do your work well. Who then can overthrow you?'

21 Talk at the Central Work Conference
25 October 1966

I have just a few words to say about two matters.

For the past seventeen years there is one thing which in my opinion we haven't done well. Out of concern for state security and in view of the lessons of Stalin in the Soviet Union, we set up a first and second line. I have been in the second line, other comrades in the first line. Now we can see that wasn't so good; as a result our forces were dispersed. When we entered the cities we could not centralize our efforts, and there were quite a few independent kingdoms. Hence the Eleventh Plenum carried out changes. This is one matter. I am in the second line, I do not take charge of day-to-day work. Many things are left to other people so that other people's prestige is built up, and when I go to see God there won't be such a big upheaval in the State. Everybody was in agreement with this idea of mine. It seems that there are some things which the comrades in the first line have not managed too well. There are some things I should have kept a grip on which I did not. So I am responsible, we cannot just blame them. Why do I say that I bear some responsibility?

First, it was I who proposed that the Standing Committee be divided into two lines and that a secretariat be set up. Everyone agreed with this. Moreover I put too much trust in others. It was at the time of the Twenty-three Articles that my vigilance was aroused.[1] I could do nothing in Peking; I could do nothing at the Centre. Last September and October I asked, if revisionism appeared at the Centre, what could the localities do?[2] I felt that my ideas couldn't be carried out in Peking. Why was the criticism of Wu Han initiated not in Peking but in Shanghai?

Because there was nobody to do it in Peking. Now the problem of Peking has been solved.

Second, the Great Cultural Revolution wreaked havoc after I approved Nieh Yüan-tzu's big-character poster in Peking University, and wrote a letter to Tsinghua University Middle School, as well as writing a big-character poster of my own entitled 'Bombard the Headquarters'.[3] It all happened within a very short period, less than five months in June, July, August, September and October. No wonder the comrades did not understand too much. The time was so short and the events so violent. I myself had not foreseen that as soon as the Peking University poster was broadcast, the whole country would be thrown into turmoil. Even before the letter to the Red Guards had gone out, Red Guards had mobilized throughout the country, and in one rush they swept you off your feet. Since it was I who caused the havoc, it is understandable if you have some bitter words for me. Last time we met I lacked confidence and I said that our decisions would not necessarily be carried out. Indeed all that time quite a few comrades still did not understand things fully, though now after a couple of months we have had some experience, and things are a bit better. This meeting has had two stages. In the first stage the speeches were not quite normal, but during the second stage, after speeches and the exchange of experience by comrades at the Centre, things went more smoothly and the ideas were understood a bit better. It has only been five months. Perhaps the movement may last another five months, or even longer.

Our democratic revolution went on for twenty-eight years, from 1921 to 1949. At first nobody knew how to conduct the revolution or how to carry on the struggle; only later did we acquire some experience. Our path gradually emerged in the course of practice. Did we not carry on for twenty-eight years, summarizing our experience as we went along? Have we not been carrying on the socialist revolution for seventeen years, whereas the Cultural Revolution has been going on for only five months? Hence we cannot ask comrades to understand so well now. Many comrades did not read the articles criticizing Wu Han last year and did not pay much attention to them. The articles criticizing the film *The Life of Wu Hsün* and studies of the novel *Dream of the Red Chamber* could not be grasped if taken separately, but only if taken as a whole. For this I am responsible. If you take them separately it is like treating only the head when you have a headache and treating only the feet when they hurt, the problem cannot be solved. During the first several months of this Great Cultural Revolution – in January, February, March, April and May – articles were written and the Centre issued directives, but they did not arouse all that much attention. It was the big-character posters and onslaughts of the Red Guards which drew your attention, you could not avoid it because the revolution was right on top of you. You must quickly summarize your experience and properly carry out political and ideological work. Why are we meeting again after two months? It is to summarize our experience and carry out political and ideological work. You also have a great deal of political and ideological work to do after you go back. The Political Bureau, the provincial committees, the regional committees and county committees must meet for ten days or more and thrash out the problems. But they mustn't think that everything can be cleared up. Some people have said, 'We understand the principles, but when we run up against concrete problems we cannot deal with them properly.' At first I could not understand why, if the principles were clear, the concrete problems could not be dealt with. I can see some reason for this: it may be that political and ideological work has not been done properly. When you went back after our last meeting some places did not find time to hold proper meetings. In Honan there were ten secretaries. Out of the ten there were seven or eight who were receiving people. The Red Guards rushed in and caused havoc. The students were angry, but they did not realize it and had not prepared themselves to answer questions. They thought that to make a welcoming speech lasting a quarter of an hour or so would do. But the students were thoroughly enraged. The fact that there were a number of questions which they could not immediately answer put the secretaries on the defensive. Yet this defensive attitude can be changed, can be transformed so that they take the initiative.

Hence my confidence in this meeting has increased. I don't know what you think. If when you go back you do things according to the old system, maintaining the status quo, putting yourself in opposition to one group of Red Guards and letting another group hold sway, then I think things cannot change, the situation cannot improve. But I think things can change and things can improve. Of course we shouldn't expect too much. We can't be certain that the mass of central, provincial, regional, and county cadres should all be so enlightened. There will always be some who fail to understand, and there will be a minority on the opposite side. But I think it will be possible to make the majority understand.

I have talked about two matters. The first concerns history. For seventeen years the two lines have not been united. Others have some responsibility for this, so have I. The second issue is the five months of the Great Cultural Revolution, the fire of which I kindled. It has been going on only five months, not even half a year, a very brief span compared to the twenty-eight years of democratic revolution and the seventeen years of socialist revolution. So one can see why it has not been thoroughly understood and there were obstacles. Why hasn't it been understood? In the past you have only been in charge of industry, agriculture and communications and you have never carried out a Great Cultural Revolution. You in the Foreign Affairs Ministry and the Military Affairs Committee are the same. That which you never dreamed of has come to pass. What's come has come. I think that there are advantages in being assailed. For so many years you had not thought about such things, but as soon as they burst upon you, you began to think. Undoubtedly you have made some mistakes, some mistakes of line, but they can be corrected and that will be that! Whoever wants to overthrow you? I don't, and I don't think the Red Guards do either. Two Red Guards said to Li Hsüeh-feng: 'Can you imagine why our elders are so frightened of the Red Guards?' Then there were Wu Hsiu-ch'üan's four children who belonged to four different factions. Some of their school-friends went to his home, several dozen at a time, and this happened quite a few times. I think that there are advantages in making contact in small groups.

Another method is to have big meetings, 1,500,000 meeting for several hours. Both methods serve a purpose.

There have been quite a few brief reports presented at this meeting. I have read nearly all of them. You find it difficult to cross this pass and I don't find it easy either. You are anxious and so am I. I cannot blame you, comrades, time has been so short. Some comrades say that they did not intentionally make mistakes, but did it because they were confused. This is pardonable. Nor can we put all the blame on Comrade Shao-ch'i and Comrade Hsiao-p'ing. They have some responsibility, but so has the Centre. The Centre has not run things properly. The time was so short. We were not mentally prepared for new problems. Political and ideological work was not carried out properly. I think that after this seventeen-day conference things will be a bit better.

Does anyone else want to speak? I guess that's all for today. The meeting is adjourned.

22 Talk at a Meeting of the
Central Cultural Revolution Group
9 January 1967

At the *Wen-hui-pao* the leftists have now seized power.[1] They rebelled on the fourth. The *Liberation Daily* also rebelled on the sixth. This is the right direction. I have read all three editions of the *Wen-hui-pao* since the seizure of power. They reprinted some articles by Red Guards. Some of them are good and should be reprinted elsewhere. On the fifth the *Wen-hui-pao* issued 'A Letter to the People of the Whole City'. The *People's Daily* should reprint it[2], and the radio stations should broadcast it. Internal rebellions are fine. In a few days we can make a general report on them. This is one class overthrowing another. This is a great revolution. Many papers in my opinion would be better closed down. But newspapers must still come out. The question is by whom they are brought out. It is good that the *Wen-hui-pao* and the *Liberation Daily* have changed management. As soon as they come out these two papers will certainly influence East China and every province and city in the country.

Before you make a revolution, you must first create public opinion. 'June First' was when power was seized in the *People's Daily*. The Centre sent a work team and put out the editorial 'Sweep Away All Monsters and Demons'. I do not agree with the wholesale replacement of the staff of the *People's Daily*, but it had to be taken over. T'ang P'ing-shu replaced Wu Leng-hsi[3]. At first the masses were distrustful because the *People's Daily* had deceived people in the past, and what's more it had issued no statement. The seizure of power in two newspapers is a national question and we should support their rebellion.

Our newspapers should reprint Red Guard articles. They are very well written whereas our stuff is utterly lifeless. The Propaganda Department of the Central Committee can be done away with, though those people can continue to eat there. There are many things which the Propaganda Department and the Ministry of Culture were unable to cope with. Even you (*pointing to Comrade Ch'en Po-ta*) and I could not cope with them. But when the Red Guards came they were immediately brought under control.

The upsurge of revolutionary power in Shanghai has brought hope to the whole country. It cannot fail to influence the whole of East China and all provinces and cities in the country. 'A Letter to the People of the Whole City' is a rare example of a good article. It refers to the city of Shanghai but the problem it discussed is of national significance.

In making revolution these days people demand this and that. When we made revolution from 1920 onwards we set up first the Youth League and then the Communist Party. We had no funds, no printing press, no bicycles. When we ran newspapers we were very friendly with the workers and chatted with them as we edited articles.

We should establish links with all sorts of people, left, right and centre. I have never agreed with a unit being all that pure in its approach. (*Someone responded: 'Wu Leng-hsi's lot are now very comfortable. They have put on weight.'*) We have allowed Wu Leng-hsi to become too comfortable. I am not in favour of their dismissal. Let them remain at their posts to be supervised by the masses.

When we started to make revolution it was opportunism which we met with, not Marxism–Leninism. When I was young I hadn't even read the *Communist Manifesto*.

We must speak of grasping revolution and promoting production. We must not make revolution in isolation from production. The conservative faction do not grasp production. This is a class struggle. You must not believe that 'When Chang the Butcher is dead, we'll have to eat pork bristles and all', or that we can do nothing without them. Don't believe that sort of rubbish.

23 Talks at Three Meetings with Comrades Chang Ch'un-ch'iao and Yao Wen-yüan

February 1967

Chairman Mao invited Comrades Chang Ch'un-ch'iao and Yao Wen-yüan to come to Peking from 12 to 18 February, and met them three times within a week. Even before they had arrived at the airport the Chairman inquired whether they had arrived or not, and when the airport comrades said they would soon be there, the Chairman waited for them in the doorway. They had no sooner arrived than the Chairman asked, 'What is this with the First, Second and Third Regiments? They have come here making accusations against you.'[1]

(1) **The question of the Three-way Alliances.** The Chairman said that for the purpose of seizing power the Three-way Alliances were essential.[2] Fukien, Kweichow and Inner Mongolia did not present big problems, though there might be a little disorder there. In Shansi at present 53 per cent were revolutionary masses, 27 per cent army, and 20 per cent cadres from various organs. Shanghai ought to learn from them. The January Revolution had succeeded, but February, March and April were more crucial, more important. The Chairman said: 'The slogan of "Doubt everything and overthrow everything" is reactionary. The Shanghai People's Committee demanded that the Premier of the State Council should do away with all heads. This is extreme anarchism, it is most reactionary. If instead of calling someone the "head" of something we call him "orderly" or "assistant", this would really be only a formal change. In reality there will still always be "heads". It is the content which matters.

'There is a slogan in Honan, "The present-day proletarian

dictatorship must be completely changed." This is a reactionary slogan.'

(2) On the Shanghai People's Commune. The Chairman said: 'With the establishment of a people's commune, a series of problems arises and I wonder whether you have thought about them. If the whole of China sets up people's communes, should the People's Republic of China change its name to "People's Commune of China"? Would others recognize us? Maybe the Soviet Union would not recognize us whereas Britain and France would. And what would we do about our ambassadors in various countries? And so on. There is another series of problems which you may not have considered. Many places have now applied to the Centre to establish people's communes. A document has been issued by the Centre saying that no place apart from Shanghai may set up people's communes. The Chairman is of the opinion that Shanghai ought to make a change and transform itself into a revolutionary committee or a city committee or a city people's committee.

'Communes are too weak when it comes to suppressing counter-revolution. People have come and complained to me that when the Bureau of Public Security arrest people, they go in the front door and out the back.

'The controlling organs in schools can become cultural revolutionary committees or cultural revolutionary leading teams.'

(3) The Central Committee's Directive on the Cultural Revolution (The Urgent Directive).[3] The Chairman said: 'I have read it and it is very well-written – it is imbued with the spirit of rebellion. The last point says, "We will take the necessary steps." If that meeting is held to bombard Chang Ch'un-ch'iao we will certainly take the necessary steps and arrest people.'

(4) [Issues outstanding]. There are a number of accounts still outstanding which must be settled later. First, the demand made to the Premier by the Municipal People's Committee; second, the question of the Red Revolutionaries; third, the broadening of the revolution to oppose the military seizure of the radio stations; fourth, the opposition to military control at Lunghua Airfield.[4]

(5) [Other matters.] There is a quotation which is currently used a great deal: 'The world is ours.' This was said by the Chairman in 1920.[5] He can't altogether remember it himself and it should not be used in future.

In future do not say: 'Overthrow the diehards who persist in following the reactionary line.' Say rather: 'Overthrow those in authority taking the capitalist road.'

The Chairman asked: 'Is T'ungchi University still at the stations and docks?'[6] Comrade Chang Ch'un-ch'iao replied: 'They still are.' The Chairman then asked: 'Were they still there when you came?' Chang Ch'un-ch'iao replied: 'I'm not sure.' The Chairman said: 'That's excellent. In the past the students had not really united with the workers. Only now have they really united with them.'

[Chairman Mao said:] 'I've read Liu Shao-ch'i's *How to be a Good Communist*[7] several times. It is anti-Marxist–Leninist. Our method of struggle should now be on a higher level. We shouldn't keep on saying, "Smash their dogs' heads, down with XXX." I think that university students should make a deeper study of things and choose a few passages to write some critical articles about.'

The people in literature and the arts should return to their own units to carry out the Cultural Revolution.

[The Chairman remarked:] 'The *Wen-hui-pao* has done very well. I completely agree with their point of view on the struggle with neighbourhood cadres and I support them.' Comrade Chang Ch'un-ch'iao said: 'The *Wen-hui-pao* exerts a lot of pressure.' The Chairman said: 'We must support them.'

24 Address at the Opening Session of the Ninth National Congress of the Chinese Communist Party

1 April 1969

Comrades! The Ninth Congress of the Chinese Communist Party is now in session. (*Long and enthusiastic applause. Delegates shout: 'Long live Chairman Mao! A long, long life to Chairman Mao!'*)

I hope that this will be a good congress, a congress of unity, a congress of victory (*enthusiastic applause and cheers*).

Since the foundation of our Party in 1921, forty-eight years have already passed by. At the First Congress there were only twelve delegates. Two of them are here. One is Old Tung [Pi-wu] and one is me (*enthusiastic applause*). Quite a few have sacrificed their lives: the Shantung delegates Wang Chin-mei and Teng En-ming, the Hupei delegate Ch'en T'an-ch'iu, the Hunan delegate Ho Shu-heng, the Shanghai delegate Li Han-chün – all these laid down their lives, while four others rebelled and became traitors: Ch'en Kung-po, Chou Fo-hai[1], Chang Kuo-t'ao[2] and Liu Jen-ch'ing.[3] The latter two are still alive. There was another delegate called Li Ta[4] who died two years ago. At that time there were only a few dozen party members in the whole country and the majority of these were intellectuals. Later the Party developed. The number of delegates attending the First, Second, Third and Fourth Congresses was very small, from ten to twenty or from twenty to thirty. The Fifth Congress was held in Wuhan. The number of delegates was somewhat larger, several hundred. The Sixth Congress was held in Moscow. There were several dozen delegates, Comrade En-lai and Comrade [Liu] Po-ch'eng participated. The Seventh Congress was held in Yenan. It was a congress of unity, for there were divisions in the Party then too, caused by the mistakes of Ch'ü Ch'iu-pai, Li Li-san and Wang Ming – especially the Wang Ming Line. There were those who were against the election to the Central Committee of comrades who followed the Wang Ming Line. We did not agree and persuaded people to elect their delegates. The result? The result was that there were only a few who were no good. Wang Ming fled abroad to oppose us. Li Li-san was also no good. Chang Wen-t'ien and Wang Chia-hsiang committed mistakes. There were only these few. As for the rest of them, such as Liu Shao-ch'i, P'eng Chen and Po I-po, we did not know that they were bad. We were not clear about their political history.

From the Eighth Congress up to now we have become more clear about them. We are clearer about their political line, their organizational line, and their ideology. Therefore we hope that this Congress will become a congress of unity (*enthusiastic applause and cheers*). Can we win victory on the basis of this unity? Can this Congress become a congress of victory? After the Congress, can we win still greater victories throughout the country? I think we can. I think this will be a congress of unity and a congress of victory (*enthusiastic applause*). After the Congress we can win still greater victories throughout the country. (*Prolonged enthusiastic applause and shouts of 'Long live Chairman Mao! A long, long life to Chairman Mao! May Chairman Mao live for ever!'*)

25 Talk at the First Plenum of the Ninth Central Committee of the Chinese Communist Party*
28 April 1969

What I am going to say is old stuff with which you are all familiar. There is nothing new. I am simply going to talk about unity. The purpose of uniting is to win still greater victories.

The Soviet revisionists now attack us. Some Tass broadcast or other, the Wang Ming material,[1] and the long screed in *Kommunist* all say we are no longer a party of the proletariat, and call us a 'petit-bourgeois party'. They say we have imposed a monolithic order and have returned to the time of the bases, which means we have retrogressed. What is this thing they call becoming monolithic? They say it is a military–bureaucratic system. According to Japanese terminology it is a 'system'. In Soviet vocabulary it is a 'military–bureaucratic dictatorship'. When they see there are many military men in our lists of personnel they call us 'military'. As for the 'bureaucratic' part, I suppose they mean the batch of 'bureaucrats' comprising me, En-lai, K'ang Sheng and Ch'en Po-ta. In a word those of you who are not military are all supposed to belong to a bureaucratic network, and we are collectively called a 'military bureaucratic dictatorship'. I say let them talk. They can say what they want. But their words have one characteristic: they avoid branding us as a bourgeois party, instead they label us a 'party of the petit bourgeoisie'. We, on the other hand, say that they are a bourgeois dictatorship, and are restoring the dictatorship of the bourgeoisie.

If we are to speak of victory we must guarantee that under the leadership of the proletariat we unite the broad masses of

*Edited from a tape recording; not examined by the Chairman.

the people to win victory. The socialist revolution must still be continued. There are still things in this revolution which have not been completed and must still be continued: for example struggle–criticism–transformation. After a few years maybe we shall have to carry out another revolution.

Several of our old comrades have been to the factories for a while to see for themselves. I hope that in future you people will also go down to have a look when the opportunity arises. You should study the problems of various factories. It seems essential that the Great Proletarian Cultural Revolution should still be carried out. Our foundation has not been consolidated. According to my own observation I would say that, not in all factories, nor in an overwhelming majority of factories, but in quite a large majority of cases the leadership is not in the hands of true Marxists, nor yet in the hands of the masses of the workers. In the past the leadership in the factories was not devoid of good men; there were good men. Among the Party committee secretaries, assistant secretaries and committee members there were good men. There were good men among the branch secretaries. But they followed the old line of Liu Shao-ch'i. They were all for material incentives, they put profits in command and did not promote proletarian politics. Instead they operated a system of bonuses, etc. There are now some factories which have liberated them and have included them in the leadership based on the Triple Alliance. Some factories still have not done so. But in the factories there are indeed bad people, for example in the Seventh of February works, which is the railway locomotive and carriage repair works at Ch'ang-hsin-tien. This is a big factory with 8,000 workers and several tens of thousands if you include their families. In the past the Kuomintang had nine district branches there, the *San-min chu-i* Youth League[2] had three organizations and eight so-called special duty organs. Of course, careful analysis is called for because in those days it wouldn't do to refuse to join the Kuomintang! Some of them are old workers. Are you going to get rid of all the old workers? That won't do! You should distinguish the serious cases from the trivial. Some were nominal Kuomintang party members. They had to join the party. It is only necessary to have a talk with them. There were others who had more responsibility, while there was a small minority who were up to their necks in it, and who have done bad things. You must distinguish between their differing circumstances. Among those who have done bad things there should also be distinctions. If they are frank then we should be more lenient. If they resist we should be severe. If they make a proper self-criticism we should let them go on working – of course we shall not give them work in the leadership. If you don't let them work, what will they do at home? What will their sons and daughters do? Besides, most of the old workers are skilled, even if their skill is not of a high order.

I have brought up this instance to illustrate that the revolution has not been completed. Therefore will all the comrades of the Central Committee including alternate members please pay attention: you should undertake very detailed work. It must be done in a detailed manner, it won't suffice to do it sketchily, that will often lead to mistakes. There are some places where too many people have been arrested. This is bad. Why arrest so many? They haven't committed homicide, arson, or poisoning. I say that provided they haven't committed any of these crimes, you shouldn't arrest them. As for those who have committed the mistake of following the capitalist road, still less should they be arrested. Those in factories should be allowed to work, to participate in mass movements. The people who made mistakes have after all made them in the past. Either they joined the Kuomintang or did some bad things – or perhaps they made mistakes in the recent period such as the capitalist roaders. But they should be allowed to join with the masses. It would be bad not to let them join with the masses. Some have been shut up for two years, shut up in 'cattle pens'. They no longer know what is going on in the world. When they come out and people talk to them, they are unable to make sensible replies. They are still speaking the language of two years ago. These people have been divorced from life for two years and they must be helped. Study classes must be organized and you must talk about history with them and tell them about the course of the Great Cultural Revolution during the past two years, and enable them gradually to awaken.

Let us unite for one purpose: to consolidate the proletarian dictatorship. You should see that this is carried out in every factory, village, office and school. At first you shouldn't try to do this too comprehensively. You can do it, but you shouldn't start doing it and then not bother about it. Don't just do it for half a year or even longer, and then have nobody bother with it after that. You should summarize experiences factory by factory, school by school, organ by organ. Thus Comrade Lin Piao's report says that we must do it factory by factory, school by school, commune by commune, Party branch by Party branch, unit by unit. The question of dealing with one Youth League branch after another and with the League as a whole has also been raised.

Another thing which we have talked about before is that we should be prepared for war. We should maintain our preparedness year after year. People may ask, 'Suppose they don't come?' No matter whether they come or not, we should be prepared. Don't expect the Centre to distribute materials even for the manufacture of hand-grenades. Hand-grenades can be made everywhere, in every province. Each province can even make rifles and light weapons. This concerns material preparation, but the most important thing is to be psychologically prepared. To be psychologically prepared means that we must be spiritually prepared to fight. Not only should we on the Central Committee have this psychological preparedness, but we should see to it that the great majority of the people have it too. Those I am talking about do not include the enemies of the dictatorship, such as those landlords, rich peasants, counter-revolutionaries and bad elements, because that lot would be happy to see the imperialists and revisionists attack us. If they attacked us these people suppose that this would turn the world upside down and they would come out on top. We should also be prepared on this score; in the process of the socialist revolution we should also carry through this revolution.

Others may come and attack us but we shall not fight outside our borders. We do not fight outside our borders. I say we will not be provoked. Even if you invite us to come out we will not come out, but if you should come and attack us we will deal with you. It depends on whether you attack on a small scale or a large scale. If it is on a small scale we will fight on the border. If it is on a large scale then I am in favour of yielding some ground. China is no small country. If there is nothing in it for them I don't think they will come. We must make it clear to the whole world that we have both right and advantage on our side. If they invade our territory then I think it would be more to our advantage, and we would then have both right and advantage. They would be easy to fight since they would fall into the people's encirclement. As for things like aeroplanes, tanks and armoured cars, everywhere experience proves that they can be dealt with.

Is it not true that in order to win victory we must have more people? People from all walks of life, no matter on which mountain-top or in which province they are, whether they are in the north or the south. Which is better, to unite more people or less people? It is always better to unite more people. Some people's opinion differs from ours, but this is not a case of relationship between us and the enemy. I do not believe, to put it in concrete terms, that the relationship between Yang Te-chih and Wang Hsiao-yü[3] is of the latter kind. Is the relationship between you two one between us and the enemy, or is it a relationship among the people? In my opinion it is merely a quarrel among the people. The Centre is also rather bureaucratic; it did not pay much attention to you. Neither did you bring it to the Centre for discussion. Such a big province as Shantung has contradictions among the people. Don't you think you should take this opportunity to talk it over? I think that in East China too there is this problem of contradictions among the people. This is also the case in Shansi. You support one faction, I support another, but what is the necessity for this incessant quarrelling? There are also problems in Yünnan, Kweichow and Szechuan. Every place has a certain number of problems, but things are much better than last year and the year before. You, comrade, aren't you called Hsü Shih-yu[4]? The year before last when we were in Shanghai things were really terrible, in July, August and September. Now life is after all a bit better. I am talking about the overall situation. In that Nanking of yours there emerged a so-called 'Red Headquarters'. Work was done and as a result they decided to cooperate, didn't they? Didn't the 'August 27th' and the 'Red Headquarters' in the end cooperate?

I believe that the main problem still concerns our work. Haven't I said these two sentences before: the answer to the problem of the localities lies in the army; the answer to the problem of the army lies in political work? You are not implacable enemies in life and death, so why bother about it? And when it comes to personal gratitude or hatred, that is not of such great consequence. In a word there is nothing from either your previous or present lives to make you mortal enemies. You simply clashed, had some difference of opinion, somebody did something like criticizing you or opposing you. You counter-attacked and as a result a contradiction arose. Those opposed to you are not necessarily bad. One of the personalities whom Peking often wanted to overthrow was Hsieh Fu-chih. He later adopted the following method: to all the bodies which wanted to overthrow him he said that there was nothing wrong with them, and those who supported him were not necessarily good.

So what I say is still the same old words, which is nothing other than unite to win greater victories. In this there is concrete content. What are we going to do? And what sort of concrete victories? And how do we go about uniting people?

I have faith in some of the old comrades who have made mistakes in the past. Originally there was a long list of thirty-odd names. We thought that they should all be elected as members of the Politburo. Later someone prepared a shorter list of less than twenty. This time we thought it was too short. The majority are middle-of-the-roaders (*laughter*). Those who oppose both the long list and the short list advocate a medium list of between twenty and thirty. So the only thing to do was to elect representatives. This is not to say that the candidate members of the Central Committee are not as good as full members or Politburo members in respect of their political level, working ability, moral and intellectual qualities; this isn't the question at all. There is something unfair here. You may say that it is quite fair; I think it is not so fair, not so just. Everyone should be both prudent and cautious, no matter whether you are alternate members of the Central Committee, Central Committee members, Politburo members, you should all be prudent and cautious. Don't be impulsive and forget what's what. Since the time of Marx we have never talked about credit. You are communists, you are that part of the masses which is more conscious, you are that part of the proletariat which is more conscious. So I agree with this slogan, 'First do not fear hardship, second do not fear death'; but not the slogan, 'Even if we get no credit, we are rewarded by hard work; if we get no credit for hard work, we have the reward of being exhausted' (laughter). This slogan is the direct opposite of 'First do not fear hardship, second do not fear death.' You can see how many of us have died. All the old comrades who remain are fortunate to be alive and have survived by chance. Comrade P'i Ting-chün,[5] at that period in Hupei–Hunan–Anhwei, how many people were with you? Afterwards how many were left? At that time there were many people, now not so many remain. At that time after the Kiangsi Soviet, the Chingkangshan Soviet, North-East Kiangsi, West Hunan and Hupei, North Shensi had gone through the fighting there were very great losses, and not many of the old comrades remained. This is what is meant by 'First not fearing hardship, second not fearing death.' For years we did not have any such thing as salaries. We had no eight-tier wage system. We had only a fixed amount of food, three mace of oil and five of salt. If we got 1½ catties of millet, that was great. As for vegetables, how could we get vegetables everywhere the army went? Now we have entered the cities. This is a good thing. If we hadn't entered the cities Chiang Kai-shek would be occupying them. But it is also a bad thing because it caused our Party to deteriorate. So there are some foreigners and journalists who say our Party is being rebuilt. We raise this slogan too, but we call it rectification and Party-building. In fact the Party needs to be rebuilt. Every branch needs to be rectified among the masses. They must go through the masses; not just a few Party members but the masses outside the Party must participate in meetings and in criticism. Individuals who are no good should be persuaded to get out of the Party, to withdraw. A very small minority may have to be disciplined. Isn't this laid down in the Party Constitution? It also has to be passed by the Party branch congress and approved by the superior level. In a word we must use prudence. This must be done, it certainly had to be done, but it must be done prudently.

This National Congress seems to have been a very good one. In my opinion it has been a congress of unity and of victory. We use the method of issuing communiqués. The foreigners can no longer fish for our news (*laughter*). They say we hold secret meetings. In fact we are both open and secret. I think that the reporters in Peking are not much good. Perhaps we have cleared out most of the traitors and spies who had wormed their way among us. In the past whenever we held a meeting it was immediately leaked out and the Red Guard posters immediately published it. Since Wang [Li], Kuan [Feng], Ch'i [Pen-yü], Yang [Ch'eng-wu], Yü [Li-chin] and Chuan [Ts'ung-pi] fell, they no longer have any more news about the meetings of the Central Committee.

That's more or less that. The meeting is adjourned (*long enthusiastic applause*).

26 Summary of Chairman Mao's Talks with Responsible Comrades at Various Places during his Provincial Tour

From the middle of August to 12 September 1971

Chairman Mao said: I hope that you will practise Marxism and not revisionism; that you will unite and not split; that you will be sincere and open and not resort to plotting and conspiracy.

The correctness or otherwise of the ideological and political line decides everything. When the Party's line is correct, then everything will come its way. If it has no followers, then it can have followers; if it has no guns, then it can have guns; if it has no political power, then it can have political power. If its line is not correct, even what it has it may lose. The line is a net rope. When it is pulled, the whole net opens out.

This Party of ours already has fifty years' history, during which time we have had ten big struggles on the question of our line. During these ten struggles there were people who wanted to split our Party, but none of them were able to do so. This is a question worth studying: such a big country, such a large population, yet no split. We can only say that this means that the Party wants what the people want, and the Party members do not want a split. In view of its past history, the future of the Party is full of hope.

First came Ch'en Tu-hsiu, who went in for right opportunism. After the 'August 7th' Conference of 1927 he organized the 'Leninist left-opposition faction' together with Liu Jen-ching, P'eng Shu-chih and others, and eighty-one of them issued a statement. They aimed to split our Party but they did not succeed. They then fled to the Trotskyites.

Next Ch'ü Ch'iu-pai committed mistakes of line. His people

came across a pamphlet of mine in Hunan which contained my remark, 'Political power comes from the barrel of a gun.' This infuriated them. How could political power possibly come from the barrel of a gun? So they stripped me of my position as alternate member of the Politburo. Later Ch'ü Ch'iu-pai was captured by the Kuomintang, wrote his 'Superfluous Words', betrayed us, and went over to the other side.[1]

After the Sixth Congress of the Party in 1928 Li Li-san started to put on airs. From June to September 1930 he followed his Li-san Line for over three months. He advocated attacks on big cities, and first winning victory in one or several provinces. I did not agree with all this. At the Third Plenum of the Sixth Central Committee Li Li-san fell.

From 1930 to 1931 Lo Chang-lung's rightist faction set up a separate Central Committee and engaged in splitting activity.[2] But they did not succeed either.

The Wang Ming Line had the longest life-span. He had formed a faction in Moscow, and organized the '28½ Bolsheviks'. Relying on the might of the Third International they seized power in the Party and held it for a full four years. Wang Ming called the Fourth Plenum of the Sixth Central Committee in Shanghai, and published his pamphlet, *Fight for the Greater Bolshevization of the Chinese Communist Party,* in which he criticized Li Li-san for not being 'left' enough. He was not satisfied until he had made a clean sweep of the bases, as in the end he practically did. During the four years from 1931 to 1934 I had no voice at all at the Centre.[3] The Tsunyi Conference of January 1935 corrected mistakes of Wang Ming's line and he fell.

During the Long March, after the meeting of the First and Fourth Front Armies, Chang Kuo-t'ao carried out a split and set up a separate Centre, but he did not succeed. Before the Long March the Red Army had 300,000 men. On its arrival in North Shensi only 25,000 remained. In the Central Soviet Area there had been 80,000. Of these only 8,000 arrived in North Shensi. Chang Kuo-t'ao did not want to go to North Shensi and carried out a split. But what way out was there at that time, other than to go to North Shensi? This was a question of political line. Our political line at that time was correct. If we had not gone to North Shensi, how could we have later gone to the North China Region, the East China Region, and the Central China Region, the North-East Region? How could we have built so many bases in the Anti-Japanese War? When we arrived in North Shensi, Chang Kuo-t'ao fled.

After nationwide victory Kao Kang and Jao Shu-shih created an anti-party alliance, with the intention of seizing power, but they did not succeed either.

At the 1959 Lushan Conference P'eng Te-huai colluded with a foreign country to seize power. Huang K'e-ch'eng, Chang Wen-t'ien, Chou Hsiao-chou popped up and opposed the Party. They formed a military club, though they did not discuss military affairs, but said such things as: 'The people's communes were set up too soon,' 'Our gains do not compensate for our losses,' etc. P'eng Te-huai also wrote a letter which was an open declaration of war. His intention was to seize power, but he did not succeed.

Liu Shao-ch'i and his lot also wanted to split the Party, but they did not achieve their ambitions either.

Then came the struggle at the 1970 Lushan Conference.[4]

At the 1970 Lushan Conference they made a surprise attack and carried out underground activity. Why did they not dare to act openly? Clearly they had something to hide. So they first dissembled and then made a surprise attack. They concealed things from three of the five members of the Standing Committee of the Politburo. They also concealed things from the great majority of comrades on the Politburo apart from their own few big generals. These big generals included Huang Yung-sheng, Wu Fa-hsien, Yeh Ch'ün, Li Tso-p'eng, and Ch'iu Hui-tso, as well as Li Hsüeh-feng and Cheng Wei-shan.[5] Before they launched their surprise attack they did not let out a whisper. They caused trouble not merely for a day and a half, but from 23 August right through the 24th and up to midday on the 25th – altogether two days and a half. This kind of behaviour shows that they had some aim in mind! P'eng Te-huai formed a military club and issued a declaration of war. They were not even up to P'eng Te-huai's level. This only shows how low their style of work was.

In my view, behind their surprise attack and their underground activity lay purpose, organization and a programme. Their programme was to appoint a state chairman, and to extol 'genius': in other words, to oppose the line of the Ninth Congress and to defeat the three-point agenda of the Second Plenum of the Ninth Central Committee. A certain person was anxious to become state chairman, to split the Party and to seize power. The question of genius is a theoretical question. Their theory was idealist apriorism. Someone has said that to oppose genius is to oppose me. But I am no genius. I read Confucian books for six years and capitalist books for seven. I did not read Marxist–Leninist books until 1918, so how can I be a genius? Didn't I put circles round those adverbs several times over?[6] The Party Constitution was settled at the Ninth Congress. Why not take a look at it? I wrote 'Some Opinions',[7] which specially criticizes the genius theory, only after looking up some people to talk with them, and after some investigations and research. It is not that I do not want to talk about genius. To be a genius is to be a bit more intelligent. But genius does not depend on one person or a few people. It depends on a party, the party which is the vanguard of the proletariat. Genius is dependent on the mass line, on collective wisdom.

Comrade Lin Piao did not discuss that speech of his[8] with me, nor did he show it to me. When they had something to say they did not disclose it in advance. Probably this is because they thought they had a grip on things and were likely to succeed. But as soon as they were told that their ideas were not acceptable, they became jittery. At first they were as bold as brass, giving the impression they could raze Lushan to the ground or stop the earth revolving. But after a few days they hurriedly withdrew the draft.[9] If it was right, why withdraw it? This shows that they were devoid of ideas and in a panic.

The struggle with P'eng Te-huai at the 1959 Lushan Conference was a struggle between two headquarters. The struggle with Liu Shao-ch'i was also a struggle between two headquarters. The struggle at this Lushan Conference is yet another struggle between two headquarters.

The struggle at Lushan this time was different from the nine previous struggles. On the previous nine occasions we drew some conclusions, while this time we have shielded Vice-Chairman Lin and have not drawn conclusions concerning an individual. He must, of course, assume some responsibility. What are we to do about these people? We should still operate a policy of educating them, that is, 'learning from past mistakes to prevent future ones and curing the disease to save the patient'. We still want to protect Lin.[10] No matter who it is who has made mistakes, it is not a good thing to forget unity and the line. After I return to Peking I must seek them out again to have a talk. If they do not come to see me I will go to see them. Some of them may be saved, others it may not be possible to save. This depends on their actions. They have two possible futures: they may reform or they may not. It is difficult for someone who has taken the lead in committing major errors of principle, errors of line or direction, to reform. Looking back, did Ch'en Tu-hsiu reform? Did Ch'ü Ch'iu-pai, Li Li-san, Lo Chang-lung, Wang Ming, Chang Kuo-t'ao, Kao Kang, Jao Shu-shih, P'eng Te-huai or Liu Shao-ch'i reform? They did not reform.

I spoke to Comrade Lin Piao and some of the things he said were not very accurate. For example he said that a genius only appears in the world once in a few centuries and in China once in a few millennia. This just doesn't fit the facts. Marx and Engels were contemporaries, and not one century had elapsed before we had Lenin and Stalin, so how could you say that a genius only appears once in a few centuries? In China there were Ch'en Sheng and Wu Kuang, Hung Hsiu-ch'üan and Sun Yat-sen,[11] so how could you say that a genius only appears once in a few millennia? And then there is all this business about pinnacles and 'one sentence being worth ten thousand'.[12] Don't you think this is going too far? One sentence is, after all, just one sentence, how can it be worth ten thousand sentences? We should not appoint a state chairman. I don't want to be state chairman. I have said this six times already. If each time I said it I used one sentence, that is now the equivalent of sixty thousand sentences.

But they never listen, so each of my sentences is not even worth half a sentence. In fact its value is nil. It's only Ch'en Po-ta's sentences that are worth ten thousand apiece to them. He talked about 'establishing in a big way', by which he gave the appearance of meaning to establish my prestige.[13] But when you get to the bottom of it, he really meant himself. They also said that the People's Liberation Army was built and led by me, and commanded personally by Lin.[14] It seems that the person who founded it cannot command it! And I did not build it all by myself either.

When it comes to questions of line, questions of principle, I take a firm hold and do not relax my grip. On major questions of principle I do not make concessions. After the Lushan Conference I employed three methods: the first was throwing stones, the second was mixing sand into soil and the third was undermining the wall. I criticized the material produced by Ch'en Po-ta which fooled a great many people. I approved the report of the Thirty-eighth Army and the report of the Tsinan Military Region which opposed arrogance and complacency.[15] Then there was the Military Affairs Committee which held such a long discussion meeting without a word of criticism of Ch'en. I inserted a few critical notes about that in a certain document.[16] My method was to pick up these stones, write a few remarks on them, and let everyone discuss them. This is what I call throwing stones. When soil is too compressed it cannot breathe. If you mix in a little sand, then it can breathe. The staff of the Military Affairs Committee was too uniform in its composition, and needed to have some new names added. This is mixing sand in the soil. The reorganization of the Peking Military Region was undermining the wall.[17]

What is your opinion of the Lushan Conference? For instance, is the Sixth Brief Report of the North China Group really revolutionary, semi-revolutionary or counter-revolutionary? I myself regard it as a counter-revolutionary report.[18] You were all present at the meeting of the ninety-nine, when the Premier made the summing-up speech and the self-examinations of the five big generals were issued, as well as those of big generals Li Hsüeh-feng and Cheng Wei-shan, so that everyone thought that the problem had been solved.[19] But in fact the Lushan affair had not finished, the problem had not been solved. They wanted to suppress it. They did not even let cadres of the rank of head of the General Command and the General Staff departments know about it. This would not do!

What I have been saying are my own personal opinions, which I am giving you informally. I shall not draw formal conclusions now, this must be done by the Central Committee.

*

You should be prudent. First of all the army must be prudent and secondly the regions must be prudent. You must not be arrogant, if you are arrogant you will commit errors. The army must be unified; it must be rectified. I just don't believe that our army could rebel. I just don't believe that you, Huang Yung-sheng, could order the Liberation Army to rebel! Under [each] army are divisions and regiments and the judicial, political and support units. If you try to mobilize the army to do bad things, do you think they will obey you?

You should pay attention to military affairs. You should not only be civil officials but also military officials. Grasping army work means studying the line and rectifying incorrect styles of work. You should not go in for mountain-top-ism or sectarianism, but pay attention to unity. I approve of the army's traditional style of quick and decisive action. But this style cannot be applied to questions of ideology, for which it is necessary to make the facts known and reason with people.

I added my approval to the document of the Canton Military Region on the 'three supports and two militaries'[20]. In order to get people to give it their attention I appended the words, 'To be studied seriously', to the Central Committee's endorsement. Now that the regional Party Committees have been established, they should exercise unified leadership. It would be putting the cart before the horse if the matters already decided by regional Party committees were later turned over to the army Party committees for discussion.

In the past the military training given to our armed forces

included unit-by-unit coaching. From individual coaching to battalion coaching took five to six months. Now that they only go in for civil and not military matters, our army has become a cultural army.

When 'one good' leads 'three goods' perhaps that 'one good' of yours will lead correctly and perhaps it will lead incorrectly.[21] And then there are the congresses of representatives of activists. It is worth studying what their actual effect is. Some are successful, but many are not. This is primarily a question of line. If the line is mistaken then the activists' congress cannot be successful.

'In industry learn from Tach'ing, in agriculture learn from Tachai; let the people of the whole country learn from the PLA.' This is incomplete. We should add, 'Let the PLA learn from the people of the whole country.'

*

You should study the article written by Lenin on the twenty-fifth anniversary of the death of Eugene Pottier. Learn to sing 'The Internationale' and 'The Three Great Rules of Discipline and the Eight Points for Attention'. Let them not only be sung but also explained and acted upon. 'The Internationale' and Lenin's article express throughout a Marxist standpoint and outlook. What they say is that slaves should arise and struggle for truth. There never has been any supreme saviour, nor can we rely on gods or emperors. We rely entirely on ourselves for our salvation. Who has created the world of men? We the labouring masses. During the Lushan Conference I wrote a 700-word article which raised the question of who created history, the heroes or the slaves.[22] 'The Internationale' says we must unite until the day comes when Communism will certainly be realized. If you study Marxism you will see that it teaches unity and not splitting. We have been singing 'The Internationale' for fifty years but people have tried to split our Party ten times. I think it possible that they will do it another ten times, or twenty times, or thirty times. You don't believe it? Maybe you don't but I do. When we reach Communism will there be no struggles? I don't believe that either. When we reach Communism there will still be struggles, but they will be between the new and the old, the correct and the incorrect, that is all. After tens of millennia have passed by, the incorrect will still be no good and will fail.

The Three Great Rules of Discipline and the Eight Points for Attention must be 'remembered clearly, each and every one' and 'the people of the whole country welcome and support them'. Yet there are a few of the rules and points for attention which are not clearly remembered, especially the first of the Three Rules and the first and fifth of the Eight Points. These are not remembered clearly. How fine it would be if they could all be clearly remembered and put into effect. The first of the Three Rules is that in all actions orders must be obeyed, for only if we march in step can we win victory. If we are not in step we cannot win victory. Then there are the first and fifth of the Eight points which say that towards the people, and towards fellow soldiers and subordinates, we should always be polite. We must not put on airs; warlord ways must be rooted out. These are the points of emphasis. If there were no points of emphasis there would be no policy. I hope that we will use the Three Great Rules of Discipline and the Eight Points for Attention to educate the army, educate the cadres, educate the masses, educate the Party members and the people.

*

The Lushan Conference called for the study of books by Marx and Lenin.[23] I hope you will read more books from now on. It just won't do if high-ranking cadres don't even know what is materialism and what is idealism. What do we do if we find the books of Marx and Lenin difficult? We can ask a teacher to help us. You are all secretaries, but you ought to be students too. I myself become a student every day. I read two volumes of *Reference Material*[24] daily, and that's why I know a little about international affairs.

I never approved of one's wife becoming the office manager in one's own work unit. Over at Lin Piao's, it is Yeh Ch'ün who manages his office. When the four of them want to ask Lin Piao about anything they have to go through her. In doing any work one should do it oneself and read and endorse papers oneself. One should not rely on one's secretary. One shouldn't let one's secretary wield so much power. My secretary is only responsible for receiving and dispatching papers. I select the documents myself, read them myself, and when something has to be done I do my own writing so that no mistakes are made.

*

The Cultural Revolution dragged out Liu Shao-ch'i, P'eng, Lo, Lu, and Yang. This was a big achievement. There were also some losses. Some good cadres have still not been able to re-emerge. The great majority of our cadres are good. The bad ones are a very small minority. Those who have been cleared out only comprise one per cent, while those who have been suspended are less than three per cent. The bad ones must be given appropriate criticism. The good ones must be praised, though not to the skies. It does a person under thirty no good at all if you call him a 'super-genius'. At the recent Lushan Conference some comrades were deceived and hoodwinked. The problem does not lie in you but in Peking. It does not matter if you have made mistakes. Our Party has a rule that those who made mistakes should first make a self-examination, and then they should be permitted to correct their mistakes.

We must take care to educate people in our ideological and political line. Our principle must still be 'learning from past mistakes to avoid future mistakes', and 'curing the disease to save the patient'. Unite to win still greater victories.

Notes

Text 1

1. The term 'centre' (*chung-yang*) in Chinese Communist parlance has a considerable range of meanings. In many instances, it is an abbreviation for 'Central Committee' (of the Chinese Communist Party), but it is also used more narrowly to identify an organ such as the Politburo or the Standing Committee of the Politburo (or perhaps even its Chairman), acting on behalf of the central Party apparatus. It is also employed more broadly to designate the whole range of decision-making bodies in Peking, including the state bureaucracy as well as the Party. In this volume, it is generally translated simply as 'Centre' (with a capital when it means a central authority, and with a small letter when it means the geographical centre as opposed to the regions), leaving it to the reader to decide on its exact meaning from the context.

2. Hsiao Ch'u-nü, despite his lack of formal education, had audited courses at a university in Wuhan, where he taught at a school and edited a newspaper. He participated actively in Communist Party and Kuomintang work at the time of the first united front of 1924–7, serving as political instructor at the Whampoa Military Academy, and also working with Mao Tse-tung in the Peasant Movement Training Institute in the summer of 1926. He was killed by the Kuomintang in Shanghai in April 1927.

3. i.e. since the beginning of the world, as described in traditional Chinese cosmogony.

4. The 'three stabilizations' – literally, 'three fixed' (*san ting*) – involved fixing quotas for grain production, for compulsory sales to the state by grain producers, and for supply of grain by the state to grain-deficient peasants, and maintaining these unchanged, in so far as possible, for a period of three years.

5. In *Wan-sui* (1969), this point and the following one are inverted.

6. Both the provisional institutions adopted in 1949, and the Constitution of 1954, provided for the existence, side by side with the Communist Party, of a number of minor parties, the most important being the Revolutionary Committee of the Chinese Kuomintang, and the China Democratic League. Though clearly subordinate to the Communist Party, these organizations provided a mechanism for the participation in the political system of groups such as non-communist intellectuals, pre-1949 political officials and military men, 'national bourgeois', etc. For details about their composition and role, see Lyman P. Van Slyke, *Enemies and Friends. The United Front in Chinese Communist History* (Stanford: Stanford University Press, 1968), Chapters 10 and 11.

7. At the first session of the National People's Congress, which adopted the Constitution on 20 September 1954.

8. A long story, the best-known work of Lu Hsün, the greatest Chinese writer of the twentieth century. For an English translation, see *Selected Stories of Lu Hsün* (Peking: Foreign Languages Press, 1960, reprinted 1972), pp. 65–112.

9. Hero of the celebrated novel *Journey to the West,* translated by Arthur Waley under the title *Monkey* (Penguin, 1961).

10. For the context, see D. C. Lau's translation of *Mencius* (Penguin, 1970), p. 201 (Book VII, Part B, Ch. 34).

Text 2

1. In 1898, the Empress Dowager Tz'u-hsi (1835–1908) resumed control of the administration, which she had relinquished to her nephew the Kuang Hsü Emperor in 1889, and crushed the 'Reform Movement'; she encouraged the Boxers in their attacks on foreigners.

2. This passage refers primarily to the defeats suffered by the Chinese Communists in 1933–4, which ultimately led them to abandon their bases in Kiangsi and neighbouring provinces and embark on the Long March. Mao blamed these reverses on the faulty tactics imposed by the Moscow-trained 'Returned Student Faction' in the Chinese Communist Party, and on the Comintern military adviser Otto Braun (Li Te), and their failure to take account of differences between Chinese and Soviet conditions. Lurking in the background is, of course, the memory of the bloody catastrophe to which policies dictated by Stalin had led in 1927.

3. There is a Chinese proverb: 'A half bottle of vinegar shakes; a full bottle does not.' Here, Mao is obviously using this metaphor to indicate that what China needs is a true synthesis of Chinese and

European elements, not simply the juxtaposition of disparate ideas and styles.

4. Traditional Chinese novels, such as *Water Margin, The Romance of the Three Kingdoms*, or the *Dream of the Red Chamber* (translated by David Hawkes under the title *The Story of the Stone,* Penguin, 1973), grew out of the story-teller's art. The chapters therefore tend to be broken at a high point in the action, and to conclude with some such sentence as: 'If you want to know how the hero got out of this fix, read (or listen to) the next instalment.'

5. Literally, to writing eight-legged essays. This highly artificial, stilted form in which candidates in the imperial examinations were obliged to cast their compositions from the fifteenth century onwards, has become a metaphor for pedantry and formalism in general. For Mao's most extensive attack on this vice, see his speech of 8 February 1942, 'Oppose Stereotyped Party Writing', in *Selected Works* (Peking: Foreign Languages Press, 1961–5), Vol. III, pp. 53–68.

Text 3

1. At this time, and earlier, the 'four pests' which the entire population was mobilized to destroy included rats, flies, mosquitoes, and sparrows. The following year, sparrows having been found to play a useful role in controlling insects, they were replaced on the list by bed-bugs.

2. *'Ta-ta yu'*. Mao is here making fun of a characteristic peculiarity of Japanese speakers of Chinese, the repetition of the adjective or adverb.

3. The *mu* or *mou* is a traditional Chinese unit of area, about 0·15 acre.

4. Put forward by Mao in January 1956. For his speech at that time, see H. Carrère d'Encausse and S. Schram, *Marxism and Asia* (Allen Lane, 1969), pp. 291–3.

5. In Text 4, Mao identifies the culprit.

6. This is a quotation from Sun Yat-sen's political testament to his comrades of the Kuomintang.

Text 4

1. Ch'en Tu-hsiu (1879–1942) was Secretary-General of the Chinese Communist Party from its foundation in 1921 until August 1927, when he was made the scapegoat for the failure of Stalin's policies. Prior to his conversion to Communism he had been an eloquent advocate of Western democratic and scientific thought as

the remedy for China's ills. In recent decades, Chinese Communist authors have acknowledged his contribution to the intellectual revolution of the May Fourth period, but have denied that he ever really accepted or understood Marxism. They characterize him as a bourgeois radical who had wormed his way into the Party thanks to the ideological confusion prevailing in the early 1920s. Mao himself, talking to Edgar Snow in 1936, dismissed Ch'en Tu-hsiu as bourgeois not only in his ideas, but in his instinctive reactions: 'Ch'en was really frightened of the workers and especially of the armed peasants. Confronted at last with the reality of armed insurrection, he completely lost his senses. He could no longer see clearly what was happening, and his petty-bourgeois instincts betrayed him into panic and defeat.' (*Red Star over China*, enlarged edition, Penguin, 1972, pp. 190–91).

2. The official view regarding the errors committed by Mao's rivals during the period 1927–35 had been laid down in the 'Resolution on Certain Questions in the History of our Party' adopted by the Central Committee of the Chinese Communist Party in April 1945. The text is included in Volume III of the *Selected Works* (Peking, 1965), pp. 177–220. Since the onset of the Cultural Revolution, the resolution of 1945 has not been considered wholly orthodox, and it no longer appears in the *Selected Works*. As for the three 'left' lines, however, the view put forward by Mao as recently as September 1971 remains basically the same (see below, Text 26). For other statements of the 'Great Leap' period about this question, see Texts 6 and 7.

3. Abram Deborin (1881–1963), a leading Soviet philosopher who stressed the omnipresence of contradictions and the link between dialectics and the natural sciences, was condemned by Stalin in December 1930 for his 'Menshevizing idealism', and subsequently forced to recant.

4. This name is transcribed as 'P'i-k'o-fu', which might be an error for Rykov, though the latter occupied an important position in the Soviet state apparatus rather than in the Comintern. It could also stand for Pieck, or Piatnitsky, who were members of the Secretariat of the Executive Committee of the International in the early 1930s. In any case, Mao's picture of the Comintern leadership is rather approximate, for Bukharin was removed from all work in the International in mid-1929, and Zinoviev had disappeared well before. Regarding the personnel more directly concerned with China, he was better informed. Kuusinen, a member of the Executive Committee and of the Secretariat, was influential in drafting

many Comintern directives on China and on the non-European countries generally. Pavel Mif's title was Deputy Head of the Eastern Secretariat, which Mao calls the Eastern Bureau (*tung-fang pu*), but his main responsibility was China. (There does not seem to have been a separate Far Eastern Department, though details regarding the organization of the Comintern are hard to come by. The above information about Mif is from his biography in *Vidnye Sovetskie Kommunisty – Uchastniki Kitaiskoi Revolyutsii* [Moscow: 'Nauka', 1970], p. 92.)

5. It is hard to guess who the 'good comrade' referred to here might be. Mao speaks of him as if from personal knowledge, but Mao himself did not go abroad until 1949, and of those representatives of the Comintern who had visited China in the 1920s and 1930s, there were few with whom he had come in direct contact, and even fewer of whom he had anything good to say. Because of the way 'XXX' is contrasted with Mif, it is just possible that it stands for Kuusinen, who had attacked Mao and the Chinese very rudely in 1964 (see *Marxism and Asia*, pp. 330–35), so that any favourable comment would have been removed, or made anonymous, by the editors of *Wan-sui* (1969). Perhaps any other Comintern figure, even if known only at second or third hand, would have been imagined by Mao to be more likeable than Pavel Mif, who came to China at the end of 1930 and personally installed as the leaders of the Chinese Communist Party the very 'dogmatists' about whom Mao is complaining here.

6. Wang Ming (pseudonym of Ch'en Shao-yü) (1904–74) was the leading figure in the group of 'Returned Students', trained in Moscow, with whom Mao contended for the leadership of the Chinese Communist Party in the 1930s and 1940s. He resided in the Soviet Union from 1957 until his death; during the Cultural Revolution, he published two vitriolic attacks on Mao (see below, Text 25, note 1).

7. Mao would appear to be concerned here rather with the uniform introduction of a system of education ill-adapted to Chinese rural reality than with the precise length of the primary course, which was not necessarily five years in the 1950s. For a detailed discussion of the educational system, including the curriculum and the length of schooling, see below, Text 10.

8. Kao Kang (*c.* 1902–*c.* 1954) was one of the leaders in setting up the base in Shensi to which Mao Tse-tung and his comrades retreated after the Long March. In the late 1940s, he emerged as the dominant figure in the North-east Region, where he cumulated

all the top Party, government, and army posts. As the leader of China's most highly industrialized area, he played an important role in Peking as well, and in 1952 he became the first Chairman of the State Planning Commission. He was publicly denounced in 1955, and at that time it was stated that he had committed suicide in February 1954. His fall undoubtedly resulted in part from personal rivalries, but it has also been commonly assumed that he was regarded as too close to the Soviets.

9. In the mid-1950s, Chiang Hua was First Secretary of the CCP in Chekiang, and Sha Wen-han was governor of the same province. In December 1957, in the context of the 'anti-rightist' campaign which had begun during the summer, Sha was violently attacked for corruption, immorality, and anti-Party activities, and also for his provincial and sectarian viewpoint, and removed from office. Chiang Hua delivered the main report at the meeting held to denounce Sha and other leading Chekiang officials; he also called for more rapid development in industry and agriculture, and referred to a 'leap' in production. Thus, his attitude towards questions of policy was indubitably correct in Mao's eyes. As the previous sentence, 'Every province now has examples of this' – linking the relationship between Chiang and Sha to the case of Kao Kang – makes plain, Mao is talking here about two things: the correctness or incorrectness of leadership; and loyalty to the nation as a whole rather than to one's own province or region – or to the Soviet Union. The two issues of the tempo of economic development, and of the manner and extent to which decision-making power should be decentralized, were central to the debates on policy going on in the spring of 1958, on the eve of the formal proclamation of the Great Leap Forward at the Second Session of the Eighth Party Congress in May. As Mao makes plain, they had to be fought out in every province, as well as at the national level.

10. The purge of Kao Kang, Jao Shu-shih (c. 1901–   ), First Secretary of the CCP East China Bureau, and seven others in 1955, on the charge of having formed an anti-Party group with the aim of seizing power, was indeed an earthquake – by far the most serious upheaval in the Chinese Communist Party from the Rectification Campaign of 1942–3 to the fall of P'eng Te-huai in 1959.

11. The *Bolshevik* and *True Words* (*Shih Hua*) were theoretical organs edited in the early 1930s by the Moscow-trained leaders of the Chinese Communist Party, which often criticized Mao's guerrilla tactics. Since a complete run of *Shih Hua* is not available,

it is impossible to say which 'five big mistakes' are referred to here.

12. In 1962, Mao put forward a periodization of the history of the Chinese People's Republic which dated the establishment of an independent and creative line for building socialism from 1958, i.e. from the beginning of the Great Leap Forward (Text 8, pp. 176–8). This is complementary rather than contradictory to the statement here; Mao began to sketch out a new policy in 1956, and the process came to fruition in 1958.

13. Mao here confirms that, apart from the terms of the Treaty of Friendship, Alliance and Mutual Assistance signed on 14 February 1950, and the thorny question of the Sino–Soviet border, two main issues on which his position clashed with that of Stalin were the arrangements for the control of the Chinese Eastern Railway, and the joint Sino–Soviet stock companies in certain key industries, both of which gave Moscow a degree of economic and political leverage within China all too reminiscent of the old colonial days.

14. The supplementary agreement of 27 March 1950 between China and the Soviet Union provided for joint-stock companies to develop oil and non-ferrous metals in Sinkiang. There was no provision such as Mao cites, but it was widely believed at the time to contain secret clauses.

15. Here Mao deliberately applies to Stalin the term 'old ancestor' (*lao tsu-tsung*) which was employed in his own youth to designate the Dowager Empress Tz'u-hsi. Clearly he wishes to suggest that these two individuals (both of whom had at one time stood in authority over him) inspired in him a similar mixture of distaste and grudging respect.

16. The Hangchow conference of early January 1958, and the Nanning conference of late January, were attended, like the Chengtu conference at which Mao made this speech, by provincial Party secretaries and some Politburo members; it was at the two January meetings that the Sixty Articles on Work Methods, which constituted the veritable blueprint for the Great Leap Forward, were drafted. (See the text of this document in CB 892, pp. 1–14).

17. The Seventh Congress of the Chinese Communist Party, in April 1945, in fact advocated the establishment of a coalition government with the Kuomintang, as is indicated by the title of Mao Tse-tung's own report on that occasion. ('On Coalition Government', *Selected Works*, III, pp. 255–320.) It did, however, lay the foundations for an effort on the part of the communists, in the new political context which would grow out of Japan's defeat, to establish themselves as a political (as well as a military) force

which would have to be reckoned with. In particular, it marked the formal consecration of the ideological independence and maturity of the Chinese Communist Party by the elevation of 'Mao Tse-tung's Thought' to the status of guide in all the Party's work. (See Liu Shao-ch'i's report on this theme in *Marxism and Asia*, pp. 259–61.)

18. The Ten-Point Programme, or Ten Great Policies, of the CCP for Anti-Japanese Resistance and National Salvation put forward on 15 August 1937 laid down a policy line mid way between the two extremes of excessive secretarianism and abject submission to the Kuomintang. (For the text, see Brandt, Schwartz and Fairbank, *A Documentary History of Chinese Communism*, pp. 242–5.) Wang Ming, who had displayed leftist tendencies in the early 1930s, has been accused since 1945 of rightist and capitulationist errors following his return to China from Moscow in 1937, but I know of no document in sixty points summarizing his views at this time.

19. This refers to Dulles's speech of 28 June 1957, two weeks after the *New York Times* report of 13 June on Mao's February speech.

20. For a brief discussion of the problems raised by the effort to improve agricultural implements and techniques in the course of the Great Leap Forward, with extracts from the 'Opinions' regarding agricultural mechanization adopted at the Chengtu meeting, which spell out some of the implications of what Mao is saying in this paragraph, see Jack Gray, 'The Two Roads: Alternative Strategies of Social Change and Economic Growth in China', in *Authority, Participation, and Cultural Change in China*, pp. 139–43.

21. The expression *chien-t'iao*, 'to carry on a pole over the shoulder', is used here both in a literal sense, to evoke images such as the building of dams by the massive use of labour-power, and as a symbol of traditional Chinese ways of doing things in general. In the remainder of this paragraph, Mao sketches out the approach, characteristic of the Great Leap Forward and of his economic thinking ever since, of 'walking on two legs', i.e. of combining modern and traditional methods.

22. According to Mao's speech of 13 October 1957 (*Wan-sui* (1969), p. 141), 'four, five, eight' was used as shorthand for the goals for grain production originally put forward in point 6 of the Twelve-year Programme for Agricultural Development (see p. 93 and note 4 to Text 3). This called for yields of 400 catties per *mu* in areas north of the Yellow river, 500 catties per *mu* between the Yellow and Huai rivers and 800 catties per *mu* south of the Huai, to be achieved by the end of 1967. In October 1957 Mao still accepted

this target date. Now, although he does not endorse the extreme optimism of the Honan leadership, he has been carried away by enthusiasm for the emerging 'Great Leap' to such an extent as to suggest that it might well be possible to attain these goals in one third to one half of the period previously stipulated. He adds, however, that even if the original schedule were adhered to, China would still have done far better than the Soviet Union. The targets set in 1956 amounted to two or three times existing yields (see above, p. 92).

23. The *chuang-yüan* or 'number one palace graduate' was the highest-ranking successful candidate in the triennial examinations for the *chin-shih* degree (see below, note 18 to Text 10). True beauty, according to this proverb, is rarer still.

24. The 'General Line' for building socialism, symbolized by the four characters *to, k'uai, hao, sheng* (more, faster, better and more economically), had been put forward by Mao in 1956, and has been regarded ever since, both by Mao and by his opponents, as summing up the essence of his approach to economic development. From mid-1956 to mid-1957 it had been seldom mentioned, though not explicitly repudiated; for Mao's resentment at this, see his speech of 22 March 1958, p. 122. In 1958 it burst forth again and became one of the 'Three Red Banners' of the Great Leap.

25. Chou Hsiao-chou (*c.* 1912–   ) was, at this time, First Secretary of the Chinese Communist Party for Hunan Province, and concurrently Political Commissar of the Hunan Military District. At the Eighth Party Congress in September 1956, he had presented a written speech on the strengthening of agricultural cooperatives. During the year 1958, he played an active role in Party affairs, but after the Eighth Plenum in December 1958 he dropped from view, and in 1959 he was relieved of his post as provincial secretary, and purged as a member of the 'anti-Party group' headed by P'eng Te-huai (see below, Texts 6 and 7). This would indicate that, like P'eng, he came to have doubts about the communes, but it was not previously known that Mao had been dissatisfied with his attitude at the time of cooperativization in 1955–6.

26. This presumably stands for Li Ching-ch'üan (1905–   ), ranking Party secretary for Szechuan province (in which the city of Chengtu is located) from 1952 to 1965, and by 1958 the leading figure in the Party organization for the whole of South-West China. At the time when Mao made this speech, his star was definitely on the rise, and in fact Mao's reference, two days later, to Khrushchev as an example of those vigorous elements which come to the Centre from the provinces (see the speech of 22 March 1958, p. 114)

may well be meant as a compliment to Li, who was elected to the Politburo in May 1958 at the Second Session of the Eighth Party Congress. Li Ching-ch'üan's name – assuming that it is he who is meant – would have been omitted by the editors of the 1969 volume because he was attacked and removed during the Cultural Revolution. He reappeared at the Tenth Congress in 1973.

27. The organization of the Party and of the state administration on a regional basis had been abolished in 1954. Regional Party bureaus were publicly re-established only in the early 1960s, but Mao here confirms that they had already been set up in 1958, in the context of the decentralizing policies of the 'Great Leap'.

28. As indicated here, Mao clashed with the Moscow-trained leadership of the Chinese Communist Party in the early 1930s not only on political issues, but on military tactics. For his own criticism of previous errors in this domain, see 'Problems of Strategy in China's Revolutionary War', *Selected Works*, I, pp. 179–249.

29. This remark was actually made by a minor character in Chapter 26 of the *Dream of the Red Chamber*; Wang Hsi-feng said the same thing, in different words, in Chapter 13 (*The Story of the Stone*, pp. 257, 509).

30. I have not been able to find the source of this quotation.

31. For a more extended discussion of why the death of older people is a cause for rejoicing, which reveals the roots of this attitude on Mao's part in the Chinese tradition, see below Text 11, p. 227, and note 40.

32. This dictionary (*Chien-ming che-hsüeh tz'u-tien*) is, in fact, a Chinese translation, first published in 1940, and reprinted in 1949 and 1951 by the San-lien Shu-tien in Peking, of a Soviet reference work, the *Kratkii Filosofskii Slovar'*, by Rozental' and Yudin, which had appeared in Moscow in 1939. I have not been able to find in it the statements quoted by Mao, but he was no doubt correct in his judgement that the Soviet understanding of dialectics in the late 1930s was different from his.

33. Because of the way numbers are written in Chinese, the figure 'twelve' in this sentence could easily be a typographical error for 'ninety-two'. If Mao really meant to say 'twelve', I am unable to identify the source from which he could have taken this theory.

34. *Wan-sui* (1969) has here 'classes' (*chieh-chi*) instead of 'stages' (*chieh-tuan*), but this appears to be a typographical error, for *Wen-hsüan* has 'stages', which makes better sense and is in accord with similar statements in some of Mao's other writings, for example in Text 11, p. 228.

35. The term translated here as 'system' (*hsi-t'ung*) is that commonly used in Chinese communist parlance to refer to one organization or apparatus among many; by 'all the various systems', Mao means the Party apparatus, the state bureaucracy, the PLA, etc.

36. This refers, of course, to the Marxist–Leninist classics, not to the Confucian canon.

37. The 156 key industrial projects scheduled to be built during the first five-year plan, 1953–7, with Soviet aid.

38. The 'emergence of the question of Stalin' refers, of course, to Khrushchev's secret speech of February 1956; the slogan 'oppose adventurism'was the rallying-cry of those who,in 1956–7, opposed Mao's economic policies.(See below, p. 138, his comments on this group, which apparently included many top leaders in the Party.)

39. The meaning here is obviously that Marxism lays down only general historical tendencies, not the precise sequence of events.

40. In the autumn of 1957, during the anti-rightist campaign, ceremonies were held in schools and elsewhere, at which participants swore to give their hearts to the Party.

41. i.e., it is not like some other places of worship where one goes every Sunday out of habit.

42. A celebrated thirteenth-century drama.

43. *ta ming, ta fang, ta-tzu-pao.* The first two phrases (sometimes translated 'great blooming and contending') summarize the slogan of the 'Hundred Flowers' campaign of 1956–7: 'Let a hundred schools of thought contend, let a hundred flowers bloom.' Big-character posters, or wall newspapers, which reached their utmost development during the Cultural Revolution, have long been familiar in China; Mao wrote one as a student at the time of the 1911 revolution.

44. Ch'en Po-ta (1904–   ). Once the leading interpreter of Mao Tse-tung's thought, and Mao's former political secretary, Ch'en rose to high eminence when he became the head of the 'Cultural Revolution Group' under the Central Committee in 1966. He disappeared from the political scene in 1970, in the course of the purge of the 'ultra-leftists'. Whatever his precise role in the events of the Cultural Revolution, he had indeed distinguished himself by his enthusiasm for the 'Paris Commune' model, which Mao repudiated in February 1967. (See the Introduction, and Text 23 below.)

45. In fact, this passage refers to the abandonment of conclusions which are 'antiquated' or no longer 'correspond to historical con-

ditions'. *History of the Communist Party of the Soviet Union* (Moscow, 1954), pp. 553–4.

46. Emperors in traditional China were referred to by their dynastic titles; their names were taboo to such an extent that even the characters composing them could not be used in other contexts.

47. *Ta t'ung* or 'great harmony' is a very ancient utopian vision which has continued to inspire many Chinese thinkers down to the present day. (See, for example, Mao Tse-tung's 'On the People's Democratic Dictatorship', *Selected Works*, Vol. IV, p. 412.) The work on this theme by K'ang Yu-wei, the intellectual leader of the reformers of 1898, has been translated by Laurence Thompson under the title, *Ta T'ung Shu: The One-World Philosophy of Kang Yu-wei* (Allen & Unwin, 1958).

48. Wu Ching-ch'ao, a disciple of Hu Shih and a contributor to his magazine *Tu-li p'ing-lun*, was a Kuomintang civil servant in the 1930s and 1940s.

49. The literary critic Hu Feng, the philosopher Liang Shu-ming, the interpretation of the *Dream of the Red Chamber* by Yü P'ing-po, and the novelist Ting Ling all came under attack in the period 1953–5. (For a general account of the context see Merle Goldman, *Literary Dissent in Communist China* (Cambridge, Mass.: Harvard University Press, 1967), Chapters 6 and 7.) Mao himself was directly involved in several of these campaigns, especially in that against Hu Feng; he also wrote an anonymous editorial in 1951 attacking the film, *The Life of Wu Hsün.* (This campaign is also discussed by Mrs Goldman, *op. cit.,* pp. 89–93.) In 1967, in the course of the Cultural Revolution, Mao's comments on two of these themes were published among the 'Five Militant Documents on Art and Literature', translated in *Peking Review*, No. 23, 1967, pp. 5–8.

50. See the extract from Mao's speech of 7 May 1937, in S. Schram, *The Political Thought of Mao Tse-tung* (Penguin, 1969), p. 226–8.

51. The use of the term 'sprouts' ('*meng-ya*') here echoes the controversy which took place in the 1950s about 'sprouts of capitalism under the Ming dynasty', i.e. as to whether elements of a new social system were developing in the 'feudal' society of China at that time, before the impact of the West.

52. Capital of the Chinese Soviet Republic in 1931–4. The 'mutual aid teams', which were formed both at that time and during the Yenan period, as well as in the early 1950s, represented the lowest stage in the development of agricultural cooperatives.

53. Mao defines these below on p. 216. As can be grasped from

the context, they relate to policies for encouraging the pursuit of individual economic interest at the expense of the collective economy.

54. Chang T'ai-yen (also known as Chang Ping-lin) was an influential intellectual of the early twentieth century, politically radical but conservative in cultural and literary matters.

55. Liu Shih-p'ei (1884–1919) was a scholar active in the revolutionary movement prior to 1911. Thereafter, he became a conservative and an advocate of restoration.

56. As his dates indicate, Wang Pi (A.D. 226–49) did indeed die early, after leaving commentaries on Lao-tzu and on the *Book of Changes*.

57. Yen Yüan (Yen Hsi-chai) was one of the Ming loyalist philosophers who refused to bow to the Manchus when they conquered China in the early seventeenth century. They had great influence on Mao's generation, and on Mao in particular; Yen is mentioned in Mao's first published article, which appeared in 1917 (*The Political Thought of Mao Tse-tung*, pp. 24, 155).

58. Li Shih-min (597–649) overthrew the Sui dynasty and placed his father on the throne as the first T'ang emperor in 618. He was, in fact, slightly older than Mao indicates when, in 626, he became emperor himself with the dynastic title T'ai-tsung.

59. Ch'in Ch'iung, also known as Ch'in Shu-pao (6th–7th century A.D.), distinguished himself as a military commander under both the Sui and the T'ang dynasties.

60. Lo Ch'eng and Wang Po-tang were political adventurers of the late Sui dynasty (early 7th century), who made their mark at a very early age.

61. Disciple of K'ang Yu-wei, perhaps the most influential polemicist among the Reformers of 1898; Mao read him while an adolescent.

62. Yüan Shih-k'ai, a high official who helped Tz'u-hsi to repress the Reform Movement of 1898, betrayed his imperial masters to become President of the Republic in 1912; he died in 1916 after an abortive attempt to restore the monarchy with himself as emperor. Tuan Ch'i-jui, one of his lieutenants, played an important role during the early years of the 'warlord era', which opened with Yüan's death.

63. Wang He-shou (*c.* 1908–   ) and P'eng T'ao (1913–61) were respectively Minister of Metallurgical Industry and Minister of Chemical Industry at this time. It is not certain what articles Mao is referring to.

64. Chang Hsi-jo (*c.* 1889–   ), a political scientist educated at Columbia University in New York and at the London School of Economics, where he studied under Harold Laski, was Minister of Education until February 1958, when he became chairman of the Commission for Cultural Relations with Foreign Countries. A non-communist, he made the criticisms to which Mao is referring on 15 May 1957, at a forum called by the United Front Department.

65. Ch'en Ch'i-t'ung, Vice-Director of the Cultural Section of the General Political Department of the People's Liberation Army, together with three other senior army political workers, published an article in *People's Daily* on 7 January 1957, at a time when the scope of the 'Hundred Flowers' campaign was a subject of dispute within the leadership, some members of which opposed Mao's policy of 'opening wide' the floodgates to criticism from outside the Party. (Ch'en I is a homonym of the late Foreign Minister.)

66. Wei Chung-hsien (*d.* 1627), a self-made eunuch who enjoyed the favour of the emperor Hsi Tsung, was the real ruler of China until the death of his protector. He was notorious for the cruelty with which he disposed of his opponents.

67. Yang Shen (1488–1529), who came first in the palace examination in 1511, was exiled in 1524 when he wept so loudly to indicate his disapproval of two proposed appointments to the Han-lin academy as to be heard all over the palace.

68. Pi Kan (twelfth century B.C.) remonstrated with the tyrannical last ruler of the Shang dynasty upon his excesses, and was disembowelled before the Emperor as a result.

69. Ch'ü Yüan (340–278 B.C.), one of China's greatest poets, is celebrated not only for his literary talents, but for drowning himself in despair when, his advice having been neglected, the state of Ch'u, of which he had formerly been a leading minister, came to ruin. For a selection of his poems, see *Li Sao and Other Poems of Chu Yuan* (Peking: Foreign Languages Press, 1955), with an introductory sketch by Kuo Mo-jo.

70. Chu Yün (first century A.D.) had a chequered career; his life was in fact spared by the Emperor in his most celebrated adventure.

71. Chia I (second century B.C.) became a member of the Imperial Academy at such an early age that he aroused great jealousy, and was finally exiled. In his article of 1917 on physical education, Mao cited his example to make a different point: that too much study at an early age was destructive to health. See my complete French

translation of this text, *Mao Ze-dong: Une Étude de l'éducation physique* (Paris: Mouton, 1962), p. 46.

72. Ch'u An-p'ing, editor of the *Kuang-ming jih-pao*, organ of the China Democratic League, took the lead in criticisms of the Party in April 1957, when the 'blooming and contending' was in full flood. He came under sharp attack in June 1957. See *Literary Dissent in Communist China*, pp. 192, 198, 205–6.

73. See John Lust's translation, *Tsou Jung: The Revolutionary Army, a Chinese Nationalist Tract of 1903* (Paris: Mouton, 1968). This pamphlet was extremely influential at the time, and Mao certainly read it as an adolescent.

74. The two most famous poets of China's literary golden age, during the T'ang dynasty. For a recent appreciation of their work, see the extracts from Kuo Mo-jo's book on the subject in *Chinese Literature*, No. 4, 1972, pp. 61–94.

Text 5

1. Chang Tsung-hsün (c. 1898–   ), who had participated in the Autumn Harvest Uprising organized by Mao Tse-tung in 1927, and accompanied him to the first base on the Chingkangshan, was in 1958 a Deputy Chief of Staff of the P L A. Liu Ya-lou (1910–65) was then commander of the P L A Air Force; he had long been closely associated with Lin Piao.

2. At the conference of Communist Party organizations in the Red Army, held at Kut'ien in Fukien Province in December 1929, Mao presented a resolution on political and organizational problems in the army which has been regarded ever since as the classic statement of his views on these matters.

3. Hsiao K'e (1909–   ), a veteran of the Nanchang Uprising and of the Chingkangshan, was director of the P L A General Training Department in early 1958. Shortly thereafter, he was shunted into a subordinate post as Vice-Minister of State Farms and Land Reclamation, and his thirty-year military career came to an end.

4. The title given to Lin Piao here, 'Chief' (*tsung*), an abbreviation for 'Commander-in-Chief' (*tsung ssu-ling*), does not correspond to any precise function, since he did not replace P'eng Te-huai as Minister of Defence until September 1959. This term is frequently used loosely in Chinese writings to designate a high-ranking officer; prior to 1954, both Lin, and Ch'en I, to whom the same title is given later in this speech, had been commanders, respectively, of the Fourth and Third Field Army.

5. Ts'ao Ts'ao (155–220), known posthumously as Emperor Wu of

the Wei dynasty, was an outstanding statesman and military leader of the period of the Three Kingdoms. For Mao's attitude towards him, see *The Political Thought of Mao Tse-tung*, pp. 162, 166.

6. K'ai Feng (1907–55), also known as Ho K'ai-feng, was a member of the 'Returned Student' faction in the 1930s. It was therefore natural that Mao should charge him with lack of knowledge of Chinese culture, and of respect for things Chinese.

7. Sun-tzu, who flourished about 500 B.C., is undoubtedly, with Clausewitz, one of the two most celebrated military writers in world history. His *Art of War* has been most recently translated by General Samuel B. Griffith (Oxford University Press, 1963), who also includes a selection of the commentaries by Ts'ao Ts'ao, Tu Yü, and others, which this text, like all other classical Chinese writings, has accumulated over the centuries. It is to these that Lin Piao is referring in calling it a 'collective work'.

Text 6

1. Wu Chih-hui (1864–1954) was a leading figure in the anarchist movement at the beginning of this century, and perhaps the most famous Chinese eccentric of modern times. Sun Fo (also known as Sun K'o) was Sun Yat-sen's son, an insignificant politician.

2. Mao is obviously referring here to the 'Great Hall of the People' and other edifices built during the Great Leap Forward, flanking the square in front of the T'ien An Men (Gate of Heavenly Peace), not to the gate itself, which dates from Ming times and was rebuilt in its present form in 1651.

3. Lo Lung-chi (1896–1965), a political scientist educated at the London School of Economics and Columbia University, was a leading member of the China Democratic League. He was Minister of Timber from 1956–8, when he was removed after being denounced for over-zealous criticism of the Party during the Hundred Flowers of 1957. Ch'en Ming-shu (1890–1965), a leader of the Kuomintang faction which chose to collaborate with the Communists after 1949, was also criticized in 1957.

4. The Cha-ya-shan Commune (also known as the Wei-hsing or 'Sputnik' Commune) in Suip'ing *hsien*, Honan Province, was one of the first communes set up on an experimental basis in the early summer of 1958; its draft regulations, adopted on 7 August 1958, served as a document for study throughout the country following the decision of the Central Committee at a meeting in Peitaiho on 29 August 1958. (For the Peitaiho resolution, and the Cha-ya-shan regulations, see *Communist China 1955–1959* [Cambridge,

Mass.: Harvard University Press, 1962], pp. 454–6, 463–70.) Ch'i-li-ying Commune in Hsin-hsiang *hsien*, Honan, and communes in Hsü-shui *hsien*, Hopei, were also among the earliest models, set up in the summer of 1958.

5. i.e., the Chinese monk who, in the seventh century, brought Buddhist scriptures from India. See below, note 34 to Text 10.

6. Mao says below (p. 145) that he himself felt, in the summer of 1958, as though he had 'found a treasure' in the regulations of the Cha-ya-shan Commune. Here he suggests that visitors came to the three model communes in the same reverent spirit as Buddhists burning candles on the mountains at dawn.

7. Chu Te, who occupied this position most of the time from the union between his forces and Mao's in 1928 until 1954.

8. A slogan prevalent among the peasantry in the summer of 1958, reflecting their understanding of communism as sharing wealth, rather than collective organization for production.

9. The Shanghai underworld in the 1920s was dominated by gangs which had grown out of secret societies with names such as this.

10. Sung Chiang was the leader of the outlaw heroes of the novel *Water Margin*, translated by Pearl Buck under the title *All Men are Brothers* (New York: John Day, 1968). The incident of the birthday tribute occurs in Chapters 14–16; this episode is translated in Cyril Birch (Ed.) *Anthology of Chinese Literature* (Penguin, 1967), pp. 448–84. For a similar comparison between the ideals of the Communist Party and those of traditional defenders of the underdog, see Mao's appeal of 1936 to the secret society called the Ko Lao Hui: *The Political Thought of Mao Tse-tung*, pp. 260–61.

11. The Chinese text here says 'that this kind of wealth was ill-gotten'. This must be a misprint, since Mao is criticizing leftist errors of confiscating things that ought not to have been confiscated, and is making the cadres responsible for these excesses.

12. K'o Ch'ing-shih (1902–65), a member of the Politburo, was then Mayor of Shanghai, and head of the Shanghai Party organization, as well as being First Secretary of the Eastern Bureau.

13. Ts'ao (457–508), who had originally distinguished himself by his prowess as a hunter, helped to establish the Liang dynasty in 502. In the poem, he identifies himself with Huo Ch'ü-ping, a general of Han Wu Ti who distinguished himself against the Huns.

14. As already indicated (see above, Text 4a, note 2), the official viewpoint at the time of this speech regarding lines in the 1930s is given in the 'Resolution on Certain Questions in the History of Our Party', adopted on 20 April 1945, in *Selected Works*, Vol. III, pp.

177–225. The 'Li Li-san Line' of 1930, and the 'Left Opportunist Line' promoted by Wang Ming and the other representatives of the 'Returned Student Faction' in the years 1931–5 are discussed both there and in the many Western accounts of this period. The Kao–Jao Line is discussed in Mao's speech of 10 March 1958 (Text 4a and notes 8 and 10 to that text). The juxtaposition of these three deviationist lines with the General Line of building socialism 'more, faster, better, and more economically', put forward by Mao in 1956 and with which he continued to identify himself, is slightly odd.

15. Folk songs and dances adapted to carry a political message, widely promoted in the Yenan base area beginning in 1942.

16. The custom of parading people in dunce caps in order to humiliate them has a long history in China; its modern manifestations extend from the activities of the Hunan peasants, chronicled by Mao in 1927, to the Cultural Revolution.

17. Chang Po-chün, Minister of Communications and leader of the China Democratic League, criticized the Chinese Communist Party severely in the spring of 1957, and then recanted in July. His case thus paralleled that of the editor of his party's newspaper, Ch'u An-p'ing (see note 72 to Text 4). He was removed as minister in early 1958.

18. General George C. Marshall organized a number of meetings on Lushan while US mediator in China in 1946–7.

19. Wu Chih-p'u (c. 1906–   ), at this time First Secretary of the Chinese Communist Party for Honan province, who had taken the lead in establishing communes in the summer of 1958. For the background to Mao's remarks here, see his discussion of the role of Honan as the vanguard of social change in his speech of 20 March 1958 (Text 4b, pp. 104–5). He was demoted in 1961 for 'adventurism'.

20. Tseng Hsi-sheng (c. 1905–   ), a graduate of Whampoa who participated in the Long March, was elected to the Central Committee in 1956. He was also First Secretary of the CCP for Anhwei province, from 1952 to 1960, and in that capacity he showed himself a strong supporter of the Great Leap Forward. He faded from the political scene in the early 1960s.

21. Teng T'u-tzu, a high official of the state of Ch'u, offended in this way Sung Yü, a nephew of the famous poet Ch'ü Yüan, who attacked him in return (fourth century B.C.).

22. A quotation from Book I, Part A, Ch. 4 of Mencius (p. 52 of D.C. Lau's translation) referring to the practice of burying wooden figures with the dead so they might be their servants in the hereafter. According to another passage from the classics (Li Chi, IV, 19),

Confucius regarded this custom as inhuman because it suggested metaphorically the idea of burying actual human beings for the same purpose. In subsequent Chinese usage the expression 'he who first made burial puppets' has come to designate the author of any diabolical invention, or more generally the bringer of misfortune.

23. The two referred to are Mao's sons by his first wife, Yang K'ai-hui. The eldest, Mao An-ying, born in 1922, was killed in 1950 in Korea. The younger, Mao An-ch'in, was left with a 'bourgeois' family following his mother's execution in 1930, and was so mistreated, according to Red Guard sources, that his mind was affected.

24. A good-hearted but exceedingly short-tempered figure in *Water Margin*, whose personality is conjured up by his nickname, 'Black Whirlwind'.

25. T'an Chen-lin (1902–   ), Politburo member and the Party's top agricultural spokesman in 1958, had espoused radical policies in the countryside at the time of the Great Leap Forward. He was made a vice-premier of the State Council in April 1959, and was regarded as a spokesman for Mao Tse-tung.

26. P'eng Te-huai (1898–   ) Minister of Defence, who launched a sharp attack on the Great Leap policies at the Lushan meetings. In his 'Letter of Opinion', dated 14 July 1959, P'eng had excused his frankness by saying that he was a simple fellow like Chang Fei (one of the heroes of the *Romance of the Three Kingdoms*), but shared only Chang's roughness, not his subtlety. Mao's remark echoing this sentence is an obvious warning to his adversaries that he possesses both a subtle tactical sense, and the firmness (or harshness) to act as circumstances may require.

27. The abortive uprising in Cànton in December 1927, ordered by Stalin and quickly repressed with great loss of life.

28. Mao himself shortly produced some comments on Stalin's last work, as well as a much more detailed analysis of the Soviet manual on political economy published after Stalin's death. See his (undated) remarks on Stalin's 1952 essay, followed by notes (dated 1960) on the Soviet textbook in *Wan-sui* (1967), pp. 156–66 and 167–247. Another version of the latter, dated 1961–2, appears in *Wan-sui* (1969), pp. 319–99.

Text 7

1. Huang K'o-ch'eng (1902–   ), PLA Chief of Staff from October 1958 to September 1959, was regarded as P'eng Te-huai's principal accomplice and dismissed from office at the same time. The link

between the 'P'eng–Huang' (or 'P'eng–Huang–Chang [Wen-t'ien]–Chou [Hsiao-chou]') group and that of Kao and Jao was further elaborated on at the time of the Cultural Revolution. See below, Text 20.

2. i.e., the left line of the Russian Returned Students, mentioned above (Text 6, note 14), and Wang Ming's line of the Yenan period, which was denounced as right opportunist or capitulationist, not stressing sufficiently the independence of the Chinese Communist Party *vis-à-vis* the Kuomintang.

3. For Mao's criticism of P'eng's line in the 1940s, see his 'Letter Criticizing P'eng Te-huai's Talk on Democratic Education', 6 June 1943, in *Chinese Law and Government*, Vol. I, No. 4, Winter 1968–9, pp. 7–9.

4. Chang Wen-t'ien (*c.* 1898–   ), pseudonym Lo Fu, a member of the 'Returned Student Faction', succeeded Ch'in Pang-hsien (Po Ku) as Secretary-General at the Tsunyi Conference of January 1935. He was Chinese Ambassador to Moscow from 1951 to 1955, and thereafter a vice-minister of Foreign Affairs until his fall in September 1959.

5. Lo Ping-hui (1897–1946) was an important military leader from the time he joined the Chinese Communist Party in 1929 until his death. It is not known how he exposed himself to Mao's criticism, but it may have been in connection with his participation in the New Fourth Army Incident of January 1941, in which he commanded a detachment.

6. *Analects*, Book XIX, Ch. 21.

7. According to Chinese mythology, eclipses occur when the celestial dog eats the sun or the moon.

8. Wan Li was Minister of Urban Construction from May 1956 to February 1958, and thus responsible for projects such as this. Subsequently he became a secretary of the Peking Party Committee and Vice-Mayor of Peking. His name (presumably a pseudonym) means literally 'ten thousand *li*'; hence Mao's pun.

Text 8

1. The work style of the PLA, defined by Mao Tse-tung in 1960 in three phrases calling for a correct political orientation, an industrious and thrifty work style, and flexible and mobile strategy and tactics, and in eight characters (four pairs) meaning unity, earnestness, seriousness and liveliness. The use of precisely these figures echoed the 'Three Main Rules of Discipline and the Eight Points for Attention' originally laid down in 1928, which guided the con-

duct of the Red Army during the struggle for power, and thus represented an attempt to establish a symbolic link with the past. For the earlier rules, see Mao Tse-tung, *Selected Works,* Vol. IV, pp. 155–6.

2. Ssu-ma Ch'ien (*c.* 145–90 B.C.) was China's first great historian, who compiled the *Shih-chi* (*Historical Records*) relating the history of China from the origins to his own day. The foregoing passage is from his autobiography, appended to that work.

3. This reading, 'even more impossible' (*keng pu-hsing*), is that of *Wen-hsüan* and of *Wan-sui* (1969). The version in *Wan sui!* says merely that it is 'also impossible' (*yu pu-hsing*) without centralism.

4. This story is indeed recounted in the *Shi-chi* in the biographies of Li I-chi and Chu Chien, and also in that of Liu Pang, the founder of the Han dynasty. See Burton Watson's translation, *Records of the Grand Historian of China* (New York: Columbia University Press, 1961), Vol. I, pp. 86–7, 269–70, and 283. Mao has drawn on all three versions, taking some picturesque details (such as the remark, 'I am a drinking man') from the biography of Chu Chien, which is commonly regarded as a later interpolation and is therefore not translated by Watson.

5. A Peking opera, based on the account in the *Shi-chi* (Watson, *op. cit.,* pp. 70–71) about Hsiang Yü's farewell from his favourite, the lady Yü, on the eve of his final defeat. Mao alluded with admiration to the first two lines of the poem composed by Hsiang Yü on this occasion in his own first article of 1917: *The Political Thought of Mao Tse-tung*, pp. 157, 160.

6. The reference is, of course, to the sharp criticism of the Party and the régime in April and May 1957, before a halt was called to the policy of 'blooming and contending'.

7. This is the reading in *Wen-hsüan*. *Wan-sui* (1969) has rather 'did not understand very well' (*pu hen liao-chieh* instead of *hen pu liao-chieh*).

8. Chia Pao-yü is the chief male character in the *Dream of the Red Chamber*. Mao's criticism of Yü P'ing-po's interpretation of this novel related precisely to the point that, in his view, the book should be regarded as a condemnation of feudal society as a whole, and not, as Yü held, simply as a lament about individual misfortune. The new garden was created for the use of the imperial concubine on the occasion of a visit to her family (*The Story of the Stone*, Ch. 18), and it is here that much of the subsequent action takes place. Regarding the relationship between the novel and the author's own family background, see David Hawkes's introduction, especially pp. 22–32.

9. For the revised text of the sixty articles on rural work adopted at the Tenth Plenum in September 1962, and a summary of the seventy articles on industrial work drafted in December 1961, see *Documents of the Chinese Communist Party Central Committee, September 1956–April 1969* (Hong Kong: U R I, 1971), pp. 689–725. For the regulations on middle and primary schools drafted in 1963, see the article by Susan Shirk in *China Quarterly*, No. 55, July–September 1973, pp. 511–46.

10. A reactionary Kuomintang faction led by the two Ch'en brothers, nephews of Chiang Kai-shek's first patron Ch'en Ch'i-mei, who played a role in creating the quasi-fascist 'Blue Shirts' in the 1930s.

11. For details on Wang Shih-wei, see *Literary Dissent in Communist China*, pp. 25–7 and *passim*.

Text 9

1. A Japanese 'revisionist' who founded a new party in the aftermath of de-Stalinization.

2. The term 'encircle and annihilate' (*wei-ch'ao*) is the same as that employed in the 1930s to designate the campaigns of extermination launched by Chiang Kai-shek against the communists. Its use here vividly reflects the degree of hostility which Mao perceived in his erstwhile comrades.

3. The *cheng-feng* or 'rectification' movement of 1942–5 was the first great campaign for the ideological remoulding of the Chinese Communist Party, and for the establishment of Mao Tse-tung's thought as the standard of orthodoxy. For the documents studied at the time, see Boyd Compton (ed.), *Mao's China* (Seattle: University of Washington Press, 1950). The most recent account of the political context as a whole is contained in Mark Selden, *The Yenan Way in Revolutionary China* (Cambridge, Mass.: Harvard University Press, 1971), pp. 177–276. For my own interpretation, see the introduction to *Authority, Participation, and Cultural Change in China* (Cambridge University Press, 1973), pp. 17–22.

4. Li Wei-han (1897–   ), a Hunanese, played a leading role in the Chinese Communist Party from its foundation in 1921. From 1944 until his eclipse in December 1964, he was Director of the Party's United Front Work Department. It is not clear exactly why he was criticized by Mao in 1962, but the charge was probably related to the 'capitulationism' of which he was accused two years later.

5. The last Manchu emperor, deposed in 1911, and restored by the Japanese in the 1930s as the emperor of the puppet country of

'Manchukuo'. For his own story, see *From Emperor to Citizen: the Autobiography of Aisin-Gioro Pu Yi,* 2 vols. (Peking: Foreign Languages Press, 1964–5.)

6. i.e., they have had their social dignity restored by the removal of the dunce-caps, real or metaphorical, which they had been wearing.

7. P'an Han-nien, a former Comintern representative, was Vice-Mayor of Shanghai from 1949 until 1955, when he was expelled from the Party and arrested.

8. In the early 1960s, in the tense conditions created by the economic difficulties which arose after the Great Leap Forward, Kuomintang commando raids on the coast and other subversive activities were a particularly serious problem.

9. Yeh Chien-ying (1898–   ), a professional soldier who joined the Chinese Communist Party in 1927 and participated in the Nanchang Uprising, became a member of the Central Committee in 1945. During the early stages of the Cultural Revolution, in 1966–7, he was appointed to the Secretariat and the Politburo. At the Tenth Congress in August 1973, he became one of the five vice-chairmen of the Central Committee.

10. Chu-ko Liang (181–234), prime minister of the Shu Han or Minor Han dynasty, was one of the most famous military strategists of ancient China. He is a central character in the *Romance of the Three Kingdoms*, and was, as Mao says, known throughout his career for his great prudence and foresight. Lü Tuan was a minister of Emperor T'ai Tsung of the Sung dynasty in the tenth century, who used to say of him that he was a fool in small matters, but not in great ones.

11. Four of these men have long been known as members of the 'P'eng–Huang–Chang–Chou Anti-Party Group'. (See above, Text 7, note 1.) The other person named, Hsi [Chung-hsün] (1903–   ), remained in public view as a vice-premier until 1962, but had lost all his posts by 1965. This reference confirms that, as some observers had guessed, his fall was linked to that of P'eng Te-huai, with whom he had been closely associated in the early 1950s.

Text 10

1. In all the available versions except that in *Wan-sui* (1969), this text contains exclusively passages dealing with education, and is described as a talk or directive at the Spring Festival on Education. As will be evident from what follows, the meeting in question was clearly called primarily for the purpose of discussing education, but

before turning to the business of the day, Mao Tse-tung talked informally with some of those present about a variety of subjects.

2. In addition to the 'minor parties' referred to above (Text 1, note 6), the institutions of 1949 and 1954 provided for the participation of 'democratic personages', not affiliated with any party, in the political life of the country. The most famous of these was Sung Ch'ing-ling, Sun Yat-sen's widow. Some of the non-communists present at the forum of February 1964 belonged to this category; others were representatives of the minor parties.

3. This refers to a series of directives put out by Chiang Kai-shek beginning in January 1939, with the aim of limiting the political and military freedom of action of the communists.

4. Chang Shih-chao (1881–1973) had been active in the revolutionary movement as a journalist from the early years of the twentieth century. He was evidently one of the non-party 'democratic personages' Mao was addressing in his opening remarks.

5. According to a note in Mao's *Selected Works* (Vol. IV, p. 79, note 1), Kao Shu-hsün, Deputy Commander of the Kuomintang's Eleventh War Zone, brought with him one corps and one column when he came over to the communists on 30 October 1945. The communists subsequently gave his name to a movement for encouraging other Nationalist commanders to emulate this example. The note in the *Selected Works* does not mention the fact, noted by Mao here, that the Nationalists thereupon turned on Kao and smashed his forces.

6. Both the Kuang Hsü emperor (reigned 1875–1908) and his successor the Hsüan T'ung emperor had occupied the throne during Mao's lifetime. In the language he uses to recall this fact (*Kuang Hsü Hsüan T'ung, tou shih wo ting-t'ou shang-ssu*) there is perhaps a hint of a suggestion that he regards them as predecessors and colleagues.

7. Tsai-t'ao was in control of the imperial guards at the time of the 1911 revolution; it is thus natural that Mao, who spent six months in the republican forces at that time, should have identified him (in the next sentence) as 'a high military official'. He was regarded, during the last years of the dynasty, as one of the more liberal-minded among the imperial clansmen.

8. On 24 December 1946, Shen Ch'ung, a girl student at Peiping University, was raped by an American Marine. This incident led to widespread anti-American demonstrations by students in many Chinese cities, and to demands for the immediate withdrawal of all US military forces.

9. That the Soviets always 'kept something back' (*liu i shou*), i.e. that they kept certain key plans or information, or even a key piece of machinery, under the control of the Soviet experts so the Chinese would not be able to complete or operate a plant without their assistance, was a common complaint in China in the late 1950s and early 1960s.

10. In 1964, Mao was to launch the slogan, 'In industry learn from Tach'ing, in agriculture learn from Tachai', and since that time both of these have generally been regarded as 'Maoist' models. Here Mao credits the Petroleum Ministry with the achievements of the Tach'ing oil-fields in Heilungkiang Province.

11. Kuan Yü (also known as Kuan Kung, the God of War) and Chang Fei (see above, Text 6, note 26) were the two principal companions-in-arms of Liu Pei, the founder of the Shu Han Dynasty, during the period of the Three Kingdoms in the third century A.D. In the *Romance of the Three Kingdoms*, the celebrated novel from which Mao has said he learned some of his military tactics (see below Text 14, p. 238), they are described as wielding the weapons referred to here. Huang Chung, Chao [Yün], and Ma [Su] were the remaining three of Liu Pei's 'five tiger generals'. Although Liu Pei, like his two rivals, claimed to be the rightful ruler of the whole empire, the territory actually controlled by him was primarily that of the Kingdom of Shu, centering on present-day Szechuan, where Mao and his comrades were meeting.

12. Huang Yen-p'ei, an advocate of American-style vocational education, had been a leading figure in the Democratic League during the civil war of 1946–9, and was Minister of Light Industry from 1949 to 1954. In 1964, he was Chairman of the China Democratic National Construction Association, as well as being a member of the Standing Committee of the Democratic League. 'Old Ch'en' is apparently Ch'en Shu-t'ung, Chairman of the All-China Federation of Industry and Commerce since 1953. Both 'Old Huang' and 'Old Ch'en' were thus 'democratic personages', who had worked with the new régime since 1949.

13. The 'Second Revolution' was the attempt, in 1913, by forces under the leadership of Ts'ai Ao, to overthrow Yüan Shih-k'ai and halt the movement away from genuine republicanism towards a restoration of the monarchy. On the other hand, the government of which Chang Shih-chao was a minister in 1925 was that of the warlord-dominated régime in Peking. Mao deliberately mentions these two contrasting episodes in Chang Shih-chao's life in order to evoke the wide variety of experience through which his

generation has passed in its search for an answer to China's problems.

14. Hsü Te-heng (1895–   ) was a student leader during the May Fourth Movement. He has been Chairman of the Chiu-san (September third) Society, referred to below by Mao, since its foundation in 1945. (The Society, named for the date of Japanese surrender, is one of the minor parties participating in the united front). The 'industrial ministry' about which Mao asks here is the Ministry of Aquatic Products, which Hsü had headed since 1956.

15. The Association for Promoting Democracy was another of the minor parties, founded originally in Shanghai in 1945, which included mainly intellectuals in its ranks.

16. Kuo Tzu-i (697–781), a celebrated general of the T'ang Dynasty, had eight sons and seven sons-in-law; his grandchildren and great-grandchildren are reported to have been so numerous that he could not recognize them, and had to be content with bowing when they came to pay their respects.

17. It will be seen from what follows that Mao's 'directives' on education at this forum, which are commonly presented in other texts of this item as a series of oracular utterances by the Chairman, who is presumed to have occupied the centre of the stage, were in reality comments on a speech by someone else. The XXX who gave the main report may well have been Yang Hsiu-feng (1898–   ), at the time Minister of Education, and a frequent spokesman on educational affairs. The XX who intervenes later in the discussions might be Ho Wei (c. 1910–   ), who succeeded Yang Hsiu-feng as Minister of Education in June 1964 when this ministry was split into two and Yang took over responsibility for Higher Education. Both of these names are, however, mere speculation; the principal speaker could also have been drawn from the Party spokesmen on cultural affairs, such as Lu Ting-i, at the time Director of the Propaganda Department, and XX might stand for P'eng Chen or Chou Yang.

18. *Chin-shih*, a successful candidate at the highest ('metropolitan', followed by 'palace') examinations, according to the system established at the end of the sixth century, which had survived, with relatively limited modifications, until the early years of the twentieth century. *Han-lin*, a member of the Han-lin Academy, which became from Ming times the preserve of those who had achieved special distinction in the palace examinations. The most convenient and accurate summary of the extremely complicated structure of the examination system as it existed in Mao's boyhood is to be found in Wolfgang Franke, *The Reform and Abolition of the Traditional*

Chinese Examination System (Cambridge, Mass.: Harvard University Press, 1968). See also the appendix to Wu Ching-tzu's novel *The Scholars* (Peking: Foreign Languages Press, 1964), pp. 717–22. This latter work, by a contemporary of Ts'ao Hsüeh-ch'in, the author of the *Dream of the Red Chamber* (see, above, note 8 to Text 8), gives a vivid picture of the seamier side of the imperial bureaucracy, illustrating the venality, cowardice, and ignorance of the literary class, as well as the point mainly stressed by Mao: their lack of contact with reality.

19. Han Yü (768–824) and Liu Tsung-yüan (773–819) were friends as well as contemporaries, distinguished poets and essayists who both experienced periods of banishment in the course of their official careers. Han Yü especially is regarded as one of the greatest prose writers in the history of China; as a student in Changsha, Mao was taught to take him as a model in writing essays.

20. Wang Shih-fu and Kuan Han-ch'ing were celebrated dramatists of the Yüan dynasty, who flourished towards the end of the thirteenth century. Wang is the author of the *Story of the Western Chamber*, cited by Mao in Text 4c.

21. Lo Kuan-chung (14th century A.D.), was the author of the *Romance of the Three Kingdoms*, the historical novel from which Mao, according to his own statement, learned something of military tactics as well as statecraft.

P'u Sung-ling (b. 1622) is known for a celebrated collection of tales of the supernatural.

22. *Hsiu-ts'ai*, literally 'cultivated talent', popular name for a successful candidate at the lowest or prefectural examinations, more correctly known as a *sheng-yüan* or 'licentiate'. Though he 'received promotion' by imperial favour to the rank of senior licentiate, he failed to pass the next higher stage in the examination system proper, the provincial examination, and therefore did not obtain the corresponding title of *chü-jen* ('selected man'), or the opportunity to sit the metropolitan examination.

23. Ming T'ai-tsu, the founder of the dynasty, reigned from 1368 to 1399; Ch'eng-tsu, the third emperor of the dynasty, reigned from 1403 to 1425. The Chia-ch'ing reign extended from 1522 to 1567.

24. Han Wu Ti, the 'Martial Emperor' of the Han dynasty, reigned 140–86 B.C.

25. Liu Hsiu (4 B.C.–A.D. 57) overthrew the usurper Wang Mang in A. D. 25 and founded the Later Han (or Eastern Han) dynasty. Liu Pang (247–195 B.C.), who founded the original Han dynasty in 206 B.C., was praised by Mao in Text 8.

26. The Department (*t'ing*) referred to here is presumably that of the Peking municipal government.

27. The character read *shu* may be either a noun, meaning book or written document (in this case, a book of history) or a verb meaning to write, especially in the sense of writing out in a fine hand. Normally, in Confucius' list of six subjects or arts, it is taken to mean calligraphy.

28. The *Shu Ching* ('Historical Classic') is one of the 'Thirteen Classics', together with the Confucian *Analects*, the *Book of Odes*. etc. The *Han Shu* is the standard history of the Han dynasty.

29. 'Walking on two legs' was one of the principal slogans of the Great Leap Forward of 1958–9. It was used primarily with reference to economic development, to characterize a policy combining large-scale modern technology and the use of small-scale, indigenous methods. Here it is used to suggest a similar approach to education, combining schools (mainly in the cities) with modern equipment and an elaborate curriculum, with simpler and more basic schools adapted to the needs and possibilities in the countryside.

30. XXX, whoever he is, offers only a rather half-hearted defence of the 'Great Leap' policies: the downgrading of expertise, he argues, though useful as a corrective to the Soviet-style technocratic attitudes prevalent earlier, went much too far, and would have led to unfortunate results if the pendulum had not swung back again. His emphasis contrasts sharply with that of Mao Tse-tung in the next paragraph.

31. Li Shih-chen (1518–98) was the author of the *Pen-ts'ao kang-mu* (*Index of Roots and Herbs*), a treatise listing more than 1,000 plants useful for medicinal purposes.

32. A mathematician of the tenth century.

33. A stringed instrument similar to a lute; skill in playing it was part of the general culture expected of the literati.

34. It is hard to know what Mao is talking about here. On his return to China in 645, after a pilgrimage of sixteen years to India, whence he brought back a quantity of Buddhist scriptures, the monk Hsüan-tsang (602–64) presided over the translation of no less than 1,338 chapters in the course of the remaining years of his life. (He figures, under the name of Tripitaka, in the novel *Journey to the West* (*Monkey*), mentioned in Text 1.)

35. Kumarajiva (350–413), a Buddhist scholar who had studied in Kashmir, was brought to the imperial capital of Ch'ang-an in 401, and placed in charge of the translation of Buddhist scriptures. These versions, the best of their time, were later superseded by the 'new

translations' of Hsüan-tsang and his successors, not because of their length, but because they were insufficiently precise.

36. Obviously the figure of 40 million *yüan* refers to the total annual bill for subsistence, while the figure of 2 to 4 *yüan* indicates the corresponding increase in the monthly amount per student. According to the best available estimates, there were, at this time, approximately three quarters of a million students in Chinese institutions of higher education. Thus the two figures are roughly consistent.

37. Hsiao Yen (464–549) occupied Nanking in 501 and was proclaimed the first emperor of the Liang dynasty in the following year. A student of Buddhism and lover of books, he was unable to implement his good intentions by reforming the administration. When T'ai Ch'eng fell to a rebellious ally in 549, he was allowed to die of hunger and despair in a monastery to which he had retired.

Text 11

1. As distinguished by Lenin in 1913 in his article 'The Three Sources and Three Component Parts of Marxism', in Karl Marx and Frederick Engels, *Selected Works* (Moscow, 1970) pp. 23–7.

2. This appears to be a very much oversimplified summary of the evidence from parliamentary inquiries and from the reports of H. M. factory inspectors presented by Marx in *Capital* (Vol. I, Part III, *passim*). Marx does make the point that it is not in the interests of the capitalists to impose such long hours that the workers are exhausted and their hourly output falls sharply, but obviously no official body, at a time when the ten-hour day was regarded as a daring and radical innovation, would have suggested that an eight-hour working day would be equally profitable for the capitalists.

3. Peking University, jointly descended from the old Peking University which launched the May Fourth Movement in 1919, and from the American-endowed Yenching University, has continued since 1949 to enjoy the highest prestige in China for general intellectual excellence. People's University (Jen-min ta-hsüeh), also located in Peking, was specially set up to provide courses more accessible to students from worker and peasant backgrounds.

4. Among the Confucian classics, the Four Books represent the core studied by beginners, the Five Classics a somewhat larger corpus.

5. Among his varied educational experiences, Mao Tse-tung has long singled out the six months he spent reading in the Hunan Provincial Library, in the winter of 1912–13, as one of the most

valuable. See S. Schram, *Mao Tse-tung*, pp. 35–45, and Mao's own account, as told to Edgar Snow, in *Red Star over China.*

6. The first sentence is from the *Doctrine of the Mean*, XX, 5; the second is from *Mencius*, Book IV, Part B, Ch. 28 (p. 134 of D. C. Lau's translation).

7. The quotation is from the Confucian *Analects*, XV, Ch. 1. The incident in which the people of K'uang detained Confucius and wanted to kill him is referred to in the *Analects*, Book IX, Ch. 5; see also Legge's note on this passage.

8. Mao's reasoning is apparently that, whether or not he went there, Confucius had nothing *against* Ch'in (a state which existed in the first millennium B.C. in present-day Shensi, whose ruler ultimately conquered the whole of China and founded the Ch'in dynasty in 221 B.C.), since he included in the *Book of Odes*, which he is supposed to have edited, a number of poems from that area, including the two mentioned by Mao.

9. The translation of the above poem, and of the titles of the two mentioned previously, are taken from Legge's version of the *Book of Odes*, Part I, Book XV, Ode i; Book XI, Ode vi; Book IX, Ode vi.

10. Love poems have traditionally been interpreted by Chinese critics as an allegory for the relations between an official and his prince; Chu Hsi (see below, note 44 to Text 11) held that they should be taken at face value. Mao puts the commonsense view that they should sometimes be taken literally, and sometimes not.

11. Wei Chuang (*c.* 858–910) was an eminent poet of the late T'ang and early Five Dynasties (began 907) period. Mao is arguing that the same principles of interpretation should be applied to the *Book of Odes* and to all classical poetry.

12. The 'Socialist Education Movement', launched by Mao after the Tenth Plenum in the autumn of 1962, was known as the 'four clean-ups' in the countryside, and as the 'five antis' (*wu-fan*) in the cities. On the first aspect, see the monograph of R. Baum and F. Teiwes, *Ssu-ch'ing: the Socialist Education Movement of 1962–1966* (Berkeley, Calif.: Center for Chinese Studies, 1968). There is no corresponding work on the urban movement.

13. On the *Kuang-ming jih-pao* see above, Text 4, note 72. The *Wen-hui pao*, published in Shanghai, was a non-Party organ which had been criticized by Mao for its bourgeois tendencies in 1957. In November 1965, it was to serve as the channel for the opening shot in the Cultural Revolution (see below, Text 14, note 6).

14. Chou Ku-ch'eng was the author of numerous works on Chinese

and world history. Since 1950 he had been a professor at Futan University in Shanghai. In 1962 he published an article on history and art, in which he expressed ideas on the *'Zeitgeist'* which were said to be an expression in the realm of esthetics of Yang Hsien-chen's philosophical theories (see below, note 18 to this text).

15. Sun Yeh-fang was at this time Director of the Institute of Economics of the Academy of Science; he was dismissed in 1966. As K'ang Sheng's remark indicates, he had adopted the ideas of some Soviet and Eastern European economists with whom he had been in professional contact about the role of the profit motive in a socialist economy.

16. In the summer of 1955, just before Mao's speech of 31 July gave a new impetus to the formation of agricultural producers' co-operatives, the Party's Rural Work Department (at the instigation, it is now claimed, of Liu Shao-ch'i) had disbanded a number of co-operatives which were said to have been hastily and prematurely formed. From then onwards, Mao had been often at odds with this organization, which was formally abolished in 1961.

17. Teng Tzu-hui (1895–1972) had been head of the Rural Work Department since 1952, though his influence had declined since the late 1950s, because of his share of responsibility for the 'disbanding' or 'weeding out' of cooperatives in 1955. It would appear, however, that he still possessed sufficient status to put his views energetically in opposition to those of Mao when, in the early 1960s, the policies enumerated here by Mao were a subject of dispute within the Party. As a symbol to cover this whole spectrum of policies, emphasizing the role of material stimulants, the private plot, etc., the expression 'four great freedoms' is less common, in documents published since the beginning of the Cultural Revolution, than *'Sanzi yibao'* ('three freedoms and one fix, or guarantee'). On this concept, which is supposed to sum up the reactionary line of Liu Shao-ch'i and his sympathizers in the countryside, see the article 'Struggle between Two Roads in China's Countryside', *Peking Review*, No. 49 (1967), pp. 11–19.

18. The view that 'two combine into one' was put forward in the early 1960s by Yang Hsien-chen (*c.* 1899–   ), who had been, since 1955, President of the Higher Party School. Beginning in July 1964, this formulation was violently attacked in the press on the grounds that it minimized the importance of struggle and contradiction, and contrasted with Mao's view that 'one divides into two', i.e. that struggle, and in particular class struggle, constantly re-emerges, even when particular contradictions have been resolved. The 'outline of

an article' referred to in the stenographer's note was presumably a summary of one of the forthcoming attacks on Yang, submitted to the Chairman in advance for his approval.

19. It would appear that Mao is here confusing A. Bogdanov, who was, with Lunacharsky, one of the leaders of the 'Proletarian Culture' movement in the early 1920s, and P. Bogdanov, the author of *A Short Course of Economic Science*, who was also, for a brief time, the head of the Supreme Council of the National Economy.

20. The point of this criticism is obviously not that the Spanish republicans fought to the end, but that they failed to grasp the axiom that territorial strong points are not in themselves decisive.

21. See above, Text 4a, note 2.

22. Mao began his activity at this institute in 1925, but it was in 1926 that he actually served as principal and made his main contribution. See *Mao Tse-tung*, pp. 79, 85–92.

23. Mao's own attitude to this episode was, in fact, ambiguous. See *Mao Tse-tung*, pp. 22–3.

24. See Mao Tse-tung, p. 22, and the fuller acount in *Red Star over China*.

25. The quotation is from *Mencius*, Book VI, Part A, Ch. 15 (p. 168 of D. C. Lau's translation).

26. This is presumably a reference to Chang Ping-lin's celebrated article, published in 1903, entitled 'A Refutation of K'ang Yu-wei's Letter on Revolution'. In this article, Chang sharply attacked K'ang not only on the issue of revolution versus gradual reform, but on the importance of racial differences between the Chinese and the Manchus, which K'ang tended to minimize. The Manchus, Chang argued, were an alien and decadent race, totally unfit to rule China. It was in this context that he discussed evolution, indicating that the existing racial differences were the product of history. (For a brief summary of Chang's article, see Michael Gasster, *Chinese Intellectuals and the Revolution of 1911* [Seattle: University of Washington Press, 1969], pp. 195–6.)

27. Fu Ying is apparently a Chinese scientist who was alive in 1964, since Mao says he wants to look him up. I have not been able to identify him more precisely.

28. Lu P'ing (c. 1910–) was President of Peking University at this time; he was removed and 'struggled against' in June 1966. See Victor Nee, *The Cultural Revolution at Peking University* (New York: Monthly Review Press, 1969), pp. 52–66.

29. Ai Ssu-ch'i (c. 1910–66) was, at the time of his death, Vice-

President of the Higher Party School. He was one of the Party's leading philosophical spokesmen, who had translated works on dialectical materialism from the Russian, and written many books and articles which aimed to make Marxism accessible to the masses. On 1 November 1964 he published an article in *People's Daily* attacking Yang Hsien-chen, the 'bourgeois' philosopher Mao refers to earlier in this talk in connection with the principle of 'two combining into one'.

30. The metaphor of 'dissecting a sparrow', put forward in 1958 in point 32 of the 'Sixty Articles on Work Methods' (CB 892, p. 10), and frequently used thereafter, designates a method of work in which general principles are derived from the careful examination of a limited number of examples. Here, Mao makes the point that, in the broader international context, China as a whole is a microcosm of the problems of revolution in the world today.

31. Leng Tzu-hsing discourses on the mansion of the Duke of Jung-kuo in Chapter 2 of the book (*The Story of the Stone*, pp. 72–5). The 'Talisman for Officials', or, as David Hawkes translates it more freely and pungently, the *'Mandarin's Life Preserver'*, was a list of the rich and influential families in the area which the former novice from the Bottle-Gourd Temple said every official should carry in order to avoid offending them and thereby wrecking his career (*The Story of the Stone*, p. 111).

32. For Mao's criticism of Yü P'ing-po see above, Text 8, note 8. Wang K'un-lun was Vice-Mayor of Peking in the 1950s.

33. Ho Ch'i-fang (1911–   ), a lyric poet and powerful figure in the literary world, had defended Yü P'ing-po up to a point at the time of the campaign against him in 1954, saying that Yü was wrong in his interpretation of the *Dream of the Red Chamber*, but politically loyal. He himself came under attack at the time of the Great Leap Forward.

34. Wu Shih-ch'ang's work on this subject has been translated into English: *On 'The Red Chamber Dream'* (Clarendon Press, 1961.)

35. It is ironic that Mao should say Hu Shih's interpretation of the novel was more correct than that of Ts'ai Yüan-p'ei (1876–1940) for one of the main grounds for criticism of Yü P'ing-po had been precisely that, as a student and disciple of Hu, he shared his teacher's belief in research for its own sake. Mao's statement here concords, however, with the views of Lu Hsün. See his *Brief History of Chinese Fiction* (Peking, 1964), pp. 311–12.

36. The figures Mao gives here, as he shifts to the historical

present and calls to mind the final showdown with the Kuomintang, are rather those at the beginning of the Anti-Japanese War than those at the beginning of the renewed civil war in 1946, when the People's Liberation Army had grown to at least half a million men.

37. In January 1949, General Fu Tso-i, commanding the nationalist garrison in Peiping (as it was then called), surrendered the city without a fight to avoid useless destruction. He subsequently became Minister of Water Conservancy in the Peking government.

38. The legendary Emperor Shen Nung is said to have taught the art of agriculture in the third millennium B.C., and in particular to have discovered the medicinal properties of plants.

39. The Lung Shan and Yang Shao cultures, located respectively in north-eastern and north-western China, were the two most remarkable cultures of the neolithic period. As Mao indicates, they are particularly noted for their pottery. For a general account, see William Watson, *China before the Han Dynasty* (Thames & Hudson, 1966), pp. 37–56.

40. The book called the *Chuang-tzu,* which was probably composed only in part by the man of the same name who lived in the second half of the fourth century B.C., is not only one of the classic texts of Taoism (with the *Lao-tzu* and the *Book of Changes*), but one of the greatest literary masterpieces in the history of China. The passage to which Mao refers here can be found in Cyril Birch (ed.), *Anthology of Chinese Literature*, p. 108.

41. Sakata Shiyouchi, a Japanese physicist from the University of Nagoya, holds that 'elementary particles are a single, material, differentiated, and limitless category which make up the natural order'. No doubt because of Mao's enthusiasm for his ideas, an article by him expounding these views was published in *Red Flag* in June 1965. For the above quotation, and a discussion of the relation between Sakata's ideas and Mao's own 'monism', see Frederick Wakeman, *History and Will: Philosophical Perspectives of Mao Tsetung's Thought* (Berkeley: University of California Press, 1973), p. 227.

42. Mao is apparently referring to a collection of essays published by Jen Chi-yü in 1963, and reprinted in 1973: *Han T'ang fo-chiao ssu-hsiang lun chi* (*Collected Essays on Buddhist Thought in the Han and T'ang Dynasties*) (Peking: Jen-min ch'u-pan-she, 348 pp.) In these studies, he quotes from Lenin at considerable length regarding dialectics.

43. T'ang Yung-t'ung (1892–1964), whom Jen Chi-yü acknowledges as his teacher, was the leading historian of Buddhism, who

had written on Chinese Buddhism under the Han, Wei, Chin, and Northern and Southern dynasties, on the history of Indian thought, etc. He was Dean of the Humanities at Peking University from 1948 until he fell ill in 1954.

44. Under the influence of Ch'an Buddhism (better known under its Japanese name of Zen), Chinese philosophers of the Sung and Ming dynasties, of whom Chu Hsi (1130–1200) is the most famous, developed a synthesis between Confucianism and Buddhism in which a central role is played by the concept *li* (principle or reason), commonly known as Neo-Confucianism. For a Chinese view of the relations between these schools basically similar to Mao's, see Hou Wai-lu, *A Short History of Chinese Philosophy* (Peking: Foreign Languages Press, 1959), pp. 33–51. For an interpretation by a Western specialist, see H. G. Creel, *Chinese Thought from Confucius to Mao Tse-tung* (Chicago: University of Chicago Press; and London: Eyre & Spottiswoode, 1953), Ch. 10.

45. Han Yü and Liu Tsung-yüan are mentioned above (Text 10, note 19). Han Yü sought to recreate the simplicity of the classical period, while avoiding excessive archaism. The slogan about 'learning from their ideas' quoted by Mao refers to this aim of seeking inspiration from the ancient Confucian sages, while avoiding outmoded forms of expression. He adopted a critical attitude towards Buddhism, but none the less borrowed some ideas from it. Liu Tsung-yüan, whom Mao calls here by his literary name of Liu Tzu-hou, was a close friend of Han Yü. While he was deeply influenced by Buddhism, Hou Wai-lu characterizes him, like Mao, as a 'materialist'. (*Short History of Chinese Philosophy*, pp. 42–3).

46. Liu Tsung-yüan's essay *T'ien Tui* (*Heaven Answers*) undertook to answer the questions about the origin and nature of the universe raised by Ch'ü Yüan in his poem *T'ien Wen* (*Heaven Asks*). The latter is translated under the title 'The Riddles' in *Li Sao and Other Poems of Chu Yuan*, pp. 79–97. It is, as Mao says, suggestive but extremely obscure.

Text 12

1. This text is, in fact, a paragraph from Chou En-lai's report of 21–2 December 1964 on the work of the government. (See *Peking Review*, No. 1 (1965), p. 11.) Unlike certain other passages in the same speech, it is not attributed to Mao. On the other hand, the Red Guard compilers of *Tui P'eng* must have had some reason for ascribing it to the Chairman, and in style and substance it is very much in Mao's vein. Moreover, at a central work conference on 20 Decem-

ber 1964, Mao Tse-tung declared: 'You people didn't even dare to include in the Premier's report the words "catch up with"; I have added for you the words "catch up with and surpass". I have [also] added a passage, "Sun Yat-sen said already in 1905 that [China could] surpass [the West]." ' (*Wan-sui* [1969], p. 578.) Although the language is not the same as that used by Chou the next day, Mao thus took responsibility for the reference to Sun Yat-sen's prophecy.

Text 13

1. Here, and later in this paragraph, the term translated as 'gentlemen' is *lao-yeh*, which also means an official, in particular a district magistrate. Mao is using it ironically of the 'new class' of Party cadres, etc.

2. Hua T'o (d. A.D. 220), a celebrated physician and surgeon who served as court physician to Ts'ao Ts'ao; the latter had him executed when he proposed to open his skull to cure him of headaches.

3. On the 'four clean-ups', see above, Text 11, note 12. It is odd that Mao should have said in mid-1965 that it was 'basically completed' (the year xx presumably stands for 1964), since he had just turned it in a new and radical direction with his directive of January 1965. Perhaps the answer lies, as I have suggested in my introduction to *Authority, Participation and Cultural Change in China*, in the fact that he saw the latest metamorphosis of the 'four clean-ups', which Liu Shao-ch'i had opposed, as the beginning of the Cultural Revolution to be launched a few months later, rather than as the tail end of the previous campaign. See Edgar Snow, *The Long Revolution* (New York: Random House, 1972; and London: Hutchinson, 1973), pp. 17 and 84.

Text 14

1. Wu Han (b. 1909) was at this time Vice-Mayor of Peking. He had contributed to the series of articles published in 1961 and 1962 in the Peking press under the title 'Notes from Three-Family Village', which contained thinly veiled attacks on Mao's 'great empty talk' and failure to listen to advice. Above all, he was the author of the play *Hai Jui Dismissed from Office*, published in January 1961, which was in fact a defence of P'eng Te-huai camouflaged as an upright official removed from office by the emperor in Ming times because he had defended the right of the peasants to their land. Yao Wen-yüan's attack on this drama in November 1965 (see note 6, below) gave the signal for the beginning of the Cultural Revolution. For Yao's hostile summary of the articles published in the early

1960s, see 'On "Three-Family Village"', *Peking Review*, No. 22 (1966), pp. 5–18.

2. A leading historian who also came under attack in the Cultural Revolution; at the time of Mao's speech he was head of the History Department at Peking University.

3. I have not been able to identify this author, or to locate his article.

4. Mao denounced this film as early as March 1950, and demanded that it be criticized. (See his 'directive' of this date, quoted by Ch'i Pen-yü in his article 'Patriotism or National Betrayal – on the Reactionary Film *Inside Story of the Ching Court*', translated in *Peking Review* No. 15 (1967), pp. 5–16. Date of the directive as given in *Mao Chu-hsi lun wen-i yü-lu*, p. 93.) Ch'i Pen-yü was purged as a member of the ultra-leftist faction half a year after he wrote the article just cited, but at the time it was an authoritative statement of Mao's views; indeed, the Chairman actually went over the manuscript and added some passages of his own. The publication of this article in March 1967 gave the signal for attacks on Liu Shao-ch'i (designated as 'China's Khrushchev') who had differed with Mao in his estimate of the film. Mao's letter of 1954 regarding the *Dream of the Red Chamber* also contained a sentence complaining that this film had not yet been criticized.

5. Ch'i Pen-yü was, like Wang Li and Kuan Feng, who came to grief with him at the end of 1967, an editor of *Hung-ch'i*. The article to which Mao refers here was entitled 'Wei ko-ming erh yen-chiu li-shih' ('Study History for the Sake of the Revolution'), and appeared in issue No. 13 of that journal, which was published on 6 December 1965, pp. 14–22. As Mao says, it did not name names; it attacked disciples of Hu Shih who had denied the relevance of class struggle to the study of history, and called for a 'supra-class viewpoint' and 'absolute objectivity', but did not identify them except by saying that they had expressed such ideas openly in 1963.

6. Yao Wen-yüan had first attracted attention by an article of June 1957, attacking the bourgeois tendencies of the Shanghai *Wen-hui pao*. Ironically, his article entitled 'On the New Historical Play *The Dismissal of Hai Jui*' appeared on 10 November 1965 precisely in that paper – because, as Mao stated in October 1966 (see below, pp. 270–71), it was not possible to get it published in the Peking press, which was tightly controlled by the Party bureaucracy. It appeared in *People's Daily* only on 30 November, apparently after Mao had put pressure on the Peking Mayor and Party Secretary P'eng Chen.

7. The standard commentary on the *Spring and Autumn Annals,* written in the third century B.C.

8. The *Tzu-chih t'ung-chien* of Ssu-ma Kuang (1019–86), written between 1072 and 1084, is a general history of China from 403 B.C. to A.D. 959. It is, with the *Shih-chi* (already mentioned), one of China's most famous historical writings.

9. The communists applied the treatment which Mao characterizes in Hegelian terms as '*Aufhebung*' (*yang-ch'i*) to the Kuomintang general Tu Yü-ming by defeating him in battle and taking him prisoner after he had refused to surrender. See Mao's 'Message Urging Tu Yü-ming and Others to Surrender' of 17 December 1948, *Selected Works,* Vol. IV, pp. 295–7.

10. For Mao's criticism of Bertrand Russell's ideas in 1920, see *The Political Thought of Mao Tse-tung,* pp. 296–8.

Text 15

1. In *Wan-sui* (1969) the first of these talks is dated March 1964. This seems inherently improbable, since the 'Ninth Reply' to the Soviets, which Mao discusses here with his nephew, would probably not have been available so early, even in draft form. I have therefore preferred the date 5 July given in another source (translated in CB 888, p. 14).

2. At this time, Mao was intensely preoccupied with the problem of bringing up successors to the revolutionary cause to which he had devoted himself for half a century. The five requirements or criteria for such successors were first publicly stated in mid-July 1964, in the editorial entitled 'On Khrushchev's Phoney Communism and its Historical Lessons for the World', translated in *Peking Review,* No. 29 (1964) pp. 7–27. (The 'five requirements' appear on pp. 26–7.) They must be 'genuine Marxist–Leninists and not revisionists'; they must be 'revolutionaries who wholeheartedly serve the majority of the people of China and the whole world'; they must be 'proletarian statesmen capable of uniting and working together with the overwhelming majority'; they must be 'models in applying the Party's democratic centralism', and must master the 'mass line' method of leadership; they must be 'modest and prudent and guard against arrogance and impetuosity'.

3. It was in 1964 that Chiang Ch'ing began in earnest her efforts to remedy this situation by developing modern revolutionary Peking opera to replace the old plays about emperors, generals and concubines.

4. I have not been able to identify this culprit.

5. Mao's brother, Mao Tse-min, served in Sinkiang from 1938 to 1942 as head of the finance department of the government controlled by the local warlord, General Sheng Shih-ts'ai, who was then collaborating with the Soviet Union. When General Sheng shifted his allegiance from Moscow to the Kuomintang, Mao Tse-min was arrested in September 1942 and executed in 1943.

6. In September 1960, Lin Piao presented to a meeting of the Party's Military Affairs Committee a report on what he called the 'four relations', shortly to be reformulated and re-baptized as the 'four firsts': priority of men over weapons, of political work over other work, of ideological work over routine political work, and of living ideology over ideas from books. These points were developed in a resolution revised by Mao himself before being adopted by the Military Affairs Committee. See J. Chester Cheng (ed.), *The Politics of the Chinese Red Army* (Stanford: Hoover Institution, 1965), pp. 33, 66–94. This is a translation of the PLA *Work Bulletin* (*Kung-tso t'ung-hsün*), a secret periodical for cadres at the regimental level and above, of which twenty-nine issues for the period January–August 1961 fell into the hands of the US Government and were subsequently released through the Library of Congress.

7. A Kuomintang general, who fought against the communists in the civil war of 1946–9, and subsequently served as a member of the National Defence Council in Peking in 1959–60.

8. i.e., Li Po and Tu Fu, referred to above, Text 4, note 74.

9. Mao's enthusiasm for this paper, which was the organ of the Communist Youth League, was natural enough at the time, for it was at the Ninth Congress of the League in June 1964 that the problem of 'bringing up successors' for the revolutionary cause had just been extensively discussed for the first time (see *Peking Review*, No. 28 (1964) pp. 6–22). It appears slightly ironic, however, in the light of what came after, for the Youth League was smashed at the beginning of the Cultural Revolution, and restored only after the Party had been rebuilt.

10. Such methods of teaching, involving field work to take down the reminiscences of old people, etc., were common in China at the time.

11. Legendary rulers supposed to have ascended the throne respectively in 2356, 2255, and 2205 B.C. The first two especially are regarded as models of what a sage–king should be.

12. Mao was acting head of the Propaganda Department of the Kuomintang Central Executive Committee in 1925–6.

13. K'ang Tse was one of the leaders of Chiang Kai-shek's Blue

Shirts, with particular responsibility for the Special Task Force which was engaged in the 1930s in propaganda, security, and combat support activities in areas where the Kuomintang was fighting the communists.

14. Mao Yüan-hsin was a Red Guard leader at the Institute in Harbin during the early stages of the Cultural Revolution. In January 1967, when a Revolutionary Committee was set up in Heilungkiang Province, he became director of the Propaganda Department. In the spring of 1967, he moved to Liaoning Province, and became Vice-Chairman of the Liaoning Revolutionary Committee in May 1968. At the Tenth Congress in August 1973, he was a member of the presidium.

Text 16

1. The new-style army under the control of Yüan Shih-k'ai during the last years of the Empire was known as the *Pei-yang lu-chün* or Northern Army. The term 'Pei-yang Warlords' is employed both of Yüan and his subordinates during the period 1911–16, and more loosely as a collective designation for the several cliques into which his epigones split up during the decade following his death. Mao is probably thinking here in particular of the warlord-dominated government in Peking in 1919, which suppressed the May Fourth student demonstrations.

2. Judging from another speech by Mao which has only recently become available ('Talk of 4 August 1966 before an Enlarged Meeting of the Standing Committee of the Politburo', *Wan-sui* (1969), pp. 650–51), this distinction between 'inner' and 'outer' probably refers broadly to the drawing of rigid boundaries in a variety of contexts, ranging from Party and non-Party at one extreme to Chinese and foreigners at the other. The crucial point at issue in the summer of 1966 (and indeed subsequently, throughout the whole of the Cultural Revolution) was, however, that of the status of the Communist Party as an order set apart from the rest of society.

Text 17

1. K'ang Sheng (1899–) spent considerable time in the Soviet Union in the 1930s, and was long regarded above all as a specialist in intelligence and security matters. Beginning in the mid-fifties, he began to play a role both in higher education, and in liaison with foreign Communist parties, participating in several important delegations for discussions with the Soviets. He became a member of the Secretariat of the Politburo in September 1962, at the Tenth

Plenum. His closeness to Mao, and his interest in cultural matters, are underlined by his participation in Mao's talks with Ch'en Po-ta about philosophy in 1964 (Text 11). In mid-1966 he became a member of the Standing Committee of the Politburo, and he played an important role thereafter throughout the Cultural Revolution.

2. Wang Jen-chung (*c.* 1906–) became first secretary of the Hupei Party organization in 1954; he actively supported the Great Leap, and was often in Mao's company when the Chairman visited Wuhan in the late 1950s and early 1960s. In 1961 he became second secretary of the Party's Central–South Bureau under T'ao Chu. His fortunes during the Cultural Revolution followed those of T'ao (see below, note 5 to Text 20): a rapid rise to prominence in the summer of 1966, when he was made deputy head of the 'Cultural Revolution Group' and then sudden elimination from all positions of power in December.

3. The leading Party organization in Chingkangshan days.

4. The 'Group of Five' was set up in early 1966, under the leadership of P'eng Chen, and produced a report dated 7 February which sought to orient the Cultural Revolution in the direction of academic and ideological debate rather than 'class struggle'. (For the text, see *CCP Documents of the Great Proletarian Cultural Revolution 1966–1967* (Hong Kong: Union Research Institute, 1968), pp. 7–12.) This was revoked by a circular of the Central Committee dated 16 May, drawn up under Mao's personal guidance, which also dissolved the 'Group of Five' and set up the new 'Cultural Revolution Group' directly under the Standing Committee of the Politburo. (This document was published only the following year; see *Peking Review* No. 21 (1967), pp. 6–9.) K'ang Sheng had been a member of the 'Group Five', but it was later claimed that P'eng Chen had misused his name and put the circular out without his knowledge.

5. Three days later, Chiang Ch'ing, in a talk at Peking University, declared that in the Chairman's view this incident was not counter-revolutionary, but revolutionary. He had arrived at this opinion after studying all the relevant documents in Wuhan, where he was at the time. According to the Red Guard editors, the incident arose when the students at Peking University 'brought their righteous indignation into play and spontaneously waged struggle against those in authority taking the capitalist road and other demons and monsters'; in the process, 'some people were beaten up' (*Current Background*, No. 892, p. 39). Those 'in authority' obviously included both Lu P'ing and the university administration, and the 'work

team' sent to the university by the Party organization. It is there-fore not surprising that Mao should have regarded the beating up of such people as revolutionary. For more on the 18 June Incident, see Victor Nee, op. cit.

Text 18

1. See above, the Introduction, p. 15.

Text 20

1. Li Hsüeh-feng (*c.* 1906–   ), First Secretary of the CCP North China Bureau, had replaced P'eng Chen as First Secretary of the Peking Party branch in June 1966. He disappeared from the politi-cal scene in December 1970; Mao subsequently identified him as one of Lin Piao's co-conspirators (Text 26, pp. 292, 295).

2. Liu Lan-t'ao (1904–   ), First Secretary of the CCP Northwest Bureau, and political commissar of the Lanchow Military Region.

3. Li Ching-ch'üan (see above, note 26 to Text 4), First Secretary of the CCP Southwest Bureau since 1961, was thus the direct superior of Liao Chih-kao, about whom Mao asks him here.

4. San-niang refers to Wang Ch'un, the heroine of the Peking opera *San-niang chiao-tzu* (*San-niang Teaches her Son*). Third wife of a Ming dynasty official wrongly thought to have died, she refused to remarry and devoted her life to educating her husband's son by his second wife, who eventually became a *chuang-yüan*.

5. T'ao Chu (*c.* 1906–   ) became First Secretary of the CCP Central–South Bureau in 1961. In the early stages of the Cultural Revolution he enjoyed a meteoric rise to power, becoming head of the Central Committee's Propaganda Department in July 1966, and ranking fourth, immediately after Mao Tse-tung, Lin Piao, and Chou En-lai, at the Eleventh Plenum in August 1966. In late De-cember 1966, he fell into disfavour and was officially denounced.

6. Here *Wen-hsüan* has '1949'; this may be a copyist's error.

7. Li Fu-ch'un (1899–   ), a Hunanese, has been a long-time close associate of Mao Tse-tung. He worked with Mao at the Peasant Movement Training Institute in 1925–6, and is married to Ts'ai Ch'ang, the sister of Mao's best friend, Ts'ai Ho-sen. He has been Chairman of the State Planning Commission since 1954. His star has dimmed somewhat in recent years, and he ceased to be a Politburo member in 1969, but he remains a Vice-Premier.

Li Hsien-nien (*c.* 1907–   ), Minister of Finance, Vice-Premier, and member of the Politburo.

Po I-po (1907–), Vice-Premier and Chairman of the State Economic Commission; he was not re-elected, even to the Central Committee, in 1969, and was extensively criticized during the Cultural Revolution for espousing the type of economic policies favoured by Liu Shao-ch'i.

For T'an Chen-lin, see note 25 to Text 6. He fell from power during the Cultural Revolution, but came back in 1973 at the Tenth Congress as a member of the Central Committee; he is also currently a Vice-Premier.

8. Hsiang Ying (1898–1941), a former labour leader, and Vice-Chairman of the Chinese Soviet Republic in the early 1930s, was political commissar of the New Fourth Army created by the Communists in central China beginning in 1937. (Among the commanders was the late foreign minister, Ch'en I.) Regarding the clash with Nationalist forces in January 1941, known as the 'New Fourth Army Incident', see S. Schram, *Mao Tse-tung* (Penguin, 1967), pp. 205–6, 217–19.

9. The 'Hundred Regiments Offensive' launched by P'eng Te-huai in August 1940 inflicted very extensive damage on the Japanese forces, but provoked a reaction which was ultimately very costly to the Communists themselves. During the Cultural Revolution P'eng has been accused of undertaking this adventure without consulting Mao.

10. In the spring of 1947, obeying the fundamental principle of guerrilla tactics, as laid down by Mao, that the aim of war is to destroy the enemy's forces rather than to hold territory for its own sake, the Communists abandoned their capital of Yenan without a struggle. This resulted in the separation of the top leadership into two groups, as enumerated by Mao, which lasted from March 1947 until May 1948.

11. Jen Pi-shih (1904–50) was a member of the Politburo at the time of his death, and had been closely associated with Mao since the 1940s.

12. Lo Jui-ch'ing (*c.* 1906–) was Minister of Public Security from 1949 to 1959. Thereafter he was Chief-of-Staff of the PLA until he suddenly fell from power at the end of 1965.

13. Lu Ting-i (*c.* 1901–), head of the CCP Propaganda Department until his fall in mid-1966, in the early stages of the Cultural Revolution.

14. Yang Shang-k'un (*c.* 1905–), at this time an alternate member of the CCP Secretariat, fell from power during the Cultural Revolution.

15. Ch'en Ch'i-han (*c.* 1898–   ), a member of the CCP Central Control Commission, who retained his position on the Central Committee in 1969, was active in military and intelligence work at the time of the Seventh Congress in 1945.

16. Wang Chia-hsiang (1907–74) was, like the other people Mao is discussing here, a member of the 'Returned Student' faction. He was China's first ambassador to the Soviet Union in 1949–51, and participated in the Chinese delegation to the Moscow meeting of November 1957, led by Mao Tse-tung, but he faded from the scene in the early 1960s. He was, however, re-elected to the Central Committee at the Tenth Congress in 1973.

17. The reading 'Tungku' is from *Wan-sui* (1969); other sources have Tungkang. Although the character for 'ku' is slightly different from that commonly used for this name, the reference may well be to the revolt of December 1930 against Mao's authority, commonly known as the Fut'ien Rebellion, which began in the town of Tungku. Wang Chia-hsiang, an adversary of Li Li-san, would presumably have supported Mao against the rebels, who were partisans of Li.

18. In August 1932, at the Ningtu conference, Mao was stripped of his control over the Red Army. He suggests here that Lo Fu (Chang Wen-t'ien – see note 4 to Text 7) wanted to expel him from the Party as well, but that Chou En-lai and Chu Te opposed this.

19. At the Tsunyi Conference of January 1935, where Mao achieved *de facto* supremacy in the Party, Ch'in Pang-hsien was replaced as Secretary-General by Chang Wen-t'ien. Without the co-operation of some of the Moscow-oriented faction, and of Chang in particular, Mao could obviously not have achieved as much as he did on this occasion in reorganizing the leadership of the Party.

20. Nieh Jung-chen (1899–   ) was Lin Piao's chief political officer during the Long March; after 1949, he occupied important positions in military and scientific work. He remains a Vice-Premier, and a member of the Central Committee.

21. Chang Chih-chung (1891–   ), a Nationalist general who had occupied many high posts under Chiang Kai-shek, was director of the Generalissimo's north-west headquarters from 1945 to 1949, when he switched his allegiance to the communists. After helping the new régime establish its authority in Sinkiang, he was appointed in 1954 Vice-Chairman of the National Defence Council in Peking.

22. Li Tsung-jen (1890–1969), acting president of the Kuomintang régime in early 1949, who returned to China from exile in the United States in 1965.

23. i.e., the reformers K'ang Yu-wei and Liang Ch'i-ch'ao, who

supported the idea of a constitutional monarchy in the early years of the twentieth century.

Text 21

1. i.e., when Mao put forward his new twenty-three-point directive for the Socialist Education Campaign in January 1965, and Liu Shao-ch'i refused to accept it. See note 3 to Text 13.

2. According to an editorial published in August 1967, on the first anniversary of the Eleventh Plenum, Mao is reported to have said, at a meeting of the Standing Committee of the Politburo in September 1965: 'What are you going to do if revisionism appears in the Central Committee? This is highly likely. This is the greatest danger.' (*Peking Review*, No. 33, 1967, p. 7.)

3. On 1 June 1966, Mao ordered that a big-character poster written by Nieh Yüan-tzu, a lecturer at Peking University, be widely published and broadcast on the radio, thus giving the signal for the real beginning of the Cultural Revolution. On 5 August 1966, he wrote a poster of his own, entitled 'Bombard the Headquarters', which turned the assault against the Party leadership. See *Peking Review*, No. 37 (1966), pp. 19–20, and No. 33 (1967), p. 5.

Text 22

1. The 'seizure of power' at the Shanghai *Wen-hui-pao* was the first act in the 'January Storm', which appeared to mark the beginning of an evolution towards a new political system based on the Paris Commune. For the manifesto announcing this action, see *Peking Review*, No. 3 (1967), pp. 5–7.

2. This was in fact done on the very day on which Mao was speaking.

3. Wu Leng-hsi (*c.* 1915–) had been editor of *People's Daily* since 1957; he had participated in the deliberations of P'eng Chen's 'Group of Five'. In late 1972, he reappeared as a 'leading member' of the editorial staff, though no longer as editor. T'ang P'ing-shu was an ultra-leftist, purged in 1968 with the Wang Li faction.

Text 23

1. Chang Ch'un-ch'iao, a secretary of the Shanghai Party committee, had helped to arrange for the publication of Yao Wen-yüan's attack on Wu Han in November 1965. Thereafter he rose rapidly, becoming a member of the Cultural Revolution Group in the summer of 1966, and a Politburo Member in 1969. He and Yao Wen-yüan were the two principal leaders of the 'Shanghai Commune'

which had been formed on 5 February 1967. For the symbolic importance of their meetings with Mao in mid-February, see the Introduction, pp. 16–17.

While the general thrust of Mao's remarks on this occasion is plain enough, the rather terse record of the main points of his conversations with Chang and Yao contained in the text translated here includes allusions to a great many details of the complex and rapidly changing situation in Shanghai in January and February 1967 which require explanation. In this and the following notes I have tried to explain briefly a few of the more important of these. For a full account of events during this crucial period, see Neale Hunter, *Shanghai Journal* (New York: Praeger, 1969). The First, Second, and Third Regiments (of Workers in the Northern Expedition) were organizations loyal to Keng Chin-chang, a leader later denounced as an ultra-leftist, who was contending with Chang Ch'un-ch'iao in early 1967 for control of the situation in Shanghai. Keng was said to have visited Peking in late December 1966; in early February 1967, he sent to Peking emissaries who were received by Chou En-lai and handed to him detailed accusations against Chang and his Workers' Headquarters.

2. This was the formula put forward in January 1967 for the 'seizure of power' by 'Revolutionary Committees'. The three components were activists who had emerged from the 'revolutionary masses', PLA representatives, and Party and state cadres.

3. This refers to the urgent telegram sent to Shanghai by the Cultural Revolution Group under the Central Committee on 29 January 1967, criticizing the Red Revolutionaries (see below, note 4) for turning the spearhead of the struggle against Chang Ch'un-ch'iao and Yao Wen-yüan, rather than against the old Party leadership headed by former Mayor Ts'ao Ti-ch'iu, and threatening them with 'all necessary action' if they persisted in their errors. (Hunter, op. cit., pp. 240–41).

4. The demand by the Municipal People's Committee is presumably that criticized by Mao on p. 277. 'Red Revolutionaries' is the abbreviation for the Revolutionary Committee of Red Guards from Shanghai Schools and Universities, one of the principal signatories of the 'Urgent Notice' denouncing 'economism' put out by thirty-two 'Rebel' organizations in Shanghai on 9 January 1967 (*Peking Review*, No. 4 (1967), pp. 7–9). This group, the strongest of all student organizations in the city, opposed Chang Ch'un-ch'iao until ordered to desist by the telegram of 29 January from the Centre mentioned in note 3. The establishment of PLA control over broadcasting stations

had been called for in the Central Committee circulars of 11 and 23 January 1967 (*CCP Documents of the Great Proletarian Cultural Revolution*, pp. 172, 200–201). The second of these opened the door to possible conflict by stipulating: 'When the proletarian revolutionaries are able to control the situation, military control should end.' Military control of the civil aviation system was ordered by the State Council on 26 January 1967(ibid., p. 208). This apparently encountered opposition at Lunghua Airfield in Shanghai.

5. For the source of this quotation (in fact from 1919), and the significance of the point at issue, see the Introduction, p. 22.

6. The 'Mao Tse-tung's Thought Red Guards' "East is Red" General Headquarters of T'ungchi University' were supporters of Chang Ch'un-ch'iao.

7. Liu Shao-ch'i's work of 1939, which had been re-issued in revised form in 1962, was known under this title in English, prior to the Cultural Revolution. It was violently attacked in April 1967 as the quintessential expression of his revisionist and careerist thinking. Since that time, the title has been translated literally as *On the Self-Cultivation of Communists* (*Self-Cultivation* for short).

Text 24

1. Ch'en Kung-po (1892–1946) left the Chinese Communist Party shortly after its foundation, and joined the Kuomintang, becoming a close associate of Wang Ching-wei. He participated in Wang's Japanese-sponsored puppet government during the period 1939–45, and was executed for treason in 1946. Chou Fo-hai also collaborated with the Japanese.

2. Chang Kuo-t'ao (1897–) was highly influential in the Chinese Communist Party in the early years. In the early 1930s he established a soviet area under his own leadership on the borders of Hupei, Honan and Anhwei provinces; when his army encountered that of Mao in June 1935, in the course of the Long March, he refused to take the route northward proposed by Mao, and moved instead westwards towards Tibet. When he finally arrived in the Yenan area at the end of 1936, his forces were so weakened that he was in no position to oppose Mao effectively. Disgruntled at his lack of effective political influence, he fled in mid-1938 to Kuomintang-held territory. Since 1949, he has lived in exile, first in Hong Kong, and more recently in Canada.

3. Liu Jen-ch'ing was a delegate of the Peking Communists at the First Congress.

4. Li Ta (*c.* 1891–1967) soon left the Chinese Communist Party,

but cooperated with it episodically. In his last years, though he had not rejoined the Party, he was president of Wuhan University. He died on 24 August 1967 as a result of Red Guard persecution. According to Wuhan radio, he had sent a personal appeal to Mao to save him; Mao had responded favourably, but his message not to 'kill Li Ta by persecution' had been intercepted by the local Party leader. See Stanley Karnow, *Mao and China*, p. 371.

Text 25

1. This refers to Wang Ming's article, 'China: Cultural Revolution or Counter-Revolutionary Coup', originally published in the *Canadian Tribune* on 19 March 1969, and subsequently reprinted in pamphlet form in Moscow by the Novosti Press Agency Publishing House. It enumerates 'ten major crimes committed by Mao Tse-tung in China', and 'five major crimes committed by Mao Tse-tung in international affairs'.

2. The '*San-min chu-i*' or 'Three People's Principles' Youth League was the youth organization of the Kuomintang.

3. Wang Hsiao-yü, a PLA political commissar, was Chairman of the Shantung Revolutionary Committee from its establishment on 3 February 1967 until October 1969. Yang Te-chih (1910–   ), who replaced him at that time, had been First Vice-Chairman throughout this period. It is odd that Mao should regard the quarrel between them as a relationship among the people, for Wang, at the time of his dismissal, was denounced as a member of the 'May 16th' ultra-leftist group.

4. Hsü Shih-yu (*c.* 1906–   ) was at this time Commander of the Nanking Military Region, and Vice-Minister of National Defence. (He had been appointed to this latter post in 1959, when Lin Piao took over the Ministry from P'eng Te-huai.) At the Ninth Congress in April 1969, he had become a member of the Politburo. Mao is alluding to the military rebellion in Wuhan in the summer of 1967.

5. P'i Ting-chün (1914–   ) became a member of the Central Committee at the Ninth Congress. At that time, he was Deputy Commander of the PLA in Fukien. He was transferred to Langchou in 1970 as Commander of the PLA there; he returned to Fukien in the reshuffle of January 1974.

Text 26

1. Ch'ü Ch'iu-pai (1899–1935), a member of the Central Committee of the Chinese Communist Party from 1923 until his death, became Secretary of the Party in August 1927 and in this capacity

was responsible for the 'first leftist line' of late 1927 and early 1928. (See above, note 2 to Text 4.) He nevertheless remained influential in the Party, and also made a name for himself as a translator of Gorki and other Russian and Soviet writers. Left behind in Kiangsi at the time of the Long March, he was captured by the Kuomintang, and executed in June 1935. While in prison, he wrote an autobiographical work entitled *Superfluous Words*, which was by no means a recantation or betrayal, but the statement of a tired and disillusioned man who none the less retained his faith in Marxism. (For details and extracts in translation, see Tsi-an Hsia, 'Ch'ü Ch'iu-po: the Making and Destruction of a Tenderhearted Communist', in *The Gate of Darkness* [Seattle: University of Washington Press, 1968], pp. 3–54.) Because Ch'ü was regarded as a revolutionary martyr, this text was not accepted as authentic in China prior to the Cultural Revolution; since then, he has been denounced as a big traitor, and *Superfluous Words* has been quoted to substantiate the charge, especially by the Red Guards. Mao here ranges himself on the side of those who, in May 1967, demolished Ch'ü's 'dog's tomb'. (*T'ao Ch'ü chan-pao*, No. 3, 5 June 1967.)

2. Lo Chang-lung (1901–49?) was a founding member of the Chinese Communist Party and an important labour leader in the 1920s. In late 1930 he supported Ho Meng-hsiung's bid for control of the Party. As a result he was expelled at the Fourth Plenum in January 1931, and thereafter joined Ho in setting up a rival Central Committee. Hence Mao's charge of 'splittism'. He later became a Trotskyite.

3. There has been considerable controversy among specialists as to Mao's real position in the Chinese Communist hierarchy in 1931–4. Mao confirms the majority view that at this time he was largely a figurehead.

4. The Second Plenum of the Ninth Central Committee, held at Lushan from 23 August to 6 September 1970.

5. The five names on Mao's list of the 'big generals' making up Lin Piao's clique were all members of the Politburo. With the exception of Lin's wife, Yeh Ch'ün, they were all senior military men. Huang Yung-sheng (1906–   ) had been Chief of Staff since March 1968. Wu Fa-hsien (1914–   ) had been Commander of the Air Force since August 1965, and Deputy Chief of Staff since May 1968. Li Tso-p'eng had been First Political Commissar of the Navy since June 1967. Ch'iu Hui-tso was Director of the PLA General Logistics Department, and had been Deputy Chief of Staff since February 1969. Of the other two, Li Hsüeh-feng (see above, note 1 to Text 20)

was an alternate member of the Ninth Politburo, and Political Commissar of the Peking Military Region. Cheng Wei-shan (1914–   ) had been Deputy Commander of the Peking Military Region from November 1959 to March 1968, and Commander since that time. He was also Vice-Chairman of the Peking Revolutionary Committee.

6. 'With genius', 'creatively', and 'comprehensively'. These adverbs, used by Lin Piao in his foreword to the December 1966 edition of *Quotations from Chairman Mao* to characterize Mao Tse-tung's contribution to the development of Marxism–Leninism, sum up the view of the subject which he had been propagating since 1960 and especially since 1966. (For samples of his speeches on this theme, see J P R S 90, pp. 65–6, 78.) Mao Tse-tung, who was endeavouring in 1970 to downgrade his own cult, here attributes all the responsibility for previous excesses to Lin Piao. For a discussion of this issue, see the introduction to *Authority, Participation and Cultural Change in China*, pp. 66–7, 103–5.

7. A 700-word statement said to have been released by Mao during the Lushan Plenum. Nothing is known of its contents except for Mao's own summary here.

8. Lin Piao's speech of 23 August 1970 to the Lushan Plenum.

9. Yeh Ch'ün is said to have withdrawn the minutes of her intervention before a meeting of the Central–South Group during the plenum.

10. Various interpretations can be put on this statement. The least probable is that it should be taken literally, and that Mao still hoped his differences with Lin Piao could be resolved. It is more likely that, in view of his delicate tactical position in the autumn of 1971 and the extent of support for Lin within the army, Mao wished to deny his intention of seeking a showdown, and more broadly to stress his own generous and forgiving nature. He may also have been trying to sound out his interlocutors, by noting whether any of them suggested that Lin Piao should no longer be 'protected'.

11. Ch'en Sheng and Wu Kuang were contemporaries who jointly led an insurrection against the Ch'in in the third century B.C. Hung Hsiu-ch'üan (1814–64), the leader of the Taipings, was born only half a century before Sun Yat-sen (1866–1925). Mao attributes 'genius' to these men because they were all, in some sense, revolutionary precursors, who therefore drew on the wisdom of the masses.

12. For Lin Piao's statement that what Chairman Mao says in one sentence surpasses what others say in 10,000 sentences, see his speech of 18 May 1966, J P R S 90, p. 80.

13. This referes to efforts by Ch'en Po-ta and Lin Piao to reinsert,

in the draft Constitution of the People's Republic of China, the provision for a State Chairman which Mao had decided to strike out in March 1970. They claimed that their aim in this was further to glorify Chairman Mao, but in Mao's view their real intention was to ensure that Lin Piao should succeed Mao as the head both of the Party and of the state. On this point, and on the very complicated question of the relations between Lin Piao and Ch'en Po-ta (who appear to have concluded a tactical alliance at the time of the Lushan Plenum, but who clearly represented different factions and different viewpoints), see Philip Bridgham, 'The Fall of Lin Piao', *China Quarterly*, No 55 (July–Sept. 1973), pp. 427–49.

14. The question raised here as to who exercised real and immediate authority over the army is obviously closely related to that of Party control over the 'gun', which had become a burning issue within the leadership – and between Mao and Lin – in 1969–70.

15. 'Arrogance and complacency' was, by this time, the accepted expression for referring to the errors in Lin Piao's work style. I have not been able to trace the documents mentioned by Mao here.

16. This apparently refers to Mao's 'Open Letter to the Whole Party' of 15 September 1970, calling for a campaign to criticize Ch'en Po-ta.

17. 'Throwing stones' refers to Mao's action in compelling the 'big generals' supporting Lin to denounce Ch'en Po-ta. 'Mixing sand in soil' meant weakening Lin's control of the Military Affairs Committee by adding new members. The wall or cornerstone of Lin's power represented by the Peking Military Region was undermined by the dismissal of his supporters Cheng Wei-shan and Li Hsüeh-feng in December 1970.

18. I have not been able to find any information about this report.

19. At a report meeting called by the Central Committee in April 1971, and attended by ninety-nine responsible cadres from the Centre, the regions and PLA units, for the purpose of discussing the progress of the campaign to criticize Ch'en Po-ta and carry out rectification, self-criticisms by the 'big generals' of the Lin Piao clique (as enumerated by Mao on p. 292) were distributed.

20. This refers to the 'Summary of the Canton Military Region's Forum on Political and Ideological Work relating to the Three Supports and Two Militaries', distributed by the Central Committee on 20 August 1971. The 'three supports' ('support the broad masses of the left, support industry and agriculture') and 'two militaries' ('military control and military training') was the slogan summing up the policy of active intervention by the PLA in all aspects of politics

and society which had developed in the course of the Cultural Revolution. Mao Tse-tung, who had launched the process in January 1967 with his directive to Lin Piao to intervene in the Cultural Revolution in support of the left, had clearly regarded this as a temporary expedient, but by 1970–71 there were signs that Lin Piao and his supporters took it as setting the long-term pattern of the Chinese political system, and were using the above slogan as a standard for opposing the restoration of Party control. Presumably the Canton document adopted a more balanced position.

21. This apparently refers to Lin Piao's replacement of Mao's 'five requirements for successors' (see above, note 2 to Text 15) by 'three criteria' of his own, which he formulated as follows in his speech of 1 August 1966: '(1) Do they hold high the red banner of Mao Tse-tung's thought? Those who fail to do so shall be dismissed from office; (2) Do they engage in political and ideological work? Those who disrupt it and the Great Cultural Revolution are to be dismissed; (3) Are they enthusiastic about the revolution? Those who are entirely devoid of such enthusiasm are to be dismissed ... We must select, promote and employ cadres in accordance with Chairman Mao's five requirements and these three criteria, especially the first one' (JPRS 90, p. 17). 'One good' leading 'three goods' is Mao's summary of Lin's viewpoint according to which a correct understanding of Mao Tse-tung's thought in itself guaranteed that a person would be a good cadre. This criticism of Lin fits into the context of Mao's ongoing effort, since the Ninth Congress, to stress that political zeal must be complemented by a correct work style and, building on this, to denounce the 'arrogance and complacency' of Lin and his supporters in the army. (See Bridgham, article cited, pp. 431–4.)

22. This refers to Mao's 'Some Opinions' mentioned on p. 293. The link between Lin's glorification of the role of 'genius' and the evocation here of the 'Internationale', with its message, 'Il n'y a pas de sauveur suprême,' is obvious.

23. Whereas Lin Piao had earlier put the view that 'In the classical works of Marxism–Leninism, ninety-nine per cent of our studies must be from Chairman Mao's works' (JPRS 90, p. 65), a movement had been under way since the Lushan Plenum of September 1970 to encourage the study of the writings of Marx, Engels, Lenin and Stalin.

24. A daily bulletin (*Ts'an-k'ao hsiao-hsi*) circulated to a fairly wide audience of cadres, containing translations from foreign news services.